Method and Meaning in Polls and Surveys

Method and Meaning
in Polls and Surveys

Howard Schuman

Harvard University Press

Cambridge, Massachusetts

London, England

2008

Library of Congress Cataloging-in-Publication Data

Schuman, Howard.
Method and meaning in polls and surveys / Howard Schuman.
p.   cm.

Includes bibliographical references and index.
ISBN-13: 978-0-674-02827-2 (alk. paper)
1. Social surveys.   2. Social sciences—Research.   I. Title.
HN29.S334   2008
300.72'3—dc22   2007043357

To the memory of
Solomon Asch, Clifford Geertz,
and Samuel Stouffer

Committed to different methods,
all three sought
and contributed to
a larger meaning

Contents

Preface

During my first year as a graduate student in an interdisciplinary social science program, I wandered into Professor Stouffer's sociology course Opinion and Communication. Ever since, I have been involved in one way or another with polls and surveys, though with continued interest in two other disciplines from within that program, social psychology and anthropology.[1] This book draws on my research and writing between those ancient days and recent months to consider the nature of questions and answers in polls and surveys. In addition, relevant research by others is included in many parts of the book, though without any attempt to cover the survey literature exhaustively. I also indicate missteps I made along the way, together with lessons I hope to have learned from my mistakes. Throughout the book, methodological problems and substantive issues are joined: as the book's title is intended to imply, my goal has always been to connect method and meaning.

There are seven chapters, each with its own focus but also linked to one or more of the other chapters. The Introduction considers how, if at all, "polls" and "surveys" differ. I then explain my use of the terms "method" and "meaning" and give special attention to one method—the survey-based experiment—that plays a significant role throughout the book. A second method, the open-ended "Why" follow-up inquiry, is indicated as equally important.

Chapter 1, Ordinary Questions, Survey Questions, and Policy Questions, discusses the difference between survey questions and the kind of questions we ask in any social interaction, along with problems caused by treating surveys as referenda. In interpreting the question-answer process, we need to reject both "survey fundamentalism," which takes distributions of answers literally, and "survey cynicism," which assumes that investigators can obtain any answer they wish. The nature of bias in surveys is considered also, with a case study involving a serious charge against two noted social scientists, and a strategy is described for building fairness into the construction of questionnaires when controversial issues are investigated. The chapter ends by qualifying my own earlier advice against emphasizing referenda-type response distributions, because survey data do help us escape the egocentric assumption that we frequently hold about the views of others. Chapter 1, along with the Introduction, is basic to the rest of the book.

Chapter 2, The Primordial Distinction between Open and Closed Attitude Questions, investigates the oldest and most fundamental, yet least tractable and least studied, difference in how survey questions are asked. I show that both types of questioning can and often do constrain answers and thus limit the validity of survey inquiries, but that by putting the two types of questioning together, as often urged but infrequently done, we can construct closed questions that are both manageable and likely to be valid. At the same time, two important case studies are presented that seemed to show defects in questioning—one with open questions, the other with closed questions—but where careful analysis indicates each set of results to be valid, rather than explained by limitations in its method of inquiry. This chapter is probably the most challenging for readers less interested in detailed analysis of survey data.

Chapter 3, Interpretive Survey Research, starts from Clifford Geertz's valuable distinction between "experience-near" and "experience-distant" concepts when working in other cultures and argues that the same difference can apply to using surveys within a single population such as that of the United States. Particularly useful for this purpose are follow-up open probes of answers to closed questions that ask respondents Why they chose a particular response. Yet because polls can seldom afford to ask many Why follow-up questions, the technique of "random probing" is described as well, with illustrations from both Bangladesh and the United States. The chapter also includes an example of linguistic coding that can add further meaning to an analysis of open responses. This is my favorite chapter.

Chapter 4, Artifacts Are in the Mind of the Beholder, explores two examples of how the context of a poll or survey can shape answers: one has to do with the order in which questions are asked, and the other with the characteristics of the asker. The first example has wide substantive meaning because it draws on what seems to be a universal norm of reciprocity within and between societies. The second considers effects created when interviewers are perceived in terms of their race in America and in terms of their political sympathies in Nicaragua. Social change plays an important role in the chapter, as do also connections to other social and biological sciences.

Chapter 5, The Survey World and Other Worlds, looks at how the meaning of a primary set of survey results can be enriched by connecting it to other kinds of evidence. First, I consider comparisons of the general population with special populations; second, survey data are compared with data obtained using other, quite different methods; and third, the problematic relation between attitudes measured in surveys and behavior assessed in "real situations" is explored. The chapter ranges widely over different types of research.

Chapter 6, Hunting a Social Science Snark, describes a serendipitous discovery that seemed to promise new insight into the nature of the objects of attitudes, the disappointment that occurred during replication, and yet the clues found to understanding of the larger issue. The chapter emphasizes the difficult balance between a search for meaning, which calls for freedom to explore novel hypotheses and interpretations, and the discipline of method, which requires replications of different types to establish confidence in conclusions.

Conclusion: A Brief Look Back at Methods and Meanings, Surveys and Polls, returns once more to consider the key words in the title of the book. In addition, the propositions advanced in previous chapters are characterized as "middle range" and thus differ from broader frameworks such as "cognitive aspects of survey methodology" and "total survey error."

I thank Jean Converse for her helpful suggestions on the chapters that follow. She read several of them in their most primitive state and gave me good advice on how (and occasionally whether) to proceed. As the drafts moved toward its present shape, Amy Corning read each chapter more times than she probably cares to remember, caught errors large and small, and made recommendations that improved both content and style. Stanley Presser provided valuable thoughts on two chapters that especially connected with our past collaboration, and Norbert Schwarz gave helpful reactions to a chapter close to his own research. Karen Blu has been generous in allowing me to quote key passages from a wonderful essay by her husband, Clifford Geertz.

I am grateful to Michael Aronson of Harvard University Press for providing encouragement from an early point and shepherding the book from initial proposal to final form. Most of my research has received support from the National Science Foundation and could not have been carried out in the absence of such grants. At an early point, NSF's Sociology Program appreciated the value of achieving greater understanding of the question-answer process in surveys and polls.

I draw in various places on writing to which a number of former graduate students contributed as co-authors or in other ways. All those individuals have gone on to bigger and better things, but they will find ideas and evidence from early work we did together in some of the pages that follow, with the original articles cited also. The University of Michigan's Institute for Social Research provided a stimulating and supportive setting for much of my research. It also made possible frequent use of the regular Survey of Consumer Attitudes for my survey-based experiments and other explorations, with the further advantage of having the data archived in the Interuniversity Consortium for Political and Social Research (ICPSR) and available to others. Most of the remaining data I analyze come from the Roper Center for Public Opinion Research. Use of the Bowdoin College Library and advice by its staff has also been helpful at a number of points.

My earliest analysis of data was carried out by writing on 3×5 inch cards a few bits of information obtained from a small set of individuals, then shuffling the cards into piles for counts and the calculation of simple summary statistics. I then graduated to the use of counter-sorters, next to submitting punch cards to mysterious individuals who ran giant computers, and so on to the immensely more powerful and convenient personal computer on which I am writing these chapters—with occasional pauses to switch to programs that enable reanalysis of data to check or pursue a point. Throughout most of that personal evolution—and especially after I moved from Ann Arbor to the Maine coast—my son, Marc, once a three-year-old with whom I put together toy motors and now an electronics engineer and systems programmer, has provided expert solutions for all the ills that computers are heir to—including a few made worse by poor advice from the Help Lines of hardware and software manufacturers. Without Marc's willingness and ability to solve problems of all kinds, this book might never have seen the light of day nor the dark of night.

My greatest debt is to Jo. Her reading of the final draft of the book has led to many improvements in clarity. But beyond that, she has been important to my life in ways wider and deeper than I could possibly describe. Our relationship goes back to our days as students together at Antioch College, with our future entirely unknown:

> I ran with her upon a running path,
> Where water squidged beneath the careless grass.
> Ahead a confident squirrel sped up a tree—
> We stared through leaves to where we could not see . . .

Method and Meaning in Polls and Surveys

Introduction

Polls and Surveys,
Methods and Meanings

The first use of language in prehistoric times may well have been to utter commands: "Stop!" "Come here!" But if so, questions might have followed soon after: "Why?" "What for?" From that point, it would have been only a short step to the use of interrogatives to learn where another humanoid had seen possible food, a dangerous animal, or something else of common interest. Asking questions has continued over the ages to be a remarkably effective way to obtain information of all kinds—assuming, of course, that the person answering is able and willing to respond accurately, something we will consider carefully in succeeding pages.

This book is about the question-answer process that is basic to polls and surveys, as it is to so much social interaction. My main concern is with questions about attitudes—positive and negative evaluations of all kinds—and also about the conceptual cousins of attitudes: beliefs, values, opinions, and a host of other terms that refer to subjective phenomena.[1] Elsewhere I consider whether it is possible to make a sharp distinction between "facts" and "attitudes" and conclude that it is not. But for the moment I will use "attitude" as a shorthand term for the kinds of questions we will be considering.

We will not, however, be focusing on how to escape the snares of poor questions, such as the sensible advice to avoid double-barreled inquiries, unnecessary ambiguities, and difficult grammar (Payne 1951; Sudman and Bradburn 1982; Converse and Presser 1986). Our concern will be with the nature of questioning itself, with issues of validity and bias, and with the contributions and limitations of the meaning sought through polls and surveys—issues raised in the early days of survey research by pioneering figures like Paul Lazarsfeld and Sam Stouffer, and with us still today. The issues will be considered both theoretically, drawing ideas from the several

1

social sciences, and empirically with the use of substantive research of my own and others.

Equally essential to the development of polls and surveys, of course, is the goal of learning about one's social environment—about a population—by sampling a small part of it (Kish 1965; Kalton 1983; Lohr 1999). We will take the sampling of large populations for granted as fundamental, keeping the main focus of this book on the question-answer process. As part of that process, however, I do draw on basic principles of sampling at specific points, for example, in developing the use of "random probes" in Chapter 3. Overall, sampling and questioning are the key components of polls and surveys today, while other features such as interviewing, though also important and to be discussed at later points, are not always integral; thus self-administered questionnaires by mail or Internet can dispense with interviewers altogether.[2]

The chapters that follow this one are best read as a series of connected essays or reflections based on evidence. Although sequenced in what seems to me a logical order, readers should feel free to follow their own interests and to treat the chapters more as sectors of a circle than as points along a straight line. Each chapter draws on my published articles and unpublished research on the question-answer process over nearly five decades, together with new thinking, new writing, and often additional analysis.[3] I also make use of the ideas and research of others that bear on the same themes but without attempting a comprehensive review of all relevant survey literature. My goal in each chapter is to arrive at conclusions and recommendations that are clear enough to provoke acceptance or challenge or perhaps some of both.

Polls and Surveys

My reference to both "polls" and "surveys" may suggest that there are two different vehicles that are based on questioning. This is true only in the sense that "polls" have typically been a part of the names used by commercial and media organizations, for example, the Gallup Poll. The term "survey" has usually been associated with academic institutions (e.g., the University of Chicago's General Social Survey) and with the federal government (e.g., the Current Population Survey).[4] But does the distinction in terminology go beyond the words favored in the names of organizations?

In earlier days, academic and government surveys regularly employed some form of probability sampling, while commercial polls ordinarily used quota or other types of nonprobability sampling that were faster and less expensive. Today, however, almost all organizations, academic and commercial, have moved heavily into interviewing by telephone; the development of various forms of "random digit dialing" has largely eliminated what was once an important distinction, though differences in response rates often remain, if only because commercial polls usually operate under greater time pressure than academic and government surveys.[5] Still another distinguishing feature of surveys is a greater emphasis on multivariate analysis, frequently using more complex statistical techniques, whereas polls more often concentrate on reporting percentages for individual questions and simple two-variable relations. Yet this difference is more a matter of how data are analyzed than of the question-answer process itself: the skilled analyst can apply sophisticated multivariate techniques to Gallup items, while the academic survey investigator under pressure to respond to a grant or contract deadline may produce a report that is little more than a summary of single-variable percentages and simple relationships.[6]

These variations in sampling and analysis are important when assessing the results of social research, but it is doubtful whether such differences today go hand in hand with the distinction between "surveys" and "polls" as names. My own hypothesis is that the distinction now tells us more about the relation of language to social roles and social status than it does about differences in method.[7] It appears to be more a matter, first, of etymology, and second, of how different words are used to appeal to different parts of the population.

Our English vocabulary is generally recognized as having two major wellsprings: its original Old English or Anglo-Saxon base, dating from the first millennium after Christ, and the infusion of new words that followed the Norman Conquest in 1066. The earlier period connects English to Germanic roots; the latter derives from Latin, at first indirectly through French and then more directly as scholars and scientists went purposefully to the classical languages in search of new terms. The two lexical sources often lead to duplication in a literal sense, but with differences in connotation and usage that we all recognize, whether consciously or not. Thus our food comes from cows, pigs, and sheep, words of Anglo-Saxon origin; but once prepared, it is transformed into the French beef, pork, and mutton *(boeuf, porc, mouton)*. The barnyard character of the first three words reflects the fact that the conquered Anglo-Saxons tended the farms, while the culinary suggestion of the latter comes from the tables of the conquering Normans.

Similarly, we have a set of everyday Anglo-Saxon words for parts of the body—mouth, eye, ear, and the like—and parallel but fancier terms from Latin, such as oral cavity. Perhaps the most divergent connotations of all appear when one considers the four-letter words that make up our great store of vulgar expressions. Many of these are Old English words, whereas their polite equivalents are generally and obviously Latinate in character.[8]

As these last examples suggest, words of Anglo-Saxon descent tend to be shorter, are often blunter, and seem more ordinary in the sense of mass usage. Words coming from French or Latin convey greater refinement and have more appeal to the educated eye and ear. My hypothesis about the distinction between polls and surveys should now be evident. "Poll" is a four-letter word, often thought to be from an ancient Germanic term referring to "head," as in counting heads. The two-syllable word "survey," on the other hand, comes from the Old French *surveeir*, which in turn derives from Latin *super* (over) and *vidēre* (to look). The first is therefore an expression with appeal to a wider public, the intended consumers of results from ABC, CBS/NYT, Gallup, and other polls. The second fits the needs of academicians in university institutes who wish to emphasize the scientific or scholarly character of their work. Because academic investigators in the social sciences perceive themselves to be regarded with some suspicion by their colleagues in the traditional sciences and humanities, it especially important for them to differentiate their work from the transient poll reports that appear in the mass media. As in many other social contexts, a distinction in names is called upon to help accentuate the difference.

Other factors may be involved as well, such as the link between the polls, in the sense employed here, and the prediction of what happens at "the polls" (that is, during elections). The present hypothesis is simply that divergent social meanings play a strong role in maintaining the poll-survey distinction even when all other differences have vanished. Moreover, a test of this hypothesis may be close at hand, for recently some commercial organizations have begun to refer to their products as surveys rather than as polls—an effort at social mobility through renaming, much as occurs in other areas of life. This trend may make academic researchers somewhat uncomfortable, however, and it will be interesting to see if social necessity leads to the invention of new words, or—to translate into Latinate English—to additional refinements in terminology.

In this book, the distinction between the two terms is of no concern: the words "poll" and "survey" will be treated as interchangeable. Because I am accustomed to using the word "survey," I tend to employ it more often, but the term "poll" will also be used occasionally to emphasize that the distinction is one that makes no difference. Often both terms will be used together ("polls and surveys") to avoid seeming to focus on one connotation or the other. Furthermore, whichever term one prefers, my assumption throughout the book is that polls and surveys play an increasingly important role in society: if not as a Fifth Estate, they are certainly an essential part of the Fourth, constantly called upon even by those who express skepticism toward them. They have attained official status in some contexts, for example, influencing which presidential candidates merit Secret Service protection prior to nomination and then determining which final candidates are to be included in presidential debates. In government surveys they are, of course, more official, and the questions used are inevitably involved in defining what is meant by important social features such as race and ethnicity, and indeed what should be counted as "rooms" in a home.

But even where reported without official recognition, their influence on political thought and action is unmistakable, as with repeated polling about a current president's popularity, where the trend and even the absolute level are taken—often, reified—as fundamental measures of public support. Thus when we consider the questions that make up polls and surveys, we deal with something both pervasive and powerful in American society, and increasingly so throughout the rest of the world as well. Indeed, even under extremely difficult war-time conditions, careful surveys are being carried out in distant nations such as Afghanistan to attempt to provide systematic evidence previously impossible to imagine (e.g. Langer 2006). Soon, to be polled may be almost as important to a small nation, at least one that aspires to be treated as democratic, as to have a seat in the United Nations.[9]

Method

Less needs to be said at this point about the other key terms in the title of this book for they constitute the content of the remaining pages. The term "method" refers first to the steps involved in any serious poll or survey: defining a population, drawing a sample, presenting questions by interview or self-administration, and analyzing the resulting data. But "method" also, and of more direct importance in this book, refers to special efforts to improve our understanding of both questions and answers. One such method requires further comment at this point because it is drawn on in each of the later chapters: the survey-based experiment, where a sample is divided into two or more random subsamples, each of which receives a different version of a question or experiences some other difference in a feature of a poll or survey. Such experiments have roots in the earliest days of polling in the 1930s, where they were referred to as the "split-ballot technique." Thousands of split-ballot experiments were carried out by Gallup, many to determine whether the wording or order of questions or of alternatives within a question made a difference.[10] After the 1940s, few such survey-based experiments were done until the mid-1970s, at which point Schuman and Presser ([1981] 1996) built their entire research program around survey-based experiments—better called "split-sample" than "split-ballot" experiments—in order to compare the effects of different ways in which the form, wording, and context of questions were varied. Bishop and his colleagues (1978) began a series of experiments on some of the same issues at almost the same time.[11]

Most of this early experimental work focused on methodological concerns: question order, response order, tone of wording, and other issues that come up in the course of constructing questionnaires. However, in some instances what began as a methodological experiment clearly had implications for interpretations of substantive social issues. This connection between method and meaning was true, for example, in the Hyman and Sheatsley (1950) "Communist reporter experiment," which had shown that the order of questions could influence basic attitudes toward a significant political issue.[12] More explicit efforts at using survey-based experiments for substantive purposes were carried out as part of my consideration with Presser of gun control issues (1977–78; [1981] 1996) and with Bobo (1988) of racial attitudes toward open housing.

The primary advantage of adding split-sample experiments to traditional surveys is to provide what Campbell and Stanley (1963; Cook and Campbell 1979) called "internal validity." Thus, a difference in answers between respondents who are randomly assigned to receive two different wordings of a question can be attributed to the wording itself, unless the difference is so small as to be attributable to chance. Because of the inevitable vicissitudes of large-scale polls and surveys, internal validity is unlikely to be as great for survey-based experiments as for more tightly controlled laboratory experimentation. However, a survey-based experiment offers a unique advantage in terms of "external validity" when it starts from a good probability sample of the national population, rather than using an ad hoc sample of students or volunteers, for this allows rigorous inference to all members of the total population. It also provides variation in age, education, region, and other social background factors that is largely excluded when the sampling is restricted to college students or others available on the basis of convenience. In addition and of great importance, probability sampling of a clearly defined population allows independent replication of results, the sine qua non for trustworthy evidence, as well as being essential for serious studies of social change, as we will see in later chapters.

A second form of external validity is more problematic for survey-based experiments: the degree to which the questions used represent the more general constructs intended. Just because questions are included within an experimental framework does not mean that the variations in questioning operationalize theoretical constructs in an adequate way. Furthermore, where a split-sample experiment compares two or more versions of the "same" construct to test a larger substantive hypothesis, the challenge is compounded because the adequacy of the wordings must be judged not only singly but in relation to each other. Of course, the problematic relation between constructs and the way they are operationalized is a major issue for all experimentation, whether carried out in laboratories, classrooms, or any other setting.[13]

There are also a number of ways to gain additional information from survey-based experiments: repeating an experiment over time tests concern over nuclear weapons in Chapter 2; splitting a sample into more than two components allows a crucial comparison that rules out "acquiescence" as an explanation for a puzzling substantive finding in Chapter 6; and also in Chapter 6, asking one version of a question at time 1 and a different version at time 2 to the same sample, makes it possible to pinpoint those who changed their answers in response to two versions of a question. A still more complex addition to split-sample experimentation is the use of factorial designs, well described by Tourangeau (2004). With such designs more than one variable can be included in a single experiment, and each combination of variables can be investigated to determine if it produces an interactive effect different from summing the effects of the separate variables.

Sniderman and Grob (1996) claim that a factorial approach provides a great leap beyond the classic split-sample experiment. However, what is most important for experimentation of all kinds is not the number of variables that can be manipulated at one point, but the extent to which an experimenter operationalizes constructs in a meaningful way, addresses important theoretical issues, and is able to fruitfully pursue issues that initial findings raise. These accomplishments characterized the simple but powerful classic social psychological experiments carried out by Asch (1952), Milgram (1974), and Latané and Darley (1970). As Milgram himself stated (1974, p. 13), "Simplicity is the key to effective scientific inquiry," and Wegner and Schneider (2003, p. 328) would add that: "The classic study . . . can be summarized in a single comparison, at most two, and never, ever goes into the kinds of factorial designs that make analysis of variance teachers so proud." Indeed, the more useful experiments reported by Sniderman and his colleagues (Sniderman and Piazza 1993; Sniderman and Carmines 1997; Sniderman, Crosby, and Howell 2000) have often come down to straightforward split-sample designs, whereas a more complex experimental comparison they report appears to be misleading because of questionable operationalizing.[14] In addition, sometimes less rather than more experimentation is needed to document an important point: in Chapter 5 respondents are shown to comfortably take quite different positions on a basic issue of racial discrimination when three questions were asked in sequence, with no need to use a more complicated design that Sniderman and Piazza (1993) constructed in order to disguise what the investigators were doing.

The other major method that I emphasize at later points is the use of open questions, but only after first showing (to my own surprise) that they are often inferior to closed questions as the main form of inquiry for surveys. I believe that their greater value comes from use as follow-up Why questions, as will be developed fully in Chapter 3. Survey-based experiments and Why open questions are seemingly opposite as methods, yet together they illuminate the meaning of answers to questions in polls and surveys.

Meaning

The remaining key word in the title of this book is "meaning," and it is especially difficult to define. Any attempt at a simple definition easily leads to circularity, as suggested by Ogden and Richards' title for their 1923 book *The Meaning of Meaning*. Moreover, the meaning of "meaning" differs in different chapters of my book. In Chapter 2 "meaning" refers to an ideal situation where respondents answer a question after taking adequate time to think about it and to qualify and explain their response in whatever way they wish. In Chapter 3, however, the word "meaning" refers to the insight an investigator gains into the forces that have shaped the answers given in a survey, including forces that may not be recognized by respondents themselves. Thus in Chapter 2 "meaning" is close to what respondents themselves think they intend, conveyed using their own concepts; but in Chapter 3 "meaning" refers to investigators' interpretation of what was said, which may be different from what respondents themselves think they were saying. In addition, in Chapter 4 we consider how the meaning of an important term changes depending on what other words it follows, while at the end of Chapter 5 the meaning of a verbal symbol is compared with the meaning taken from a concrete embodiment of that symbol. In Chapter 6 I recount the pursuit of a serendipitous discovery through hope, disappointment, and a larger exploration of the meaning of attitude objects. Whether looked at from the standpoint of respondents or from the standpoint of investigators, Clifford Geertz's definition of meaning is as useful as any I have found: "the conceptual structures individuals use to construe experience" (1973, p. 313).

Method and Meaning Redux

In the pages that follow, methodological inquiries often point toward substantive construals, and substantive research often raises methodological issues. Thus meaning and method are intertwined throughout the rest of this book.

— 1 —

Ordinary Questions, Survey Questions, and Policy Questions

A fundamental paradox of survey questioning is that we use ordinary questions much like those employed in daily life, yet our results should seldom be treated like ordinary answers. This paradox in turn complicates the use of survey results in relation to policy questions in ways that neither the public nor many policy makers fully appreciate. We need to understand the paradox, consider its causes, and think of practical ways to deal with it.

In ordinary life a question is typically asked because one person wishes information from another. You might ask an acquaintance how many rooms there are in her new house, or whether she enjoyed a particular book or film, or if she supports the legalization of doctor-assisted suicide. The normal assumption on both sides of the interaction is that you are interested in her answer in and of itself. Your purpose might vary from wanting advice based on her experience to trying to get a sense of her general values, but in any case you usually evaluate her answers as such and make judgments based on them. Let us call this process "ordinary questioning" and the questions themselves "ordinary questions."

In survey interviews we ask much the same kinds of questions—that is, their form, their wording, and the manner of their asking are often hardly distinguishable from ordinary questions. We do at times use fancy formats, with names such as Likert-type or Semantic Differential; but by and large, the survey questioner cannot depart too far from ordinary questioning, for the essential nature of the survey interview is communication with people who expect to hear ordinary questions. Indeed, the major justification we give for contacting respondents and taking their time is that we seek information—whether facts or opinions or both. The whole interview is couched in the framework of ordinary questioning.

10

Not surprisingly, respondents often assume that the interviewer is directly interested in the facts and opinions they give, much as would a friend or acquaintance who asked the same questions. By this statement I don't mean that respondents necessarily assume a personal interest in their individual answers, though occasionally that does happen. What many respondents do assume, however, is that their answers will be added to those of all others who are interviewed and tallied up to give totals that are directly interpretable.[1] If opinions are asked for, the survey is seen as a kind of referendum, and the investigator is believed to be interested in whatever is at issue, for example, how many favor and how many oppose doctor-assisted suicide. If facts are being sought through the survey, the assumption is that the goal is simply a table showing, for example, how many people have what size homes, or whatever was asked about.[2]

Yet experienced survey researchers know that it is often just such tables that are most problematic to interpret. Especially when we deal with opinions, but even when we deal with what are called "facts," the results for any single question—what survey analysts sometimes refer to as the "marginals"—may be too much a function of the way the question is asked to allow for any simple interpretation. The results on doctor-assisted suicide (or on legalized abortion or on taxes or on just about any controversial issue) will depend heavily on the conditions and definitions presupposed in the question wording, and the same is true to an extent even for a question on how many rooms you have in your house. Thus attitudes toward doctor-assisted suicide can hinge on descriptions of the absence or presence of pain and its degree; the likelihood of death in what span of time; the nature of the physician's involvement; and the age, the state of mind, and other characteristics of the person contemplating such an action. "Rooms" depend on exactly how parts of a house are categorized and what is included as a distinct room. "Don't trust the 'marginals' in any absolute sense" is one of the first lessons a person should learn when working with survey data.

Instead what we often do is to hold constant the question—or the index or scale, if two or more questions are summed or averaged—and make comparisons across time, across genders, and across other variables. We may not know what 65 percent really means in terms of support for doctor-assisted suicide, but we act on the belief that if the question wording and other survey conditions have remained constant, we can say, at least within the limits of sampling error, that our results represent an increase or decrease from an earlier survey, and also that we have some sense of whether the change is large or small. Or if 61 percent is the figure for men and there is a quite different figure for women, a sex difference of approximately such and such a size exists. There are assumptions with regard to such conclusions that remain problematic, such as whether constancy of meaning is really maintained over time and across other variables, and also whether associations are really less affected by question wording than are marginals. But we believe, based on both intuition and experience, that such comparative conclusions are less likely to lead us astray than assertions based on single-item percentages.[3]

The tendency to take too literally single-variable distributions of responses (the "marginals") is essentially the same as believing that answers come entirely from respondents, forgetting that they are also shaped by the questions we ask. Looked at theoretically, this tendency can be seen as a manifestation of the "fundamental attribution error" (Ross 1977)—the human propensity to overestimate the importance of personal dispositional factors relative to situational influences. Thus, on first hearing the results of classic social psychological experiments by Asch (1952) on conformity and by Milgram (1974) on obedience, we immediately look for unusual personality factors, and we underestimate the likelihood that many people in a laboratory situation can be induced to conform to peer pressure or to the commands of an authority figure. Likewise, if 10 percent of a sample in a survey say spontaneously that they have "no opinion" on an issue, this statement does not mean that they differ categorically from the other 90 percent, for we know that by simply introducing an explicit "no opinion" alternative into the question, we can usually raise that 10 percent almost threefold (Schuman and Presser [1981] 1996). Similarly, almost any pretest experience will show that the proportion of people who place themselves in a particular category of a pro-con item can readily be altered by introducing more gradations in the set of offered alternatives. Indeed, for some questions we can shift marginals substantially merely by changing the race or the sex of the interviewers who ask the questions.

In sum, there a direct connection between what we know about survey responses and the line of experimental results in social psychology that dates back many years—at least as far back as Triplett's (1897) observation that children wind fishing rods at different speeds depending upon whether they are alone or in the presence of other children who are also winding fishing rods. "Behavior has such salient properties," wrote Fritz Heider in 1958 (pp. 54–55), "that it tends to engulf the field rather than be confined to its proper position as a local stimulus whose interpretation requires the additional data of the surrounding field—the situation."

This is not to assert that response marginals are never stable in the face of changes in form, wording, or context of questions. The term "error" in the "fundamental attribution error" is really something of a misnomer, for the intent is to say that the situation is usually a more important source of behavior than we expect but not that it is always more important. The problem with survey marginals, as with other indicators of behavior, is that we cannot know from viewing them in a single setting just how stable they are: how easy or difficult it would be to shift them by exerting some force, such as a change in the form, the wording, or the context of the question.

Problems with the Referendum Point of View

The difference between what respondents expect to be done with their answers—what we will call the "referendum point of view"—and what the sophisticated survey investigator expects to do—the "analytic point of view"—is a very large difference. The respondent in a national survey believes that the investigator intends to add up all the results, item by item, and then tell the nation what Americans think. But the sophisticated investigator knows that such a presentation is usually problematic at best and can be dangerously misleading at worst, because answers depend on questions and there is no single way to word most questions. Thus there is an important difference in the goals of the two main parties—the respondents and the investigators—in the survey process, and among other difficulties, this difference can lead to ethical problems having to do with obtaining "informed consent" to a survey. "Your Opinion Counts," says the blurb distributed by polling organizations, but often your opinion does not, and indeed should not, count in the simple referendum sense that respondents assume. Moreover, to make matters even more awkward, policy makers often have the same point of view as respondents: they want to know how many people favor and how many oppose the issue that they see themselves confronting. Yet it may be neither possible nor desirable for the survey to ask exactly the question the policy maker has in mind, and in any case such a question is likely to be only one of a number of possible questions that might be asked on the issue.

One reason sometimes given for the undependability of a focus on marginals is that answers in surveys are frequently affected by small, even trivial, changes in question wording. I do not think that this explanation is the principal one: at the very least it is exaggerated, and in some cases it may even be theoretically nonsensical. In *Questions and Answers in Attitude Surveys* (Schuman and Presser [1981] 1996), we tried in a number of split-ballot experiments to shift marginals by means of small or even not-so-small changes in wording and were often either unsuccessful or produced only minor shifts. For example, in one experiment we substituted the phrase "end pregnancy" for the word "abortion," after having been informed by pro-choice partisans that the former was a softer way of putting the matter and thus likely to yield more support for abortion. Yet the rewording produced no appreciable change at all in the distribution of responses. In another instance, we removed what seemed to be clearly loaded wording from an alternative to a question on work values and, to our surprise, found no effect. All in all, our deliberate attempts to shift marginals by variations in tone of wording or phrasing were noteworthy as much for the negligible as for the large effects produced.

These negative results are supported by the theoretical difficulty of defining exactly what is meant by a small change in wording. Does "small" refer to the size of the word changed? Or to its grammatical character? Or to what? Consider the difference between the words "a" and "the." Such words in English tend to be treated as unimportant, even trivial, yet it is really no surprise that substitution of one for the other can have large effects. For example, if we say that the Secretary of State shook hands with *the* wife of the Egyptian ambassador, this statement would imply something quite different than if we say that the Secretary of State shook hands with *a* wife of the Egyptian ambassador. The shift from *the* to *a* moves the implication from monogamy to polygamy. It would be odd to say that such a change in wording is small, just because articles are less conspicuous in English than are nouns or verbs. In the end, "small" probably refers to what are treated as synonyms, but in many such cases there are differences in connotation that affect responses in entirely appropriate ways.[4]

No, it is not usually tiny changes in wording that make marginals so untrustworthy, but several other factors about questions. I will stress two here. First, respondents feel enormously constrained to stay within the framework of a survey question. They will almost always use one of the two or three or more alternatives given by the interviewer, rather than offering a substitute of their own, even if a substitute is allowed or encouraged and would have great appeal if offered. Similarly, consistent effects on marginals occur with variations in certain formal aspects of questions (e.g., whether a "don't know" response is encouraged or discouraged).[5]

The second and related factor is that most public issues are discussed at a relatively general level, as though there is just a single issue and it has only two sides. But what is called the abortion issue, to take one example, consists of a large number of different issues having to do with the reasons for abortion, the trimester involved, and so forth. Except at the extremes, exactly which of these particular issues is posed and with what alternatives makes a considerable difference in the marginal results, and thus any single set of marginals is likely to be misleading if taken to summarize views on abortion as a general issue. And the same is true for most other serious issues. It is genuine change in question content that is responsible for most important shifts in marginals, not minor variations in wording, even though the latter can also sometimes occur and are important to recognize.

These two factors are among the most important ones in accounting for the difficulty in interpreting marginals, but they are not the only ones. On numerous issues, the public is so uninformed that the marginals have little meaning and less staying power (Delli Carpini and Keeter 1996; Bishop 2005). Some variations in marginals are due to question-order effects, probably because the meaning of the question itself varies from one context to another, as will be discussed in Chapter 4. And other marginals arc quite misleading if extrapolated beyond the present moment, because they fail to take into account the impact that an unexpected event (e.g., a natural disaster such as a hurricane) can have on opinion on a range of issues.

Furthermore, beyond problems having to do with the questions we ask, we always need comparative data to make good sense of results. Suppose that each reader of this chapter answered a simple yes/no question about whether reading it has been useful, with the yield being 60 percent yes and 40 percent no. Leaving aside all the problems of question wording and answering, the 60 percent should be interpreted against a backdrop of results based on reading other chapters in other books with similar goals. If the average for yes for the other books is only 40 percent, I might feel rather pleased; however, if the average of yes for the other books is 80 percent, I would rightly feel disappointed. We are all aware of the fundamental need for comparisons, yet it is all too easy to forget about the difficulty of interpreting absolute percentages when as investigators we feel the urge to learn about public reactions to a new event, or when as consumers of polls we read that X percent of Americans believe such and such about a new issue.

From all these considerations, it becomes clear that the presentation of univariate percentages is fraught with danger and that satisfying the public hunger for results in the form of referenda should usually be, if not avoided, then set forth with cautions and in subdued tones. An exception, of course, would be an official referendum that the survey is in fact attempting to predict word for word. In that singular case, the poll can have value in the form of "predictive validity." Moreover, any artifacts that occur in such cases inhere in the official referendum, not in the survey question used to predict its results.

It is worth asking whether the interpretive problems discussed in this section apply also to what I have called ordinary questioning in a two-person conversation. At least in part, they do. Answers to ordinary questions, if not followed up, can sometimes be just as misleading as marginals, and some of the distortion due to social pressure in the survey interview can also occur in ordinary questioning. Yet ordinary questioning in the course of a conversation often does allow a fair amount of credence to be given to answers, because a questioner is able to adapt questions to the individual answering, to probe further and deeper for meaning, and to continually synthesize the responses received. Little of this can be permitted to survey interviewers for fear of both bias and interviewer variation in the asking—a price we pay for the genuine advantages of standardization. Thus in ordinary questioning, it is possible to end up with an integrated sense of what the answerer thinks about a general issue, which is much harder to accomplish in the context of a survey interview.

There may or may not be an important exception to this conclusion with regard to relatively straightforward factual questions. Conrad and Schober (2000) have shown that what they call "conversational interviewing"—where interviewers are trained to say whatever may be needed to insure that questions are interpreted as intended—can improve the quality of responses to questions such as those about consumer purchases and about certain features of personal homes. Issues remain as to how well this form of interviewing can be implemented routinely and efficiently in large-scale surveys, how widely it can apply to a range of factual questions, and how much difference it will make in the findings and conclusions from a survey. In any case, the authors write that they "do not intend [these particular] results to extend to opinion or attitude questions" (p. 23).

Four Strategies

What can survey investigators do to take account of the inherent ambiguity of results for a single question, assuming that past time points are not available for comparison? There is no certain way to avoid confounding substantive interpretation with the unique features of a question, but there are several ways to mitigate the problem. One strategy is to include, in all important surveys at least, some open-ended questions that allow investigators and readers to appreciate, so far as possible, the frames of reference and alternatives that come most spontaneously to respondents. Open questions have limitations of their own, as discussed in Chapter 2; but they do offer one way for investigators to minimize mistaking a mirror of their own minds for a window into the minds of others. Chapter 3 is devoted to the use of open questions.

A second strategy is to ask a wide variety of closed questions about an issue, to include a spectrum of information and belief inquiries as well as pro-con attitude questions, and then to give a number of univariate results if any are to be provided at all, thus emphasizing the complexity of the issue. The exact wording of each important question should always be provided as well. This strategy may be difficult to follow in brief newspaper or other media story form, especially when there are a large number of questions, but Web sites can be used to provide additional documentation. The sequence of questions may also be needed when order effects appear at all likely, as discussed in Chapter 4. (The Pew Research Center ordinarily makes full questionnaires available on its Web site). Furthermore, this strategy of multiple questions requires a good deal of forethought in question construction if it is not to conflict with the equally desirable need to create a small set of permanent indicators that can be replicated over time to monitor social change on an important issue.

A third strategy is to include survey-based experiments with different question wordings administered to random subsamples of the total sample. Whether the different wordings change univariate and other results becomes the concern, and if so, why this occurs becomes the focus. For example, a CBS News Poll asked the following question in March 2006 in two ways to random halves of a national sample, with the wording difference shown here within the brackets: "Do you think ['the result of the war with Iraq' vs. 'removing Saddam Hussein from power'] was worth the loss of American life and other costs of attacking Iraq or not?" The response "worth it" was chosen by just 25 percent in the first case, but by 40 percent in the second. Thus how the question was worded did make a difference in this case.[6] On the other hand, the following CBS Poll question in April 2006 showed little difference despite the wording variation: "Do you think of your vote for Congress this fall as a vote for ['George W. Bush' vs. 'George W. Bush's policies'], a vote against ['George W. Bush' vs. 'George W. Bush's policies'], or don't you think of your vote this fall as being about George W. Bush's ['presidency' vs. 'policies']?" To the extent that wording does not make a difference, greater reliance can be placed on the conclusions drawn from the results.[7]

Sometimes the effect of a variation in wording is more important for key associations with another variable than for single tabulations. The CBS Poll in February 2006 compared responses to a question about whether "most people in government" take responsibility when something goes wrong and responses to a parallel question about whether "most people in the Bush Administration" take responsibility when something goes wrong. Almost 90 percent of the self-reported Democrats answered negatively to the same degree to both versions of the question, but among self-reported Republicans 80 percent were negative to the first wording ("most people in government") but only 31 percent were negative to the second wording ("most people in the Bush Administration"). The huge and highly significant difference by political party in the results is clearly meaningful and informative.[8]

A fourth strategy can be useful when planning a survey investigation into controversial issues where the different sides may not even frame important questions in the same way. The idea is to enlist representatives of opposing sides to help in negotiating questions that take into account their different perspectives. Such an approach can provide both the reality and the appearance of fairness. Reality and appearance are both important, the former for obvious reasons and the latter because otherwise any set of results on a controversial issue is apt to be attacked as biased by the side that was not consulted and that feels disadvantaged by the outcome.

An instructive example of this fourth strategy arose when a University of Michigan Medical School professor asked the university's Survey Research Center to carry out a survey about the use of animals in medical experiments—more specifically about the transfer of unclaimed dogs and cats from pounds to laboratories for use in such experiments. The Michigan legislature was soon to consider a bill prohibiting transfers from pounds for this purpose, and the Michigan Society for Medical Research wished to show the relevant legislative committee that public sentiment opposed such a bill.

Views concerning experimentation on animals are like debates about abortion and other moral issues: there are highly committed groups at both extremes, as well as a large part of the population that can easily be made aware of the issue but has not really thought it through. As director of the Survey Research Center at that time, I was reluctant to help carry out a survey for political purposes where only one side of an emotionally charged issue would be involved in the design of the questionnaire and reporting of the results. Moreover, this was a classic case where the sponsor was interested in the survey solely as a quasi-official referendum and not in its analytic use for understanding the bases of public attitudes and beliefs. I agreed to carry out the survey only if someone representing the other side of the issue was allowed to review drafts of the questionnaire and to indicate any questions the representative thought were unfairly framed. Fortunately, the sponsoring society's own representative agreed, and I obtained the cooperation of the president of the Michigan Federation of Humane Societies for this purpose, because she had recently written an article in support of the bill prohibiting transfer of animals for experimentation. In the following description, I will refer to her as "the critic," and to the medical school professor as "the sponsor."

I first talked at length with the medical sponsor, next constructed a draft set of questions, then reviewed the draft with the critic, and then repeated these steps in the course of pretesting and revision. The goal was to arrive at a set of questions that seemed desirable to the sponsor, reasonably fair to the critic, and adequate from my own standpoint as a relatively neutral observer and also from the standpoints of the pretest interviewers. I did not try to bring the two parties to the conflict together in one room because, although each was quite sophisticated, each also judged the near-immorality of the other's position too strongly to allow direct collaboration.

This kind of shuttle diplomacy worked well for a number of the questions. In some cases the critic had no serious objection to a question, whereas in other cases her objection led me to revise the question in a way that the sponsor accepted. In two instances, however, the wishes of the sponsor and the reactions of the critic could not be reconciled, even after strenuous efforts, and I decided to make use of a split-sample experimental approach to allow both versions of each question to be asked. We would see whether it made any difference if we used the original version written for the sponsor or the version preferred by the critic.

In the first case, the sponsor wished to precede a question with a sentence that the critic felt would distract people from the main moral issue. I didn't personally regard either the question itself or the disagreement over it as very important and was glad to find that the experimental administration showed no difference in distribution (or in any other way) between the two versions. However, the second question under dispute was much more crucial to the purpose of the questionnaire. It is also important because it shows how two sides can phrase a question differently—not because of minor variations in wording, but because of fundamental disagreements about the central issue under debate. The question was the first to deal directly with the release of unclaimed animals to laboratories, and the sponsor wanted the question to indicate that the animals to be released would otherwise be killed by the pound because they had not been claimed as pets—similar to the argument that stem cell research is often done on embryos left over from in vitro fertilization and due to be discarded. The critic, however, rejected this assumption entirely. Her position was that such arrangements between laboratories and public pounds tend to reduce the motivation by pounds to curb the unwanted animal population in nonlethal ways, mainly through encouraging adoption. I was persuaded that each side was sincere, that each argument was at least somewhat plausible, and that it was worth asking the question with and without the disputed assumption to see what effect it had. After all, if the distinction made no difference to the general population, it lost relevance as far as the survey results went.

As it turned out, omitting the statement preferred by the medical sponsor did lower significantly ($p < .05$) the support for release of pound animals to laboratories, but the actual percentage drop was small—from 61 percent down to 54 percent—and did not change the fact that a majority of our sample of Michigan adults appeared to support such release with or without the statement. In addition, the experimental variations produced unexpected order effects later in the questionnaire, which also reduced noticeably, though not greatly, the evidence for public support of laboratory use of pound animals. The final report for the sponsor, which was also given in draft form to the critic for comment, drew two conclusions from the split-ballot experiments (Camburn and Schuman 1985). The first was that the changes in wording we actually performed had some effect, but only a small one, on the results. Readers were alerted to the fact that percentages can change for reasons other than sampling error, but also that in the instances studied experimentally the changes did not alter broad conclusions. The sponsor was reasonably satisfied with this summary. At the same time, we noted that the question variations we used had some effect and that they were not necessarily the most powerful that might have been tried. Other nonexperimental results from the survey suggested that the main way to appeal to the majority of the population on this issue would be to emphasize that dogs and cats in medical experiments not only die but do so often with considerable suffering. Whether that would be a valid claim was not for me as the survey investigator to determine, any more than my deciding between the moral positions on the issues involved in the experiments that we actually carried out. But had the key questions included such an assumption, my guess is that the marginals—the referendum results—would have been altered much more substantially. Thus the critic may have learned something relevant to her position as well.

We can draw several broader conclusions from this unusual experience. For one thing, I believe that both the critic and the sponsor felt that our survey organization had gone to considerable lengths to avoid bias in the questions. It was also clear from their comments that both parties came away with greater respect for the need for careful questionnaire design. I in turn realized that by hearing two sides of the issue, I had gained substantive understanding that was valuable in the question construction process.

One need not assume that this approach would be easy to carry out in other settings or with other sponsors or critics. But it does seem worth considering as a possibility when issues are highly controversial, for it can help protect survey research from two of the false beliefs that most bedevil it. One belief can be labeled "survey fundamentalism": the naive acceptance of the numbers in a survey report as a literal picture of public opinion, with or without the now conventional footnote about "margin of error." The other and equally naive belief—let us label it "survey cynicism"—is that poll results are worthless because investigators can readily produce whatever numbers they wish by means of clever question wording or statistical mumbo jumbo. We need in every report, academic or commercial, to counter these two widespread views—sometimes put forth, one might note, by the same person at different times depending upon how results come out. The most effective way to steer between Scylla and Charybdis in these cases is by repeated demonstrations of scientific discipline from which both the public and the survey investigator can learn.

A Kafkaesque Charge of Bias in Survey Questioning

What I described earlier as the fundamental paradox of survey research—the referendum point of view versus the analytic point of view—lies deep within each of us, as well as between the public and the survey investigator. We all wish at times to know how "the public" as a whole feels about a breaking issue—whether the initial invasion of Iraq or the federal government's response to a natural disaster such as a hurricane. Therefore, we need both to remind ourselves and the public of the limitations of single-variable results, and at the same time to consider carefully instances where bias in question formulation or the presentation of results is claimed. The following case study illustrates the strong and weak points of an accusation of bias regarding one important survey.

Most experienced survey researchers may at some point have received a letter from a disgruntled respondent complaining about a particular question as unfair or intrusive. But such objections, though perhaps frequent enough to interviewers, do not often reach the ears of investigators, and therefore are easily ignored. Suppose, however, that such a complaint became the basis for a narrative by a contemporary Kafka. There might then be not a single letter, but a torrent of letters and calls; not from an elderly man in Peoria with time on his hands, but from an eminent mathematician at Yale and his colleagues around the country; not just aimed at the investigator, but at the foundations that support him and the magazines and journals that publish his writings. The narrative might end (but perhaps only temporarily?) with the whole file of communications being published, the investigators' casual responses included, in the form of a huge book. Indeed, since there is no logical ending to the narrative, even reviews of the book risk becoming part of some future compilation, adding further to the unwanted controversy and publicity.

Just such a Kafkaesque nightmare was visited some years ago on two well-known social scientists, Everett Ladd and Seymour Lipset, although the degree to which they were innocent victims was exactly what was at issue. Their tormentor was Professor Serge Lang, to whom (along with some 8,700 other college faculty members) they sent a lengthy questionnaire as part of the sample for "The 1977 Survey of the American Professorate." Lang did not like the questionnaire, and when, on not responding, he received a standard reminder, he initiated a spate of letters, articles, and other documents that he filed, and then published in a 700-page volume aptly titled *The File* (Lang 1981). His goal, as stated in a "dear reader" preface, was to make "people think independently and clearly"—as, for example, when they might otherwise unthinkingly respond to such a questionnaire.[9] Those who simply glance at *The File*, especially those who are themselves survey or polling researchers, may be inclined to set aside the volume as a tempest in a teapot. Within the potpourri of letters and articles, however, important questions are raised about common polling practices, though these are less often stated directly by Lang than by others with calmer heads who came to his support. Most of those who are concerned with surveys and polls are vulnerable on at least some of these issues (the present writer no doubt at some point on all of them), and it can be healthy to be exposed to criticisms from aroused respondents and other nonsurvey observers.

A number of specific problems can be identified in connection with the Ladd-Lipset survey, some easily noted and others raising much more challenging issues.[10] First, on a minor scale, the explanation that the survey offered to respondents in requesting their cooperation was somewhat misleading. It claimed to be gathering information primarily "useful to the formation of sound education policy," but a fair number of the questions, especially sections on political, social, and moral issues, were neither manifestly nor in true purpose related to that goal. Instead, they were included because of Ladd and Lipset's interest in studying the ideological views of American academics. There is nothing wrong with the latter aim, which indeed leads to much interesting data and interpretation, but evidently no mention of it was made to respondents. Not that decisions about how much to explain ahead of time regarding the goals of a particular survey are always simple: sometimes it is impossible to be wholly candid, as in the case of split-sample experiments; or impractical, as in complex omnibus surveys; or presumed undesirable because it may result in the loss of potential respondents and thus produce sampling bias, as in the common reluctance in polls to mention that questions on income will be asked. But clearly, substantial deception should be avoided except where necessitated by important scientific goals and not likely to be especially vexing to respondents if revealed. (It is also interesting to note that experimental studies suggest that greater candor in the initial description of survey content may not reduce response rates as is usually feared [Singer 1978; Singer and Frankel 1982]).

Second, the Ladd-Lipset data were not used in ways that respondents would necessarily like. Neal Koblitz, then a mathematician at Harvard and perhaps the keenest critic of the Ladd-Lipset survey, notes that when race and religion are tied to ideological responses, the results could lead to characterizations inimical to some respondents, for example, by stereotyping Jews in ways likely to make timid college administrators hesitate to hire them. Of course, this criticism is true of any study that relates attitudes to personal characteristics of respondents, even if done qualitatively, and thus provides a possible argument against almost any social science analysis—an argument that we ordinarily need to resist if we are to do serious research. But resistance will be both easier and more justifiable if we minimize actions that engender distrust, such as asking a host of sensitive questions that are not really relevant to one's stated purpose. The letter that best makes this point was by Laurence Veysey, a historian, to the *New York Review of Books* (September 24, 1978, reprinted on p. 228 of *The File*). Veysey vigorously defends the desirability of obtaining a wide range of data on the attitudes and values of academics, but objects to the investigators' lack of forthrightness in explaining their aims, as well as to the way their questions were phrased. It is also worthwhile to advise respondents initially that they should feel free to omit particular questions if they wish—an instruction fairly common nowadays, but not included regularly in surveys in earlier times.

Third, there was at least one clear instance where the particular ideological view of the world held by Ladd and Lipset does seem to have biased the phrasing of a question. As Koblitz points out, an inquiry about whether the United States should send military aid "if Rhodesia were subject to a massive invasion from the surrounding states," which occurs in the context of other questions about friendly countries being invaded by foreign enemies (e.g., Yugoslavia by the Soviet Union), failed to allow for the possibility that some black Rhodesians at that point in time might have regarded the "invasion" as a liberation or, indeed, that some respondents might have wished the United States to give aid to the outside forces. Moreover, beyond instances of clear bias, the Ladd-Lipset questions are often stated in an unnecessarily contentious way. Many are in the form of rather arbitrarily worded agree/disagree generalizations (e.g., "Too many people ill-suited to academic life are now enrolling in colleges and universities"), which may seem extreme or loaded to some respondents quite apart from their agreement or disagreement with the idea presumed to be behind the statement. Moreover, options for "don't know," "no opinion," or "middle alternatives" were not usually provided, although gradations along scales (e.g., "agree with reservations") were offered. There are sometimes analytical justifications for omitting mid-scale and nonscale options, but we may need to keep more clearly in mind the impact of this decision on respondents. Likewise, more balanced and neutrally phrased interrogative items are likely to seem fairer to respondents than catchy agree/disagree statements, and it is difficult to see why such an approach would have hampered the Ladd-Lipset research goals.

It is useful at this point to consider more fully what is meant by "bias" in question wording. There are different, though related, ways in which a question can be biased. The most obvious is that an attitude question that divides respondents in pro/con terms can include wording that clearly suggests the desirability of one of the directions. For example, a "survey" I once received from the conservative organization called "The Moral Majority" included the question: "Do you believe that smut peddlers should be protected by the courts and the Congress, so they can openly sell pornographic materials to your children?" The question writer in this case was clearly trying to influence the choice of answers.

Another form of bias is one that occurs to some degree in almost all questions and involves imposing a frame of reference, not necessarily valenced, that is not accepted by members of the population being questioned. The pervasiveness of this second type of bias is suggested by our recognition today that questions that are not intended to be gender specific but that refer only to "he" may not be as neutral as they once appeared, especially to male writers. The Ladd-Lipset questions often seemed to invite both kinds of bias by the use of phrasing that was one-sided or double-barreled, or that oversimplified a complex issue more than necessary for their well-educated academic sample. Why ask respondents whether they agree or disagree with the statement: "The peer review system of evaluating proposals for research grants is, by and large, unfair; it greatly favors members of the 'old boy network' "? Why not ask respondents, instead, whether they think the peer review system is fair or unfair, and then ask separate questions (if needed) about such features as peers knowing one another well, about alternative methods of evaluation, and so forth?

At the same time, we should recognize that not all forms of bias due to different tones of wording can be completely eliminated. For example, Britain and Argentina went to war in the 1980s over claims to ownership of islands to which they had given different names: the Falklands (Britain) or the Malvinas (Argentina). It would have been virtually impossible to ask exactly the same survey question in both Britain and Argentina, because the very names of the islands symbolized the conflict over ownership.

Finally, the initial replies by Lipset to his critics were at best strained. To Koblitz's thoughtful letter cited above, Lipset wrote that "I regret that I did not find your criticisms of sufficient technical relevancy to reply in detail." Lipset went on to refer to an "enormous literature" on "the art of asking why" and offered to provide "a detailed methodological bibliography." But there really is no "technical literature" that adequately addresses the inquiries by Koblitz and others, and what little literature there is on question construction is indeed at points violated by the investigators themselves. For example, there has long been a substantial body of thought opposed to use of agree/disagree question formats (Krosnick, Judd, and Wittenbrink 2005). In later correspondence and in an essay written especially for *The File*, Lipset and Ladd provided much more thoughtful answers, but during the first year or so of the controversy they attempted to handle complaints with a broad assertion of technical expertise in question wording that I do not think exists anywhere.

The Ambiguity of "Ambiguity"

We now come to a larger issue that has no simple solution: Lang's disdain for any ambiguity in a question. Although it is usually desirable to reduce ambiguity in attitude items, Ladd and Lipset are certainly right in their repeated emphasis on the impossibility of eliminating it completely. Moreover, the notion of ambiguity is itself far from unambiguous when considering survey questions. University of Chicago mathematician Saunders MacLane carefully notes the questions in the 1977 survey that he regards as ambiguous because they might be answered one way by members of one discipline but another way by members of another discipline—for example, whether choice of one's research problem is influenced by one's personal values. To the serious survey analyst, however, this kind of "ambiguity" is not an obstacle but an opportunity, for it constitutes part of the variation that is useful to explore. In this case, associations between answers and academic disciplines are the goal, not univariate results. But it is just this difference in orientation between investigators and respondents—an analytic rather than a referendum perspective—that makes communication to the public difficult, and it often leads investigators to focus on reports of single-item results in popular publications. Yet emphasis on separate items as an end in themselves, without serious qualification about their uncertain meaning, muddies just the distinction that needs to be transmitted to readers.[11]

George Bishop (2005, p. 15), a sophisticated survey researcher, also treats ambiguity of questions as a violation of "a cardinal assumption in survey measurement: that the question should mean the *same thing* to all respondents," arguing further that if this assumption cannot be made, then valid comparisons across respondents become extremely difficult, if not impossible. He uses as one example a question about approval or disapproval of George W. Bush's "handling of his job as president," regarding such an item as defective because some respondents may answer in terms of an international crisis and others in terms of economic matters. However, it seems to me that this critique confounds ambiguity with the different types of questions we may wish to ask. Two respondents may both have an unfavorable attitude toward the president, but for quite different reasons. The finding of dislike can be quite clear and useful to know, as are the different reasons for the dislike, but the one does not mean that the other is somehow wrong.

Indeed, even if both respondents say they dislike the president because of his foreign policy, it may turn out on closer examination that they had quite different things in mind, one thinking entirely about Iraq and the other entirely about Israelis and Palestinians. Moreover, even if they agreed completely on the Iraq war as the central issue, they might still be in serious disagreement, with one opposing the war entirely and the other strongly supporting its inception but not its execution. There probably is no end to the specification that is possible, but no matter how far we go, "like" and "dislike" remain reasonable constructs to measure, as are also the beliefs we might assess to understand better the different bases of such pro/con attitudes and their likely future course (see also Fishbein [1967] on the difference between beliefs and attitudes).

From a Fundamental Paradox to a Fundamental Dilemma

The final issue to consider in this chapter brings us full circle to the limitations of the referendum approach to polls and surveys, yet also qualifies those limitations by reminding us of their original and still important function. Perhaps the earliest and most striking contribution of polls has been to free us from our own limited, at times almost solipsistic, perceptions of the beliefs and attitudes of the general public. We tend to talk with and listen to people much more like ourselves—friends, relatives, neighbors, local media—than to people who represent a random sample of the total population. Partly for this reason and perhaps partly because of a kind of egocentric bias that inclines us to assume that our own views are so sensible that they must be shared by other reasonable people, there is a strong tendency to overestimate the degree to which the opinions of others are similar to our own (Fields and Schuman 1976–77; Ross, Greene, and House 1977).[12] Polls and surveys provide results that run counter to this propensity, offering a broader view of opinions that reflect other regions of the country, other social classes, and other racial, ethnic, and religious groups.

Thus polls and surveys that are well done in terms of sampling a general population contribute to creating a more cosmopolitan citizenry, and reports of single-variable results can therefore serve a positive social function. Yet at the same time, there is a lack of public sophistication regarding the extent to which survey results are shaped by how questions are framed and worded, how much or little they are answered carefully and knowledgeably, and how greatly they may be restricted to a particular point in time. Furthermore, as Alexander (2006, pp. 86–87) writes, "polls not only reveal but construct the public's shifting attitudes toward the continuous, fragmented, and difficult-to-interpret flow of ongoing social events." They do this by the very action of framing issues and choices.[13]

In sum, in a deeper and more ineluctable sense, the distinction between reports of absolute percentages and more analytic uses of survey data goes to the heart of the conflicting views of survey questions that have run through this chapter. To convey both the value of such results and their limitations is a formidable challenge to those responsible for providing reports to the public. In the end, there is not only a fundamental paradox to survey questioning, but a fundamental dilemma for polls and surveys when they are intended for public enlightenment.

Postscript on Facts versus Attitudes

Although for many questions, the distinction between "factual" and "attitudinal" is clear and convenient to make, it is by no means airtight and we should probably think in terms of a continuum. Some questions that are ordinarily treated as "factual" have a substantial attitudinal component. An individual born in the United States of an African father and a white mother, as in the case of Barack Obama, is usually considered "black" by others and perhaps by himself, but this categorization is more the result of attitudes than of "fact" and may well change as attitudes shift over time. Indeed, although surveys often expect interviewers to classify respondents by "race," there can be disagreement among interviewers, as well as disagreement between interviewers and their respondents. Today even one's sex, once treated as simple and categorical, has turned out to be anything but that in some lives.

An example of a similar ambiguity that involved actual behavior comes from a lengthy investigation of whether the amount of "studying" done by college students is related to the grades those students obtain (Schuman et al. 1985). At first thought, "studying" appears to be a rather straightforward behavior, but it is so mixed up with consideration of "attention" and "concentration" that it proved impossible to operationalize other than through self-report, and that approach seemed far from trustworthy. The problem of self-report was not just a matter of tendencies to exaggerate or downplay studying but uncertainty about what even the students themselves believed to be time they spent studying. At one point we decided to observe studying in the college library, but gave up after finding it impossible to determine whether a person staring off into space (or even at a book) was thinking about the academic matter at hand or daydreaming about a past or future social relationship or something else. On the other hand, some people do their most creative thinking when taking a shower, though they may not code that time as "studying." In the end, we could not be sure that our failure to find a relation between hours studied and grade-point average was not due to the profound uncertainty of the several measures of "studying" that we obtained.

Furthermore, although attitudes are sometimes thought of as more fragile to measure than facts, certain attitudes, such those toward each of two presidential candidates in the days just prior to an election, may be much less ambiguous than some "hard facts."

— 2 —

The Primordial Distinction
between Open and Closed
Attitude Questions

The most basic decision in designing or choosing an important survey question is whether it should be open or closed. Because open questions ask people to answer in their own words (and with their own thoughts), the answers appear to have substantial "face validity"—to "open a window into the mind of America," as a leading survey researcher once wrote (Stouffer 1955, p. 25). Closed questions have the quite different merit of focusing attention on specific responses chosen by an investigator (Converse and Presser 1986), as well as providing the practical advantages of greater speed and lower costs. For the practical reasons especially, closed rather than open question predominate in most surveys.[1]

The comparative advantages of the two forms of questioning were controversial in the earliest days of polling, as indicated in Jean Converse's (1987) account of an important debate between two government research units during World War II. Ironically, the leading proponent of open questions, Rensis Likert, had earlier developed what eventually became the most widely used of all formats for closed questions: sets of agree/disagree items.[2] But as head of the Office of War Information (OWI) Surveys Division, Likert used what he called the "fixed question/free answer" method: he had his interviewers record responses verbatim and probe nondirectively for clarification, and he then drew on the answers both as detailed examples and in the form of codes or categories of responses. His main opponent, Elmo Wilson, head of the OWI Polls Division, relied instead on simple closed questions, which enabled him to obtain larger samples at lower costs and to produce summary results much more quickly.

The evidence bearing on the differences and differential validity of open- and closed-question forms has been quite limited, unlike other methodological aspects of the question-answer process. For example, "response order effects" (variations in the order in which alternatives are presented to respondents) have been the subject of a large number of randomized survey-based experiments by numerous investigators, probably in part because such experiments are straightforward to construct with computer-assisted interviewing and in part because the results can be treated formally and related to other experimentally studied phenomena such as primacy and recency effects.[3] However, when it comes to decisions about whether to use open or closed questioning, the advice tends to be commonsensical (e.g., coding open questions is expensive and time-consuming) and seldom very different from the arguments offered in the early 1940s by followers of Likert and Wilson. The paucity of evidence is due to the fact that such experiments are complex to carry out and analyze, and in addition the results are laden with content difficult to divorce from the form of the questions.

Yet we do have accumulating experimental evidence, and these previously reported experimental results, plus new data and additional analysis, are brought together in this chapter.[4] My review of the evidence leads to recommendations about validity that are sufficiently clear either to accept tentatively or to challenge. Validity in this context refers to answers that reflect the attitudes of respondents in relation to an investigator's goal in posing a question. This conceptualization puts initial emphasis on comparisons of open and closed univariate results, but I will also take account of analytic relationships where practical and especially relevant to the purposes of a question. In addition, I limit consideration to survey questions that might be asked in *either* an open or a closed form, but discuss in the next chapter a different use of open-ended inquiries that is of considerable value.

The Failings of Both Closed and Open Questions

We should begin with the recognition that both closed and open survey questions have serious limitations and that our goal is to take advantage of the fact that their limitations differ, allowing each form to compensate to some extent for the weaknesses of the other.

How Closed Questions Can Fail Ignominiously

Closed questions constrain responses to those offered as part of the question, and there is strong evidence that the constraint occurs even when investigators wish to allow spontaneous answers to modify a closed set of alternatives. In October 1986 we asked a random half of a national sample in entirely open form to name "the most important problem facing this country today"— known as the MIP question. We asked the other half of the sample a specially constructed closed version of the question that deliberately listed four problems (energy shortage, quality of public schools, legalized abortion, pollution), each of which had been given by less than one percent of the American population in answer to a similar open question by the Gallup organization. Respondents in this half of the sample were not forced to choose one of the rare alternatives, for interviewers told them as part of the question that "if you prefer, you may name a different problem as most important." The results of comparing the closed and open forms of the question are shown in Table 2.1.[5]

The categories most frequently coded for the entirely open Most Important Problem question were unemployment (17 percent), general economic

Table 2.1 Constraint by a closed question

Open question: "What do you think is the most important problem facing this country today?"

Closed question: "Which of the following do you think is the most important problem facing this country today—the energy shortage, the quality of public schools, legalized abortion, or pollution?—or if you prefer, you may name a different problem as most important."

Response category	Open question	Closed question
The energy shortage	0%	6%
The quality of public schools	1	32
Legalized abortion	0	8
Pollution	1	14
All other responses	93	39
Don't know	5	0
Total	100	100
(n)	(171)	(178)

Source: University of Michigan Survey of Consumer Attitudes, October 1986.

Note: All SCA data are obtainable from the Interuniversity Consortium for Political and Social Research (ICPSR).

problems (17 percent), threat of nuclear war (12 percent), and foreign affairs (10 percent), with the remainder of the responses scattered among a dozen codes. Less than 3 percent spontaneously mentioned any of the four "rare" problems. On the closed form of the question, however, nearly 60 percent of the sample chose one of the four rare alternatives as most important, with only 39 percent taking advantage of the option to name some other problem. Moreover, unemployment, which was given by 17 percent of the respondents to the fully open MIP question, was volunteered by only 6 percent of the respondents on the closed form, though quite likely many who selected one of the closed alternatives would have chosen unemployment had it been offered.

On the basis of the closed question, a casual reader might well have concluded that the quality of public schools troubled Americans a great deal (32 percent of the sample selected it), followed by the issues of pollution (14 percent), legalized abortion (8 percent), and the energy shortage (6 percent), whereas on the open question the issues of education, pollution, abortion, and energy shortage were virtually unmentioned. (We cannot compare correlates of the latter four issues on the two question forms because there are too few cases in those categories on the open form to allow comparison.) Most observers, myself included, will assume that the issues given in response to the open MIP question provide a better picture of aggregate American concerns at that point in time and that the findings on the closed question were seriously distorted by the presentation of four preselected problems as part of the question, despite the encouragement to respondents to depart from them if they wished. Only if we are interested in the relative ranking of education, pollution, legalized abortion, and the energy shortage does the closed question have value for telling us about issues that concerned Americans during that period. Moreover, this result is not a matter of a "statistically significant" but substantively small effect, but a major impact due to the form of the question. The compelling message from the experiment is that there is no way to escape the frame of reference created by a closed question, because respondents stick closely to the alternatives provided in a question, even when they are invited to volunteer a different choice of their own.[6]

How Open Questions Can Fail to Be Truly Open

The term "open question" implies freedom on the part of respondents to express whatever they wish, but the framing of an open question also influences importantly the answers people give. There are two distinct issues. First, some quite legitimate responses tend to be precluded because they do not come to mind for respondents as within the frame of reference of the question. Second, there are uncontrolled media and other influences that bring some possible responses more readily to mind than others. There is clear experimental evidence on the first issue, and more indirect but persuasive evidence and theory on the second.

An experimental finding of open question preclusion occurred when the standard open question about "the most important problem facing this country at present" was compared with a closed version of the question that presented eight specific issues, such as crime and violence, unemployment, and inflation (Schuman and Presser [1981] 1996, pp. 83–85). Most of the issues did not show large percentage differences, but "crime and violence" yielded many more responses when offered explicitly on the closed form than when coded from free answers on the open form: 35 percent versus 16 percent ($\chi^2 = 44.73$, df$= 1$, p$< .001$ for "crime" vs. other issues combined). Since crime is usually seen as more a local than a national problem, while the other alternatives are viewed as clearly national, the most plausible interpretation of the result is that the closed question informs respondents that "crime" can be a legitimate answer to the question, whereas the open format leads people to think of unambiguously "national" issues. Quite likely the limitation in this and similar cases is not conscious but occurs because only responses suggested by the wording of the open question come readily to mind.

The previous example involved a plausible interpretation of an unexpected finding, always an uncertain step, but my second example of preclusion by an open question was predicted in advance on the basis of a study of social memories. In an earlier survey, I had asked a cross-section sample of Americans in 1985 to name one or two of the most important "national or world events or changes from the past 50 years" (Schuman and Scott 1987). To this open question, the most frequently given responses had to do with World War II (29 percent) and the Vietnam War (22 percent), and other answers referred to social changes such as the civil rights movement (8.5 percent) or scientific/technological developments like space exploration (13 percent). Much less frequent were responses referring to the invention of the computer (4 percent), which would not have seemed surprising except that concern about computers had often appeared elsewhere in the survey, for example, in response to questions about what children need to learn "to get ahead in life." This discrepancy suggested that computers had made a considerable impact on the public, but that the "national or world events or changes" open question may have missed that importance. The open question probably focuses thoughts on the broad political domain, and even where that is not the case, as with space exploration responses, dramatic events such as the 1969 moon landing may have been necessary to stimulate responses. Thus we hypothesized that the open-question wording precluded mentions of the invention of the computer.

The hypothesis was tested a year later in 1986 by repeating the open question to a random half of a national sample and asking a closed form of the question to the other half. The closed form included the four most frequently given open answers (World War II, the Vietnam War, the assassination of John F. Kennedy, and the exploration of space), plus "the invention of the computer."[7] The data shown in Table 2.2 offer strong support for the hypothesis. On the open question, the invention of the computer is the least frequently

Table 2.2 Constraint by an open question

Open question: "There have been a lot of national and world events and changes over the past 50 years—say, from 1930 right up until today. Would you mention one or two such events or changes that seem to you to have been especially important?"

Closed question: "There have been a lot of national and world events and changes over the past 50 years—say from about 1930 right up until today. Would you choose from the list I read the event or change that seems to you to have been the most important? Or if you wish you can name an event or change different from the ones I mention. Here is the list: World War II, the exploration of space, the assassination of John F. Kennedy, the invention of the computer, or the Vietnam War."

Response category	Open question	Closed question
World War II	14%	23%
Exploration of space	7	16
Assassination of J. F. Kennedy	5	12
Invention of the computer	1	30
The Vietnam War	10	14
All other responses	52	5
Don't know	11	0
Total	100	100
N	(347)	(354)

Source: University of Michigan Survey of Consumer Attitudes, July and August 1986.

mentioned (just one percent) of the five answers that are the focus, while World War II, Vietnam, the Kennedy assassination, and space exploration continue to be given frequently. However, on the closed question, the development of the computer was chosen by 30 percent of the public—more often than World War II or any of the other responses! It is also noteworthy that the space exploration category does not show a jump from open to closed forms similar to the computer alternative, which indicates that more than a shift of emphasis from political to nonpolitical answers is involved. More likely it was a shift from changes that reach public consciousness through dramatic events (such as the televised moon landing), as against changes that are more gradual and cumulative in influence such as the development of the computer.[8] In sum, unlike the experiment in Table 2.1 where the open question could be seen as more valid than the artificially constructed closed question, the experiments on preclusion by open questions point to greater validity in some cases by closed questions.

Because of the importance of these findings on open question constraint, I repeated the 1986 experiment in 2003, with the time period extended to 75 years to retain 1930 as the beginning year.[9] One change was made because the "September 11 terrorist attack" seemed certain at that point to be given frequently to the open question; hence it was substituted for the "space exploration" alternative in the closed form in order to maximize agreement between the open and closed forms, keeping the number of closed alternatives to five. Both the revised question and the results are shown in Table 2.3, and they replicate well the 1986 finding about computers. There is a large and highly significant increase in the computer response from only 6 percent mentions to the open question to 24 percent choosing it on the closed question. (This single open-to-closed change accounts for three-quarters of the total chi square of 59.5 for the table.)

In addition, however, the "JFK assassination" also shows a smaller but significant increase (from 5 percent to 10 percent), which accounts for most of the remaining total chi square.[10] We should note that for those born around the time of the event itself or later, "remembering" has to do not with autobiographical or episodic memory but with what would have been later learned in school or in other ways (a form of semantic memory), and that the closed question functions almost like a multiple-choice test for such learning. In any case, the Kennedy increase provides some evidence of an open-to-closed increase due to a specific event not remembered unless respondents are reminded of it, as well as of the much larger increase due to

Table 2.3 Replication of open/closed experiment on computers

The next question concerns how people think about the past. There have been a lot of national and world events and changes over the past 75 years—say from about 1930 right up until today.

Open question: "Would you mention the two such events or changes that seem to you to have been the most important?"

Closed question: "Would you choose from the list I read the two events or changes that seem to you to have been the most important? Or if you wish you can name events or changes different from the ones I mention."

Response category	Open question	Closed question
World War II	45%	30%
JFK assassination	5	10
9/11 attack	34	29
Invention of the computer	6	24
Vietnam War	9	8
Total	100	100
N	(297)	(597)

Source: Time-sharing Experiments for the Social Sciences, 2003. Originals are at http://www.experimentcentral.org/data/data.php?pid=94.

Notes: First mentions only. (The table is limited to categories available as closed choices, and this accounts for the smaller total N for the open question to which other answers were also given.)

The partitions tested are the following:

Total Likelihood Ratio χ^2 for the 5 by 2 table: 59.5, df = 4, p < .001;
Computer vs. other 4 responses combined: $\chi^2 = 45.4$, df = 1, p < .001;
JFK assassination vs. remaining 3 responses $\chi^2 = 11.5$, df = 1, p < .001;
WWII, 9/11 attack, Vietnam: $\chi^2 = 2.5$, df = 2, p = n.s.

listing a response such as "invention of the computer" that was precluded from the frame of reference implicitly defined by the open question.[11]

The "Availability" of Responses to Open Questions

We have seen that open questions can preclude legitimate answers that are chosen on parallel closed questions. Can we assume, however, that those responses that are mentioned to open questions are high in personal importance to the mentioners? When individuals answer an open question, they must select from what comes to mind—what is "available" to themselves, to adapt Tversky and Kahneman's (1982) terminology. Some writers have assumed that what comes most readily to mind is what is most important to respondents (Scott 1968), as with the images of food sometimes said to overwhelm people who are starved (Levi 1959), or the preoccupations of those who have fallen deeply in love, as portrayed in several of Shakespeare's plays. However, a different interpretation of the availability of responses to open questions is proposed by writers who emphasize the fleeting basis on which answers are usually produced in survey interviews (e.g., Zaller and Feldman 1992; Zaller 1992; Bishop 2005). Unlike individuals in extreme situations involving physical deprivation or mental anguish, most survey respondents are not under great internal pressure to offer a particular response, nor are they forced by the interviewing process to search their minds for deeply significant answers. Thus their spontaneous responses may reflect mostly what they happen to have heard or come upon recently, often something of temporary note because of media attention rather than of great personal significance.[12] This was Tversky and Kahneman's (1982) emphasis.

I found this uncertainty about the meaning of responses to open questions in a reexamination of Samuel Stouffer's classic study, *Communism, Conformity, and Civil Liberties* ([1955] 1992).[13] Stouffer used open questions to address two related issues: "How much personal anxiety or involvement do Americans feel [in the mid-1950s] with respect to the internal Communist threat [and] with respect to the loss of civil liberties?" (p. 87). After asking respondents: "What kinds of things do you worry most about?" which yielded only a trivial number of relevant responses, Stouffer focused on answers to the open question: "Are there other problems you worry or are concerned about, especially political or world problems?" He characterized the answers as providing "invaluable data on the depth and intensity of opinions" (p. 20), which implies availability of responses due to their personal importance. Since there were relatively few responses about either Communists (about 5 percent of all answers) or civil liberties (just 2 percent), Stouffer concluded that "Very few Americans are worried or even deeply concerned about either issue" (p. 87). He then proceeded to work almost entirely with a set of closed items, creating a Perception of the Internal Communist Danger scale, which he used to classify people into categories from great worry to little worry about the danger. Stouffer never brought together the answers to his closed and open questions, but apparently assumed that they were consistent.

Important to the present reanalysis of Stouffer's data is a comparison of his cross-section sample of Americans with his second, purposively constructed, sample of "community leaders" (e.g., mayors, political party chairs, newspaper publishers) from 123 mid-size cities. First, Table 2.4 brings together evidence of concern over Communists in response to open and closed questions by the general public and the community leaders. The comparison points up a paradoxical finding. If one regards mentions of Communists to the open question as a measure of "the depth and intensity" of concern about the Communist threat, then the leaders sample shows much greater concern than the cross-section sample (12 percent vs. 5 percent; $\chi^2=95.8$, df= 1, p<0.001). However, if one uses Stouffer's Perception of the Internal Communist Danger scale (broken into three categories), or simply focuses on responses to the single most-general closed question he employed (bottom panel of Table 2.4), then the cross-section sample shows more concern than the leaders (p<0.001 for both comparisons). For example, a much higher proportion of the cross-section sample emphasized the danger of Communists on the single closed question—21 percent in the cross-tabulation say "very great danger" and an additional 25 percent say "great danger"—than the mere 5 percent who mentioned Communists to the open question.[14] Thus there is no straightforward way to determine which sample was more worried by the Communist threat, nor which type of question, open or closed, was more useful for assessing personal concern about Communists.

However, the difference between the community leaders sample and the cross-section sample in their mentions of Communists to the open question makes more sense if it reflected, at least in part, the leaders' greater awareness of current political issues and not necessarily their greater anxiety. This interpretation gains credence when we discover that amount of education in the cross-section sample is significantly associated with mention of Communists in response to the open question (gamma = .29, p<.01) but is not associated with perception of Communist danger as measured by the general closed question in Table 2.4 (gamma = .02, p = n.s.). If education were related mainly to personal anxiety and concern over Communists, this should show up in responses to the closed questions as well—indeed, perhaps more so because the multi-item scale built from closed questions should benefit from having higher reliability than responses to a single open question.

Additional evidence that responses to the open question do not always reflect personal anxiety appears when we look at the relation between mentioning Communists in response to the open question and mentioning civil

Table 2.4 Responses to Stouffer's open and closed questions on
Communist threat

	Cross-section sample	Leaders sample
Responses to open question:		
Communist threat mentioned		
as a worry or concern	5%	12%
N	(4,933)	(1,500)
Perception of internal		
Communist threat scale:		
Relatively great danger	30%	27%
In between	51	44
Relatively little danger	19	29
Total	100	100
N	(4,933)	(1,500)
Single closed question:		
"How great a danger do you feel		
American Communists are to		
this country at the present time?"		
A very great danger	21%	15%
A great danger	25	22
Some danger	41	45
Hardly any danger	10	15
No danger	3	2
Total	100	100
N	(4,546)	(1,489)

Source: Stouffer's original 1954 data, obtained from the Roper Center.

Note: Table 2.4 is composed of three parts:

First is the open question already mentioned, which reads: "Are there other problems
you worry or are concerned about, especially political or world problems?"

Second, the Perception of Internal Communist Danger scale is based on a set of closed
questions that were combined by Stouffer using a modified Guttman procedure (see
Stouffer 1955, Appendix C, for detailed questions and construction). Percentages
have been recalculated after omitting Don't Know responses (387 in the cross-
section sample and 11 in the leaders sample).

Third, one of the questions from the Perception of the Internal Communist Danger
scale is also used separately by Stouffer and is shown here as the third part of Table
2.4 because it is simpler than the full scale and has considerable face validity taken
alone.

liberties in response to the same open question. Stouffer treated these responses as diametrically opposed, but in the cross-section sample the association between mentions of Communists and mentions of civil liberties tends to be positive, reaching borderline significance (gamma=.28, Fisher's Exact Test: p=.09). For the leaders, the association is negative, but only slightly so (gamma=−.17, Fisher's Exact Test=n.s.). Thus a coding of Communists on the open question does not necessarily indicate simple anxiety about Communists, but it can be combined for some respondents with a concern about civil liberties.

Finally, we consider the association that was most important to Stouffer's investigation: the relation between concern about Communists and his separately created scale of Willingness to Tolerate Nonconformists (e.g., Communists, atheists, socialists) more generally. In the cross-section sample, the association (gamma) between the two scales based on closed questions (the Perception of Communist Danger scale and the Tolerance of Nonconformists scale) is gamma=−.15 (p<0.001), indicating that those who say they are most worried about Communists are least tolerant of nonconformists— which was one of Stouffer's main conclusions. However, when concern about Communists is measured using responses to the open question, the relation in the cross-section sample to the Tolerance scale is slightly positive (gamma=+.07), though nonsignificant (SE=.05), suggesting there is either no relation or a trend in the opposite direction, with those mentioning Communists being more tolerant of nonconformists.

In sum, there is little support for Stouffer's assumption that mere mentions of Communists to his open question indicated "depth and intensity of opinions" about Communists, nor are such mentions a straightforward indicator of the proportions of Americans showing such concern. More likely they reflect a mixture of responses showing personal concern *and* a simple awareness (availability) of what was an important issue in terms of media attention.[15] But when the question of a Communist danger is posed directly in a closed form, nearly half of Stouffer's cross-section sample and more than a third of his leaders sample claimed that the danger was substantial. We do not have good reason to doubt these figures as approximate indicators of direct concern about Communists as an internal danger.

Moreover, further elucidation of the meaning of responses to open questions appears when we turn from mentions of Communists to the many fewer mentions of civil liberties in Stouffer's survey—just 2 percent. There is evidence that such open responses reflect personal concern about civil liberties better than mentions of Communists reflect personal concern about Communists. First, mentions of civil liberties to the open question and answers to the closed questions that form the Tolerance for Nonconformists scale both show the leaders sample to be more tolerant than the cross-section sample. Second, mention of civil liberties in response to the open question and Tolerance for Nonconformists scores are more highly associated with each other (gamma = .46 in the cross-section sample and .47 in the leaders sample) than are the mention of Communists and the Perception of the Internal Communist Danger scale (only .18 and .37 in the two samples). Third, mention of civil liberties and the Tolerance for Nonconformists scale are both related to the Perception of Internal Communist Danger scale in the same direction and to almost the same degree: gamma = −.16 and −.15, respectively, in the cross-section sample; gamma = −.26 and −.29 in the leaders sample. Finally, mention of civil liberties and the Tolerance for Nonconformists scale are positively and significantly (p < .01) related to education in both the cross-section and the leaders samples. Thus, despite (or because of) the small percentage of people who mention civil liberties in response to the open question, our results suggest that such mentions indicate genuine concern over civil liberties more than mentions of Communists indicate genuine concern over Communists. Open and closed measures of attitudes toward civil liberties give consistent and meaningful results.

This reanalysis points to an important general proposition about answers to open questions, based on the finding that the relatively infrequent open responses about civil liberties appear to be a more valid indicator of personal concern than the more frequent open responses about Communists. Rare responses, such as mentions of a need to return to the gold standard or the desirability of preserving vernal pools or other seldom mentioned issues, which are usually relegated to the "Other" category in open coding, probably do reflect intense personal involvement, because their availability to the minds of respondents cannot be due to emphasis by the popular media. The same may also be true even of issues such as legalized abortion or gun control that are better known yet are still volunteered as important by only small minorities within the national population. In sum, the smaller the number of people who give a particular response to an open question about their concerns, the more likely that such a response reflects genuine personal involvement rather than simple awareness of what is in the news. By the same token, issues mentioned in response to an open question by a high proportion of the population—for example, inflation or unemployment today—

are likely to reflect heavy media treatment and thus to be less indicative of purely personal concern for many of the mentioners than Stouffer believed.

Blaming Survey Questions for Unwanted Results

We have seen that the limitations of both open and closed questions sometimes lead to invalid results, but this does not mean that every disappointing result is due to a defective question. To what extent can the kinds of problems with open and closed questions we have considered help explain substantive findings that do not meet expectations? We will consider two important cases where investigators were tempted to blame unanticipated outcomes on the form of questioning, but where careful analysis shows their criticism to be unjustified: one case where the limitations of an open question seemed at fault, the other where the same appeared true of a closed question.

Did Open Questions Fail to Identify Public Concern about a Nuclear Threat?

The United States and the Soviet Union (USSR) had a huge number of nuclear missiles aimed at each other for many years, with the awful potential for mutual destruction. This greatly troubled knowledgeable scientists such as Freeman Dyson (1984), as it still does today when a possible nuclear attack by terrorists is contemplated. Yet if we are to judge by surveys that allowed the spontaneous mention of nuclear war relative to other public issues, concern about a devastating nuclear attack was seldom important in the minds of most Americans. Surveys conducted during 1980 and 1981 by the University of Michigan's Survey Research Center (Miller et al. 1981) and by the Gallup organization (Gallup 1982) found fewer than 10 percent of the adult population mentioning the threat of war of any kind when asked variants of the open Most Important Problem (MIP) question: "What do you think is the *most* important problem facing this country today?" It seemed possible, however, that the standard MIP question stimulated answers reflecting what was immediately available to respondents, largely as a result of current media attention, rather than eliciting judgments about issues of more fundamental importance. If so, then adding "nuclear war" as a choice to a closed set of alternatives should produce a significant open-to-closed increment, just as was the case with "the invention of the computer" discussed earlier in connection with Tables 2.2 and 2.3.

Together with two graduate students, I was able to test this hypothesis by using experimental comparisons of open and closed questions at five time points over a 21-month period in 1982 and 1983.[16] After starting a priori with "the threat of nuclear war," only three other problems were mentioned often enough in Gallup Polls at that point (February 1982) to require inclusion as closed alternatives: the high cost of living, unemployment, and budget cuts. I will use the term "common categories" to refer to the four alternatives, which were presented as choices on the closed form and also served as code categories for the open form. Other noncommon categories were developed as needed to accommodate responses that did not fit the four common categories, as shown in Table 2.5.[17]

Each of the four common categories shows an increase in percentage between open and closed forms, as will almost always be the case as one moves from an open question to a closed question that constrains most respondents to a small number of specified categories. In order to focus directly on the nuclear threat alternative, the other three common categories can be collapsed, creating a simple 2 by 2 chi square table for each of the five years: open vs. closed, nuclear threat vs. other common categories). Once this is done, in three of the five surveys there is no significant difference between the open and closed question forms. In one of the two months in which the forms do differ significantly ($p < .05$ in October 1982 and $p < .02$ in December 1983), the ratio of nuclear war responses to the other three collapsed categories is actually higher on the open form than on the closed form (December 1983). These results argue against the hypothesis that a limitation by the open question accounts for infrequent mention of the nuclear war threat on that form.[18]

In addition, looked at in more absolute terms, in none of the first four surveys does the proportion of respondents choosing nuclear war as the most important problem on the closed form ever reach one out of five, whereas unemployment is offered by almost half the respondents in two of those months. To be sure, in the fifth month the percentage choosing nuclear war on the closed form rises to 30 percent, but at that point the parallel open–form common category shows almost as high a percentage. In sum, the data in Table 2.5 clearly disconfirm an explanation of low psychological "availability" for the infrequent mention of nuclear war on the standard MIP question.

We took one further step to make certain that the standard MIP question was not inadvertently missing potential nuclear war responses. Because the

Table 2.5 Nuclear war as the most important problem: Comparisons of open and closed questions across time

Open question: "What do you think is the most important problem facing this country today?"
Closed question: "Which of the following do you think is the most important problem facing this country today—the high cost of living, unemployment, the threat of nuclear war, or government budget cuts?—or if you prefer, you may name a different problem as most important."

Response	April 1982		June 1982		October 1982		July 1983		December 1983	
	Open	Closed	Open	Closed	Open	Closed	Open	Closed	Open	Closed
High cost of living	16%	22%	15%	22%	6%	22%	5%	20%	2%	15%
Unemployment	28	43	28	39	43	46	42	45	22	28
Nuclear war	6	15	3	16	4	12	6	14	24	30
Budget cuts	2	8	3	10	1	3	0	6	1	10
Interest rates	1		3		2					
Government deficit	2		1	1	2	4	1	2	2	4
General economics	9		9	2	11	1	7	1	7	2
Soviet aggression	1				0				1	
National defense	1		2		1		1		2	1
Specific countries	1				0		2		6	
Foreign affairs	3		6	1	4		7	2	6	1
Crime	4	2	4		3	1	1	1	3	
Food, energy shortages	1		1		1		1			
Moral, religious breakdown	5	2	6	3	7	2	8	3	7	1
Distrust of government	3	2	4	2	4	0	2	1	4	
Other gov't defects	4	2	4		2	4	2	1	2	
Other	10	2	5	1	9	3	11	4	8	2
Don't know	3	1	1	1		1	3		3	5
Total	100	100	100	100	100	100	100	100	100	100
N	(186)	(197)	(174)	(189)	(191)	(189)	(207)	(170)	(282)	(261)

Source: University of Michigan Survey of Consumer Attitudes, for the months indicated.

question refers to problems facing "this country today," it is conceivable that respondents were led to think of purely national issues, whereas nuclear war may come to mind mainly within a larger international frame of reference. To check on this possibility, we carried out a further small experiment in November 1985 in which the standard open MIP question was paired with a version identical in every respect except for substituting the phrase "the world" for "this country." With this new phrasing ("What is the most important problem facing the world today?"), respondents concerned about the threat of nuclear war were provided full opportunity—in fact, almost encouraged—to give such an answer. The national sample for the new experiment was small, but the results were unequivocally negative: of the 56 people who received the "country" version, 16 percent mentioned nuclear war; of the 46 people who received the "world" version, 19 percent mentioned nuclear war—a trivial and nonsignificant ($\chi^2 = 0.2$) increase. The new version of the question did produce more world-related responses such as "hunger," and it did not elicit typically domestic economic answers like "unemployment." Yet mentions of "nuclear war" did not increase appreciably as a result of the broader international frame of reference.

If lack of wide concern about the nuclear war threat was not due to the form of survey questioning, what was the explanation? Respondents in the last two surveys who did not choose nuclear war on the closed form were asked why they made a different choice—a follow-up approach that anticipates the emphasis on Why questions to be developed in the next chapter. Putting aside those respondents (some 17 percent) who simply repeated that the problem they chose (unemployment or inflation in most cases) was a very important one, three different explanations were offered. The most frequent (38 percent) was that nuclear war is something to worry about for the distant future, but that unemployment or inflation or budget cuts is an important problem here and now. "I know nuclear war could happen, but it's not an everyday problem," said one person. The second most-frequent explanation (30 percent) was out-and-out denial that a nuclear war is possible: "Nobody is crazy enough to start a nuclear war." Finally, the third type of explanation frequent enough to call for a separate category (15 percent) was that the problem is one the respondent can do nothing about. Only this last explanation is one where nuclear war could be seen as possibly most important to the respondent, despite not being mentioned to either an open or a closed form of the MIP question.[19]

Yet between July 1983 and December 1983, the "threat of nuclear war" category did increase substantially on both question forms: by 17 percent on the open form and by 16 percent on the closed form. A series of real events reported by the media appears to have aroused public concern about nuclear war between July and December of 1983, though it would be difficult to pinpoint the effect of each: news reports about European mass resistance to nuclear missiles; the shooting down of a South Korean airliner by the Soviet Union with the deaths of 269 passengers and crew; a bomb attack that killed 241 marines in Lebanon on October 23; the U.S. invasion of Grenada on October 25; and finally the Soviet break-off of arms control talks in late November and early December. At the same time, diminished concern over unemployment and inflation left much of the public (and of the news media) freer to focus on the threat of war.

To link actual events and respondent perceptions of problems, we examined a detailed listing of the topics covered by the evening national news broadcasts for the three major television networks (ABC, CBS, and NBC) over each of the survey months, using records available from the Vanderbilt Television News Archives. Nuclear war and related issues were mentioned frequently in news reports in the first half of 1982, then dropped to a lower level, only to rise to their highest frequency at the end of 1983. It seems likely that it was the conjunction in late 1983 of the more general reports on Soviet-American tension (e.g., the Korean jetliner) and the increase in specifically nuclear-related reports (break-off of disarmament talks) that accounted for the abrupt rise at the end of that year in mentions of the threat of nuclear war on both open and closed forms.[20]

The analysis of the MIP experimental results over time supports the conclusion that except in a period of great tension, the threat of nuclear war is not seen as "most important" by more than a small percentage of the public. The same is probably true of "global warming," an issue about the distant future from the standpoint of most Americans. In terms of our present focus on the question-answer process, the results serve as a warning against blaming too quickly the form of a poll question—in this case, an open question—when findings are contrary to expectations.[21]

Did a Closed Question Distort the Meaning of the 2004 Presidential Election?

Commentary on the 2004 Bush versus Kerry election focused exquisite attention on a response obtained in the National Election Pool (NEP) Exit

Poll to the closed question: "Which one issue mattered most in deciding how you voted for president?" Immediately after Bush's victory, pundits pounced on the finding that "moral values" registered the highest percentage (22 percent) of choices among the seven alternatives offered to respondents, albeit only slightly ahead of "economy/jobs" (20 percent) and "terrorism" (19 percent). Bush's winning margin in the popular as well as electoral vote was then widely attributed to issues such as abortion, gay marriage, and whatever else "moral values" meant to the general public. Within a short time, however, a number of other commentators sharply criticized the focus on "moral values," in part because they regarded the NEP closed question as badly designed (e.g., "moral values" was said not to qualify as an "issue") and in part because further examination of both the exit poll data and the vote itself did not support the claim that "values" were decisive in Bush's reelection.

Rejection of the "moral values" response as "the" key to the outcome of the election has been supported by much later analysis.[22] However, that leaves unsettled the validity of the response as measuring something real that was one important element in support for George W. Bush, and possibly of continuing import in the future. We can consider the validity of the NEP closed question itself by taking advantage of a valuable post-election experiment carried out by the Pew Research Center that repeated the exact question as part of a split-sample comparison, with the other half asked a parallel open question.[23] I will look at the main criticisms of the closed question, using the open version as another way of approaching the meaning and limitations of the "moral values" closed response for the election. We can draw also on what has been learned from the experiments discussed previously in this chapter.

The full open and closed results from the Pew experiment are presented in the A columns of Table 2.6, with two additional columns (B) that repercentage only the comparable seven substantive categories.[24] If we restrict attention to the seven closed categories (the B columns), "moral values" is the most frequently chosen alternative on the closed question, just as it was in the NEP results, with a lead of 28 percent over the next choices of "Iraq" (23 percent) and "economy/jobs" (22 percent).[25] On the open question, the moral values code drops to 22 percent, well behind "Iraq" at 39 percent, but ahead of the other five alternatives. If all the open codes are included (as in the A open question column), "moral values" is reduced to 14 percent, still second among all the codes provided by Pew.

Thus a substantial proportion of the sample, when asked an open-ended question three to six days after the election to account for its vote, responded by giving answers that Pew considered codable as "moral values." It is useful to learn the content of these responses, which some have described as a "grab bag" (Langer and Cohen 2005). Fortunately, the Pew data set provides the actual text of the answers: 60 percent used the words "moral values," "morals," or close equivalents ("family values"), and most of the rest referred either directly to abortion, gay marriage, or stem cell research (23 percent in total), or in a few cases mentioned a candidates' religiosity (10 percent). Furthermore, we can say more about the large percentage who simply used words such as "moral values" to the open question, for after obtaining responses to the closed question, Pew asked those who chose the "moral values" alternative: "What comes to mind when you think about moral values?" Nearly half (44 percent) mentioned abortion, gay marriage, or stem cell research, while most of the rest referred to religious or traditional values. Quite likely some of the latter, especially among the preponderance who were Bush supporters, would have agreed that issues like abortion and gay marriage are part of "moral values" from their standpoint. In sum, for most respondents, the specific issues just noted and the term "moral values" and a candidate's religious commitments were all closely connected. For an open question that allowed people to say whatever they wished, the answers seem reasonably homogeneous, and "moral values" is what the majority of the respondents prefer as a summary term.

Langer and Cohen (2006) propose that the relatively large number of mentions of "moral values" to the Pew open question was due to "media priming." They report that a Nexis news archive search found 2,173 mentions of "moral values" in the seven days after the election, as compared with just 179 mentions in the week before the election, and suggest that media influence was the reason so many of Pew's post-election respondents gave such an open response. They also note that an open question quite similar in wording to Pew's question was part of a different survey some two weeks before the 2004 election, and this survey reports just 4 percent of those who claimed to be "absolutely certain" to vote coded as mentioning "moral religious values," plus another four percent in a category labeled "abortion issues." The comparison survey gives a total of 8, or perhaps 9 percent—as against Pew's 14 percent.[20] Although the difference is not huge, it may be reliable (p = .03 for moral values vs. all other open mentions combined, though the selective dichotomizing may have capitalized on chance),

Table 2.6 Closed and open responses to moral values questions

Closed question: "Which one issue mattered most to you in deciding how you voted for president?" [READ AND RANDOMIZE FIRST SEVEN ISSUES SHOWN IN TABLE.]

Open question: "What one issue mattered most to you in deciding how you voted for president?" The codes were prepared and the coding done by the Pew Research Center.

Response	A. Full responses		B. Comparable responses only	
	Closed question	Open question	Closed question	Open question
Moral values[a]	27	14	28	22
Iraq	22	25	23	39
Economy/jobs	21	12	22	19
Terrorism	14	9	15	14
Health care	4	2	4	3
Education	4	1	4	2
Taxes	3	1	3	2
Honesty/integrity	—	5	—	—
Like/dislike Bush	—	5	—	—
Like/dislike Kerry	—	3	—	—
Direction of country	—	2	—	—
Leadership	—	2	—	—
Foreign policy	—	2	—	—
Other	4	12	—	—
Don't know	1	5		
Total	100	100	100	100
N[b]	(567)	(558)	(538)	(364)

Source: Pew Research Center survey, November 5–8, 2004.

a. The open code for moral values is composed of three types of responses: the response "moral values"; three social issues (abortion, gay marriage, stem cell research); and "candidate's religiosity/morals."

b. These are the unweighted N's, but the percentages are based on Pew's report, which used a weight. See Pew Web site for details in the report.

and it is certainly possible that some Pew respondents were influenced by media discussion of "moral values." However, the response "moral values" involves the kind of devotion to an issue by a committed minority that seems less vulnerable to media priming, unlike more standard issues such as "inflation" or "unemployment," as discussed earlier (p. 42), and it is impossible to know for sure at this point. If so, presumably it added to the open code category some suggestible respondents atypical of those who would have given the response without priming, and this should show up in analysis using the open and closed versions of the question.

A closely related criticism of the closed question is that the term "moral values" biased choices because it provided a "socially desirable" alternative. However, the terms "values" and "morality" were used a good deal in the 2004 campaign, especially by those supporting the Bush effort, and it seemed appropriate to recognize this use in the questioning. In addition, we found earlier that the assumption that a particular tone of wording would attract respondents due to social desirability was not confirmed in a case where it seemed especially plausible. The point is always important to check where possible, but the criticism of social desirability should not be accepted simply because it is a possibility. In this case, with the exception of "Iraq," all the response percentages increase when going from the open to the closed form of the question in Table 2.6(A), as ordinarily happens when respondents are limited to a fixed set of alternatives, and "economy/jobs" shows almost as large a percentage difference as "moral values."[27]

Next, we consider the "moral values" closed response in light of the constraints previously shown to be created by closed forms of questions. Closed questions can preclude desired choices by not listing them as alternatives, even when the option of volunteering a different answer is encouraged (see Table 2.1). One check on whether all likely choices are included as alternatives in the closed question is to note responses given with some frequency to the comparable open question. The full open question answers on the left side of Table 2.6 do not suggest any missing issues, though "honesty/integrity" at 5 percent is a possible exception that might have been included under "moral values," which would have increased its proportion still more. A second and different type of check is available because the 2004 Los Angeles Times Exit Poll used a closed issues question with 12 alternatives, not just seven as in the NEP and Pew question. Yet none of the added alternatives yielded more than 5 percent of the total (e.g., "Social Security" registered just 5 percent, though in the 2000 election it had been at 21 percent [Keeter 2006]).[28] Putting together both of these ways of identifying additional alternatives that might have attracted respondents, it seems unlikely that the high percentage choosing "moral values" in the 2004 exit poll can be attributed to the absence of some particular response that would have appealed to respondents had it been offered. Unless such an alternative can be suggested as compelling, we can reject the claim that the NEP and Pew closed question results should be dismissed because the high percentage for "moral values" is merely a function of the specific set of issues offered to respondents.

The open form of a question can also preclude responses when the frame of reference of the question fails to bring to mind a possible answer a respondent might give if informed that it is appropriate, as was true for "the invention of the computer" in Table 2.2. That may have happened to some extent with the Pew open question because it emphasized "issues," and one criticism of the NEP closed question by Langer and Cohen (2005) was that "moral values" is not really an "issue." Thus the difference between the 22 percent who expressed a "moral values" response on the open Pew question and the 28 percent who chose "moral values" on the closed Pew question, where it was legitimized as an acceptable alternative, may have been due to question wording that emphasized "issues."[29] In this sense, the higher percentage for the NEP closed question may have provided a better estimate of preferences than the percentage for the open question, because it defined "moral values" as a legitimate response. At a theoretical level, the claim that "moral values" is not an "issue" imposes on ordinary voters a dichotomy that may make sense to political analysts, but is unlikely to be an essential division in the minds of people who move freely between issues and candidate qualities when deciding their vote. Why insist that respondents who give numerous answers to an open question that can be summarized well under the term "moral values" be prevented from hearing such an alternative as part of a comparable closed question?

This brings us to the most important reason that the original NEP closed question was included in the exit poll: as one way of asking voters to explain their preference for Bush or Kerry in the 2004 election. The most striking result from the Pew experiment is that whether one uses the open or the closed "moral values" response, the results are almost identical, and for both forms of the question they are overwhelming. Of those in the Pew Poll who chose "moral values" from among seven alternatives, Bush won 88 percent of the vote, and of those coded as giving "moral values" to the open inquiry, he won 92 percent of the vote. (For the NEP Poll, which of course differed in exact timing, sample, mode of administration, and other ways, the effect was almost as great: 82 percent voted for Bush.) These results provide a lovely example of a "form-resistant correlation": an association where the form of the question made little, if any, difference in its relation to another key variable (Schuman and Presser [1981] 1996, p. 4). Further-

Table 2.7 Relations between moral values response and background variables
(significance levels)

Variable	Closed question	Open question	Interaction with Q form
Male/female	n.s.	n.s	n.s
White/black	.01	.01	n.s.
Hispanic/non-Hispanic	n.s.	n.s.	n.s.
Age (6 categories)	n.s.	n.s.	n.s.
Education (5 categories)	n.s.	n.s.	n.s.
Region (4 categories)	.001	.10	n.s.
Protestant/Catholic	.01	.001	n.s.
Born again/not born again	.001	.001	n.s.
Attend religious services (6 categories)	.001	.001	n.s.

Notes: Responses on both question forms are dichotomized: moral values vs. six other alternatives combined. This variable was cross-classified separately with each social background variable shown in the table, with chi square values calculated where the background variable is dichotomous and tau beta calculated where the background variable is ordinal. Cell entries are resulting significance levels. Relations are shown as not significant when $p > .10$, though in almost all such cases $p > .20$.

Interactions between question form and age, education, and attendance were tested using three linear logistic regressions; no signs of nonlinearity were evident by visual inspection. Other interactions were tested using three variable tables, with likelihood-ratio chi squares calculated. For region, where the interaction involving region has $p = .11$, see also ft. 30.

For the closed question, $N = 532$; for the open question (where miscellaneous codes are excluded), $N = 358$. Actual samples are slightly smaller because of missing or Other responses on particular variables.

more, examination of five standard background variables and three additional religion variables leads to mostly similar conclusions with regard to their relations to the "moral values" response versus the other six alternatives combined for both open and closed forms, as shown in Table 2.7.[30]

One can still dispute the meaning of "moral values" responses on either form, as for example, how much to accept respondent explanations of the reason(s) for their vote as having genuine causal significance, rather than being a post-election rationalization or an epiphenomenal correlate of more fundamental factors. Furthermore, as emphasized earlier, the effect of the "moral values" choice on the outcome of the 2004 election, especially in comparison with other issues such as "terrorism" and "Iraq," is an entirely separate concern, one that the present analysis does not address. Our main interest here is in the relative merits of open and closed questions, and in terms of that goal, the findings from the Pew experiment provide a further caution against attacking the form of a question—in this case, a closed question—when results do not fit an observer's expectations.

Conclusions and Recommendations about Open and Closed Questions

1. *No Panacea.* Neither open nor closed questions provide a sure way to obtain a valid picture of respondent attitudes. On the one hand, closed questions constrain answers to the alternatives explicitly offered, no matter the added encouragement to respondents to give different responses if they wish. If an alternative is omitted that many respondents would prefer to choose, it is likely to be substantially underrepresented in the final results. On the other hand, open questions constrain answers more subtly, but in several different ways: they can imply a narrower frame of references than would be the case if alternatives are made explicit; they confound lack of recall with judgments of preferred responses; and they frequently yield answers that are ambiguous and difficult to categorize.

Yet despite the limitations of both closed and open questions, blaming unexpected results on the use of just a closed or just an open question can also be misguided, as we saw in detailed analysis of two important cases where such plausible methodological critiques turned out to be wrong. Substantive interpretations were called for instead. Thus before blaming unwanted results on defective questions, hard evidence is needed.

2. *The Preferred Solution.* If an attitude question is to play a key role in a survey, the best approach is to construct a split-sample experiment that will produce univariate and analytic results for both open and closed forms of the question. One can then determine empirically whether question form plays an important part in shaping results. If it does not, the two forms can be combined, or perhaps better, one form can be treated as a replication of findings obtained with the other, as done in the two cases examined closely in this chapter. If the two forms do lead to different findings, these become part of the outcome of the research, as occurred with my hypothesis about the kinds of problems named as important that are least likely to be the result of media influence because they are so rare (p. 42).

3. *Next Best Solution.* Because few polls or surveys are likely to include many open/closed experiments, usually a choice must be made when a question can be asked in either form, but not both. Based on the evidence presented in this chapter, a carefully constructed closed question is likely to be more valid than an open question for most purposes.[31] By "carefully constructed" is meant initial piloting with an open inquiry to discover the typical answers (and the typical words) that respondents give spontaneously, then making use of that information in the design of a final closed question. This approach was recommended long ago by Paul Lazarsfeld (1944), and it receives at least lip service from most experienced survey investigators, though how much it is actually followed is quite uncertain. (No such pilot record has been reported for the 2004 NEP Exit Poll, which precipitated the controversy over whether "moral values" was the key to Bush's victory. The exit poll questions simply appeared, as from the hand of Zeus.)

However, even agreement between open and closed forms does not provide complete assurance of validity, because both can omit a potential response, as we saw. Stouffer's metaphor about opening a window into the mind of respondents needs to be taken with a grain of salt, because those we interview are not always able to tell us in their own words what will be meaningful to them if offered as a closed choice. Since even open questions can constraint answers in important ways, investigators who wish to be certain to include all appropriate alternatives should make their preliminary open inquiry as broad and diverse in approach as possible. In addition, they need to exercise some imagination to think of answers that might not come to mind immediately, yet may turn out to be entirely legitimate and even preferred when included as closed alternatives, as was true of "the invention of the computer" in one experiment.

4. *Doubtful Reasons for Preferring Open Questions.* One argument sometimes made in favor of open questions is that closed-question alternatives can "put words into peoples' mouths." A variant of this argument is a concern that socially desirable phrasing may introduce bias. There are cases where tone of wording does affect responses—the classic example is the forbid/allow effect first reported by Rugg (1941)—but the frequency and import of the problem tends to be exaggerated. In a number of past instances such an effect was anticipated but did *not* occur.[32] Even the forbid/allow effect seems to be largely a matter of a shift in univariate distributions, with no change in trend over time and only a minor change in

associations with education. Other examples sometimes cited, such as the difference between references to "welfare" and references to "the poor," involve clearly different objects and would be unlikely to be treated as appropriate synonyms in constructing a question (Smith 1987b; Rasinski 1989). Further research on this issue is needed, but for now the available data do not seem to me to provide a compelling reason to avoid closed questions, though they do argue further for split-sample comparisons of wording where the point is important.

A second reservation about closed questions that involve multiple responses is that the results will vary depending on the number of alternatives offered. The main concern, however, should be that a question include all alternatives that have substantial appeal to respondents, rather than aiming for a large number of alternatives. Thus one goal of a well-constructed closed question should ordinarily be the elimination of minor response alternatives that are seldom chosen, unless of course the goal is to demonstrate the paucity of a certain kind of response. The inclusion or exclusion of minor categories should have little impact, though further experimentation on this issue is needed, especially as to where the approximate cutoff point occurs that defines "minor" alternatives that can be safely dropped.

Still a third reservation about closed questions concerns effects due to the order in which alternatives are presented. Although such effects have been documented with shorter items and also with long lists of choices (e.g., respondent reports of magazines they read), none of the multiple–alternative questions studied by Schuman and Presser ([1981] 1996, ch. 3) revealed artifacts due to the order of the alternatives read to respondents.[33] In any case, where these might occur, usually an adequate solution is to rotate alternatives on a systematic or a random basis, something readily done as part of computer-assisted interviewing. With this concern, as with the others, the problems posed by closed questions must be evaluated in comparison to the problems of open questions, which are often more severe and less easy to address.[34]

5. *Studying Change over Time.* The most compelling need for open questions occurs when an investigator is measuring change, or when a question might well become a baseline for assessing future change. In such cases an open question may be essential because of the possibility of entirely new kinds of answers being given, such as a new war or a new issue like global warming.

Yet sometimes a transient event can attract great attention, and whether or not to allow it to dominate results has to do with the goals of the survey. An inadvertent but dramatic example occurred in the course of what was intended to be a one-time open/closed experiment on the Most Important Problem question in February, 1977 (Schuman and Presser [1981] 1996). The closed form included five choices: unemployment, crime, inflation, quality of leaders, and breakdown of morals and religion, whereas the open form allowed any answer respondents wished to give. The best-laid plans of both the country and the investigators were disrupted when the entire eastern half of the United States was suddenly struck by the coldest winter in recent history, leading to fears of shortages of natural gas. A "food and energy shortage" code could be created for responses to the open form and it recorded these concerns by making that category the second highest (22 percent) after "unemployment" (24 percent) and well ahead of "inflation" (16 percent), which had been the leading issue in previous months (43 percent in a Gallup Poll in October 1976). The closed form of the same question, on the other hand, was impervious to the winter events: only a single person out of 592 respondents mentioned anything to do with the energy crunch, and he would naturally have been coded under "Other."

The unexpected winter crisis dominated news across the country at that point in time and was therefore highly salient to respondents, but it is doubtful that it reflected deep personal significance for most people, as against prominence because of its emphasis in the media. Evidence for this conclusion appears in a reanalysis if we cross-tabulate the energy code with the survey's classification of the United States into four regions: although the western side of the country was spared the main effects of the blizzard, mentions of an energy and food crisis versus all other responses showed little or no relation to region in the survey (for West vs. combined other regions, and food and energy response vs. all other responses, $\chi^2 = 2.90$, df $= 2$, p $= .40$).[35] Most of the impact of the winter of '77 on attitudes was probably a result of extensive and dramatic media coverage.

Had our closed question included "food and energy crisis" as a possible response, it would doubtless have registered the effect of the winter crisis also. And had the sudden event been less transient—say, a Hurricane Katrina or the 9/11 Terrorist Attack on the World Trade Center—the open question would have been essential to capture the full impact of the new event and to serve as a baseline for later measurement. Thus which of two sets of results becomes the focus of analysis—those obtained with the open question or those obtained with the closed question—depends in part on the aims of the investigator and in part on the nature of the unexpected event. Validity, we should bear in mind, has to do with responses in relation to an investigator's goals, not responses taken alone.

When we turn to more complex open questions, there can be serious difficulties of coding when assessing change over time. Duncan, Schuman, and Duncan (1973, pp. 35–39) found that conclusions about an apparent shift in answers over two decades were compromised because of evidence that understanding and application of code categories by both investigators and coders may have varied between the two time points. Unless the coding of an open question is simple and straightforward, closed questions are likely to be much more precise when tracking change, even though one must also allow for possible shifts over time in the way respondents interpret the wording of the closed alternatives.[36] Where it is highly desirable to track change using complex open questions, it is important to preserve the open responses from each time point and to code all the data at once, with coders blind to the different periods of the surveys so far as that is possible.

6. *Studies of Social Memory.* In research where measuring recall of past events is the primary goal, open questions seem ipso facto desirable. For example, recently my main use of open questions had been to discover whether experiencing a national or world event during one's adolescent or early adulthood years increases the likelihood of remembering it as especially important in later years (Schuman and Scott 1989a; Schuman and Rodgers 2004). Operationally, the ages 12 to 29 have provided the hypothesized range of maximum impact for most events, though the narrower range of 18 to 25 is also used (Krosnick and Alwin 1989). The assumption in such research is that open questions are needed not only because they can capture the effect of newly occurring events, but also because they are useful when the focus of the research is on "recall," as well as on judgments of importance. The open and closed questions presented in Table 2.3 can be used to check that assumption by graphing against birth cohort each of the five events from the table, as shown in Figures 2.1 through 2.5, with one line representing the open question and the other line representing the closed question. Based on visual inspection of these figures, the results provide modest support for the assumption with regard to World War II, the Kennedy assassination, the Vietnam War, and the September 11 attacks. In each case, the predicted birth cohort years (indicated by the bolder lines in

the figures) shows the expected effect more clearly for open than for closed questions.[37] The closed questions reflect similar trends but with more deviations and anomalies.

The one clear exception among the five figures is "the invention of the computer," perhaps because so few respondents gave that answer to the open question; but such an explanation cannot account for the good fit to prediction of the curve for memories of the Kennedy assassination—also relatively few in number. This difference suggests that the two types of preclusion (diminished availability vs. frame of reference) may not function in exactly the same way when memory itself is the issue—a distinction that invites further research. Overall, it still seems preferable to use open questions to explore remembering in the sense of recall, but the decision is not as self-evident as I had previously assumed.

7. *A Basic Qualification.* To assert that properly constructed closed questions are more valid than open questions in most cases is not to claim that the univariate findings obtained with closed questions can be treated as literally correct. As emphasized in Chapter 1, such results—the marginals—are always a function of the wording of a question—the question itself, quite apart from the alternatives included when the question is closed. The goal of this

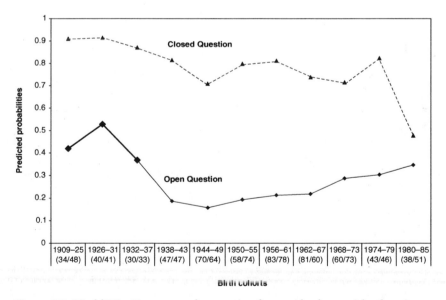

Figure 2.1 World War II responses by question form and cohort, with education, gender, and race controlled

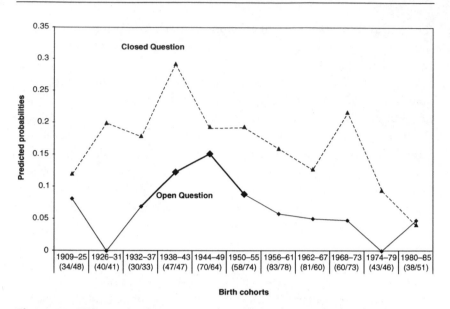

Figure 2.2 JFK assassination responses by question form and cohort, with education, gender, and race controlled

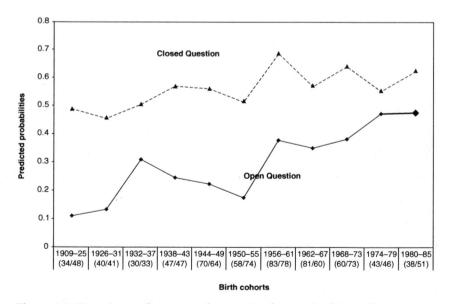

Figure 2.3 Terrorist attack responses by question form and cohort, with education, gender, and race controlled

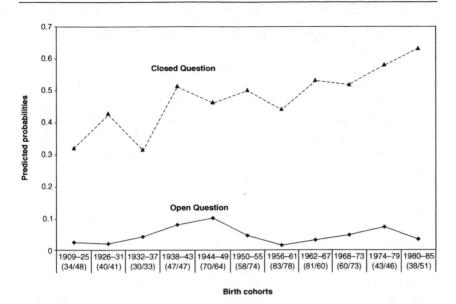

Figure 2.4 Computer responses by question form and cohort, with education, gender, and race controlled

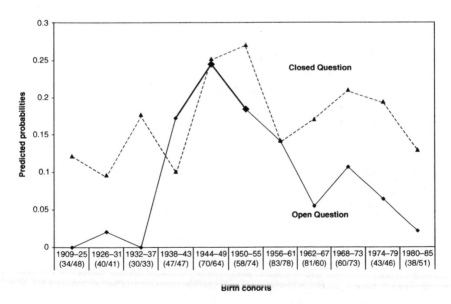

Figure 2.5 Vietnam responses by question form and cohort, with education, gender, and race controlled

chapter has been to compare open and closed question forms, not to disregard the emphasis in Chapter 1 on the limitations of all single–variable results. We need also to keep in mind the crucial distinction between the univariate distribution of responses to a question and the associations of these responses with other variables, the latter being the main concern in most social research. There are many instances, some treated earlier in this chapter, where univariate or marginal distributions vary significantly due to one or another change in wording, but where associations are not altered importantly. The principle of "form-resistant correlations" is not invariant, but it holds for a substantial proportion of the cases confronted in analyzing data from polls and surveys (Schuman and Presser [1981] 1996, pp. 302–304).

8. *Where Open Questions Shine.* Although the conclusion of the present chapter is that in most surveys an adequately constructed closed question will be superior to a parallel open question, there are other ways in which open questions serve important purposes that cannot be met at all by closed questions. First, open questions provide records of responses that can be drawn on in innovative ways. Converse's (1964) use of open responses to classify levels of political ideology was a major instance of this kind of creative use of open answers. Second, the study of beliefs about the threat of nuclear war made use of a different type of open question than those presently under examination: not an open question intended to substitute for a closed question, but a follow-up "Why" question intended to help us understand the meaning of answers to the previous closed question. This indeed is the most valuable type of open questioning in polls and surveys, and we turn to exactly such uses in the next chapter.

— 3 —

Interpretive Survey Research:
Why Questions

Open questions are important as a starting point in pilot interviews for constructing closed questions, and they may also be essential in surveys that track long-term trends where issues may change. But the richest contribution offered by open questions is interpretive: to help us understand the meaning of closed choices (or even of brief open answers such as "the economy" when given to a "Most Important Problem" question). This contribution calls for asking nondirective follow-up "Why" questions, such as "Could you tell me a little more about that?" or "Would you explain what you mean by _____?" The goal is to create a bridge between the investigator's assumptions about the meaning of words and the meanings given to the same words by the respondent—words both of questions and of answers. The bridging does not require us to believe that respondents know exactly why they say what they say, but only that their explanations can provide clues to how they interpreted our questions and what was on their minds when they responded. We as researchers can then make our own interpretations.

There is a useful connection here to the work of the ethnographer attempting to interpret concepts in a different culture, as described eloquently by Clifford Geertz (1983) in his essay "From the Native's Point of View: On the Nature of Anthropological Understanding." Geertz starts by discussing the posthumous publication of Malinowski's (1989) diary dealing with his years in New Guinea and the Trobriand Islands. The diary revealed that Malinowski had not been "a walking miracle of empathy, tact, patience, and cosmopolitanism." Geertz then asks:

if it is not, as we had been taught to believe, through some sort of extraordinary sensibility, an almost preternatural capacity to think, feel, and perceive like a native ... how is anthropological knowledge of the way natives think, feel, and perceive possible? ... What happens to *verstehen* when *einfühlen* disappears? (p. 56)

He answers by making a crucial distinction between "experience-near" and "experience-distant" concepts:

An experience-near concept is, roughly, one that someone—a patient, a subject, in our case an informant—might himself naturally and effortlessly use to define what he or his fellows see, feel, think, imagine, and so on, and which he would readily understand when similarly used by others. An experience-distant concept is one that specialists of one sort or another—an analyst, an experimenter, an ethnographer, even a priest or an ideologist—employ to forward their scientific, philosophical, or practical aims. "Love" is an experience-near concept; "object-cathexis" is an experience-distant one. (p. 57)[1]

The problem Geertz discusses is how to deploy the two kinds of concepts to obtain an interpretation that is

neither an ethnography of witchcraft as written by a witch, nor systematically deaf to the distinctive tonalities of their existence, an ethnography of witchcraft as written by a geometer. (p. 57)

People use experience-near concepts spontaneously, unselfconsciously ... they do not, except fleetingly and on occasion, recognize that there are any "concepts" involved at all ... What else could you call a hippopotamus? Of course the gods are powerful, why else would we fear them? The ethnographer does not, and, in my opinion, largely cannot, perceive what his informants perceive. (p. 58)

Instead, the goal is to

grasp concepts that, for another people, are experience-near, and to do so well enough to place them in illuminating connection with experience-distant concepts theorists have fashioned to capture the general features of social life. (p. 58)

Thus Geertz's method is to listen to the experience-near concepts with which people express themselves, then connect these to theoretical (experience-distant) concepts meaningful to anthropologists working to understand the social world. By moving back and forth between the two types of concepts, with each used to elucidate the other, he hopes to arrive at a kind of insight that neither alone could provide.

What Geertz describes is close to what the survey investigator hopes to accomplish when trying to make sense of how a sample of people—including Americans from different ethnic, regional, and class backgrounds—construe some aspect of their social world. This account does not apply to the survey administered simply to estimate which candidate in an election will have the greater number of votes. Instead, it describes a survey employed to illuminate the attitudes and beliefs of ordinary people by connecting their own words to a more abstract set of concepts that they might not employ themselves or perhaps even understand. Open-ended questioning is important for this purpose, because it invites people to express their own ideas in their own words, and it is up to the investigator to listen and then interpret these in a way that is informative. Such an approach was foreshadowed by those who first developed the research survey more than half a century ago, for example, Paul Lazarsfeld in an insightful 1935 article on "The Art of Asking Why." It can be illuminating today when we ask follow-up Why questions after closed choices.[2]

The Meaning of "Mistake"

An example from the Vietnam War period provides a striking demonstration of the value of adding an open "Why" inquiry to an important Gallup time series based on the following closed question:

> In view of the developments since we entered the fighting, do you think the United States made a mistake in sending troops to fight in Vietnam?
>
> 1. Yes, mistake
> 2. No, not a mistake
> 3. [Volunteered: Don't Know]

The loss of public support for the war can be traced in responses to the closed question by cross-section samples of Americans surveyed between early 1966, soon after the war officially began, and 1973, the year that U.S. involvement ended. As Figure 3.1 shows, less than a third of Americans in 1966 agreed that the war was a mistake, but the percentage agreeing climbed steadily over the next eight years, and by 1971 the original distribution had essentially reversed, reaching nearly 70 percent agreeing that it was a mistake.[3]

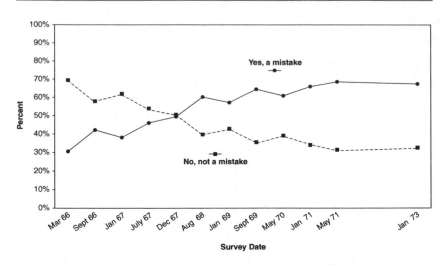

Figure 3.1 "In view of the developments since we entered the fighting, do you think the United States made a mistake in sending troops to fight in Vietnam?"

But what was meant by calling the war a "mistake"? For many of those living in college towns like Ann Arbor, Berkeley, and Madison, the answer seemed obvious: the war was increasingly seen to be a mistake because the conflict was not primarily a struggle against Communism, but rather a civil war between an unpopular government in South Vietnam and a nationalist movement that had widespread support. Moreover, as part of U.S. intervention in what was really an internal conflict, our military power was bringing death and destruction to the Vietnamese people, north and south. This was the main message of the first "teach-in" held in Ann Arbor in 1965, and it grew ever stronger on major campuses as the months passed, with opposition to the war regarded as a clear-cut moral position.[4] Yet there were signs that this stance for opposing the war did not reflect the views of the larger public—not even the views of that part of the public that was turning against the war. For example, campus protests had peaked largely in response to American military offensives, notably the incursion into Cambodia in 1970, whereas polls seemed to show no loss of public support at such points, but rather at times of apparent U.S. defeats, such as the Tet Offensive launched by the North Vietnamese and the Vietcong in 1968. In addition, much of the public rated anti-war protestors quite negatively when provided with an evaluative scale. Thus, to understand the meaning of "mistake" within the larger public, it was essential to obtain "experience-near" concepts with which members of the population explained their views.

In a 1971 cross-section survey in Metropolitan Detroit, I repeated the Gallup "mistake" question, and interviewers then asked the 1,263 people who agreed that U.S. intervention was a mistake: "Why do you think it was a mistake?" and "Is there any other reason why you think it was a mistake?"[5] Interviewers were expected to record verbatim the answers people gave to these questions.

Initially I considered the standard approach of coding first-mentioned content, but this seemed likely to lose important themes that sometimes occurred in the same answers.[6] After experimenting with different alternative coding schemes, my student colleagues and I developed what I called "thematic coding." Each response was coded in terms of ten broad themes developed partly on the basis of theoretical expectations and partly after a careful review of the content of 100 responses chosen at random. Each of the 1,263 responses was to be coded zero for a particular theme if it was not mentioned; if the theme was mentioned, the response was further categorized in terms of the way the theme was treated. Within a given theme the categories were meant to be mutually exclusive, hence a response could be coded into one category only. The ten themes themselves were not mutually exclusive: a response could be coded other than zero on as many of the themes as seemed appropriate. This thematic approach to coding seemed to capture well what was important in these sometimes complex answers.

Table 3.1 presents the results for the five themes that are most relevant for our present analysis, along with the marginal percentages for the total sample.[7] For comparison purposes, I drew on responses to the same questions by the students in three sociology classes at the University of Michigan in early 1972: two introductory classes consisting of first- and second-year students and a more advanced class for juniors. The combined student sample (initial N = 278, reduced to the 236 who answered "Yes, mistake" to the initial closed question) does not attempt to provide an adequate representation of the university, but it offers a useful contrast for the present purpose. In one sense it may be too conservative a sample, because it under-represents juniors, seniors, and graduate students who were likely to have been most fully exposed to the views of faculty and activist students who were against the war.

Table 3.2 summarizes the results for the student and Metropolitan Detroit samples on three important themes. (In later references I will sometimes refer

Table 3.1 Reasons why U.S. intervention in Vietnam was a mistake:
Five major themes

I. United States Not Winning War

0. Theme not mentioned	66%
1. The war is unwinnable	10
"It can't be won militarily; it's guerilla warfare."	
2. We are not trying to win the war	8
"Win or get out."	
3. We are not winning (stated as a fact with no additions)	1
"We're just getting beat like crazy."	
4. The war is not ending (low priority relative to 1, 2, 3)	16
"The war just goes on and on."	
Total	101
N	(1,263)

II. People Killed or Injured by the War

0. Theme not mentioned	58%
1. American soldiers killed or injured	28
"So many boys being killed."	
2. American soldiers hurt in other ways	2
"All those soldiers getting the dope habit."	
3. People killed or injured: identity ambiguous	7
"So many innocent lives have been taken."	
4. Both Americans and Vietnamese explicitly mentioned	3
"I hate violence." "Too many Americans and Vietnamese killed."	
5. Vietnamese killed or injured (includes references to any Vietnamese, on either side, either civilian or soldier)	0
"Thousands of Vietnamese killed by the mass bombing."	
6. Vietnamese people hurt in other ways	1
"We make racketeers out of the people."	
Total	99
N	(1,263)

III. Loss of U.S. Resources

0. Theme not mentioned	80%
1. U.S. resources wasted: no mention of alternative social uses	9
"It's ruined our economy."	
2. U.S. resources wasted: explicit mention of alternative social uses	3
"We send money there and there's poverty here."	

Table 3.1 (*continued*)

3. War causes polarization in the United States. "All the young people are turning against the country."	4
4. We have enough problems of our own to take care of (low priority).	4
Total	100
N	(1,263)

VII. Vietnam War Is Internal Conflict

0. Theme not mentioned	54%
1. It is a civil war	5
2. Vietnamese don't want us there "Just want to be left alone."	5
3. The war is the Vietnamese responsibility, not our war "Let them fight their own war."	16
4. Our intervention worsened the conflict (low priority) "We changed a small war into a bigger one."	1
5. Shouldn't meddle in other people's business (low priority) "Too messed up, should not get involved in other people's troubles."	19
Total	100
N	(1,263)

VIII. U.S. Goals Morally Questionable

0. Theme not mentioned	89%
1. U.S. motives wrong or questionable "Our efforts at world domination are subject to question."	3
2. We shouldn't force our way of life on Vietnam "Who are we to say what is the right way there."	6
3. North Vietnamese or Vietcong justified "North Vietnamese form of Communism is the best way for them."	1
4. The war is wrong; no further explanation (low priority)	1
Total	100
N	(1,263)

Source: 1971 Detroit Area Study (Interuniversity Consortium for Political and Social Research).

to the Metropolitan Detroit sample as the "general public.") Theme II, "People Killed or Injured by the War," is one of the two most frequently mentioned by both samples, probably because of its salience to any question about war. Students showed this concern to a greater degree than did the general public (62 percent vs. 42 percent, $\chi^2 = 34.6$, df = 1, p < .001), but the more important difference had to do with the types of victims mentioned. Even those moral critics of the war who granted some legitimacy to American political goals also argued that the costs to the Vietnamese exceeded any possible gain to them. From that standpoint, the American military effort was symbolized by a U.S. officer's widely published explanation at Ben Tre during the 1968 Tet Offensive: "It became necessary to destroy the town to save it" (Oberdorfer 1971, p. 184).[8] Our research question was the extent to which concern for Vietnamese suffering showed up in answers of those members of the general public who saw the war as a mistake. As Table 3.2(A) indicates, of those Metropolitan Detroit respondents who opposed the war and who mentioned lives lost or injured as a reason for their opposition, nearly three-quarters referred only to American soldiers. The students, on the other hand, were much more likely to refer to both Americans and Vietnamese and also more likely to refer to Vietnamese only. These responses provide one clue to the differing meanings of the word "mistake."

Theme VIII in Table 3.2 concerns a more political type of anti-war criticism, one that centered not on the destructive nature of the war, but rather on the motivations for, and goals of, American policy in Vietnam. The category includes accusations of American imperialism, support for the North Vietnamese, and more general criticisms of the war as "immoral." We did not expect anything approaching consensus among students on this more extreme position, but in fact more than a third did touch on such a theme. In the Metropolitan Detroit sample, however, only one out of nine persons gave a response classified anywhere under this theme (p < .001 for the student vs. Detroit difference). For the general public, opposition to the war seldom entailed a political-moral criticism of American goals in Vietnam.

Theme VII reveals a more subtle distinction between the student concerns and those of the general public. The theme as a whole dealt with emphasis on the Vietnam War as an internal conflict, but there were two ways of looking at this. The one represented by categories 3 and 5 focused on our staying out of "their troubles": "Let them fight their own wars" was a frequent pithy statement of this outlook. The other point of view, categories 2 and 4, carried the assumption either that the Vietnamese did not want

Table 3.2 Comparisons of general public and students on three themes

	Public (%)	Students (%)
A. *Theme II: Identity of People Killed or Injured*		
Americans only (1, 2)	73	15
Both (3, 4)	24	75
Vietnamese only (5, 6)	3	10
Total	100	100
N	(525)	(147)
B. *Theme VIII: U.S. Goals Morally Questionable*		
Theme not mentioned (0)	89	65
Theme mentioned (1–4)	11	35
Total	100	100
N	(1,263)	(236)
C. *Theme VII: Vietnam as Internal Conflict*		
They cause us trouble (3, 5)	84	43
We cause them trouble (2, 4)	16	57
Total	100	100
N	(518)	(90)

Source: See Table 3.1.

Notes: Numbers in parentheses after codes refer to specific categories in Table 3.1. All three panels show statistically significant relationships at p < .001, using χ^2 and 3, 2, and 2 df, respectively.

American involvement or that such involvement actually made the war worse for Vietnam. (Category 1, "civil war," probably belongs with the second point of view, but is omitted in the comparison because it is somewhat ambiguous.) In other words, the first perspective on the war was strictly in terms of American interests and concluded that "they cause us trouble"; the second perspective was at least partly in terms of Vietnamese interests and concluded that "we cause them trouble." Summarized under these rubrics, Table 3.2(C) shows that Metropolitan Detroiters who mentioned this theme at all did so overwhelmingly in terms of "they cause us trouble." Students, however, were much more likely to emphasize that "we cause them trouble."

Thus on all three of these themes we find sharp differences between the general public and the student sample. If a sample of students who actually participated in anti-war demonstrations would have been still more different from the Metropolitan Detroit population, we begin to get some measure of the gap between the campus-based protests and the general public's disenchantment with the Vietnam War reflected in national surveys. The gap is further validated by another code from Table 3.1 (Theme III, category 3): "War causes polarization in U.S." This category was seldom mentioned by the general public (just four percent), but 16 percent of the students referred to the fact that the war created polarization within America. For much of the Metropolitan Detroit population, polarization was probably not salient because protesters were perceived as deviants rather than dissenters. Students, however, were more likely to experience personally the conflict between the university climate of opinion and that in their homes and hometowns.

The main implication of the differences between the general public and the students is that during the Vietnam period the president had little to fear from the college anti-war movement, because the latter did not speak the same language as the larger population. Public disillusionment with the war grew despite the campus demonstrations, not because of them. The president's primary enemies were the Vietcong and the North Vietnamese, because it was their resilience and apparent successes that undermined public support for the war. The anti-war movement was not wholly ineffective: it influenced commentators and columnists, who in turn (but in different words) affected the public. But attempts by moral spokespersons against the war to proselytize the general public directly were likely to fail, or even prove counterproductive, unless carried out with more skill and less righteousness than was often the case.

The interpretive term "pragmatic" appeared to make most sense of the majority of answers by those in the general public who felt that the war was a mistake. These people did not oppose the war on principle, but for pragmatic reasons having to do with its failure to achieve its original goals and with the American losses it entailed. "Pragmatic" in this context is an experience-distant concept, one not likely to be used by ordinary respondents, but one constructed on the basis of listening to their answers. It is what happens when an investigator "hops back and forth between the whole conceived through the parts that actualize it, and the parts conceived through the whole that motivates them, [as] we seek to turn them, by a sort of intellectual perpetual motion, into explications of one another" (Geertz, 1983, p. 69). Both interpretive anthropology and "interpretive surveys" must do a lot of hopping back and forth between the concepts used by ordinary people and the concepts developed by social scientists: the goal in both cases is to explicate social expressions that on their surface are enigmatic and thus to understand what "natives" are up to wherever they may live.

Interpretive Themes and Social Background Characteristics

Age and Education

Analysis within the Metropolitan Detroit sample by age and education expands the meaning of references to the nationality of casualties in Theme II. Although the general public was much more likely to mention only American casualties than were the students, the variation by age and education in such mentions within the public was also illuminating. It was noncollege youth who focused especially on American military deaths and injuries, as indicated by the significant interaction in Table 3.3, with the highest percentage in the cell created by younger age and lesser education. This combination corresponds to the social class difference among young men who were most vulnerable to becoming casualties during the Vietnam years, for it was those youth outside of college settings who were especially likely to be drafted and thus perhaps killed or injured themselves.[9]

Gender

Women were more likely than men to mention "People killed or injured" as a reason for opposing the war, but this difference was entirely accounted for by the "Americans only" category (see Table 3.4). Men and women did not

Table 3.3 Percent mentioning American soldiers killed or injured, by education and age

	Years of education	
Age	0–12	13 and over
21–29	42% (100)	15% (85)
30 and over	33% (522)	22% (227)

Notes: White respondents only. Base N's in parentheses. Three-way interaction: $\chi^2 = 4.38$, df = 1, p < .04.

Table 3.4 Percent by gender on selected anti-war themes and subthemes

	Men (N = 535)	Women (N = 728)	Difference
Theme I: United States Not Winning War			
We are not trying to win the war (2)	11	5	6*
The war is not ending (4)	13	18	−5*
Theme II: People Killed or Injured	33	48	−15**
Americans only (1 and 2)	22	37	−15*
Both (3 and 4)	9	10	−1
Vietnamese only (5 and 6)	2	1	−1
Theme VIII: U.S. Goals Morally Questionable	15	7	8**

Notes: Numbers in parentheses refer to specific categories in Table 3.1.
*p < .05, using χ^2 for category 2 of Theme I vs. remainder of Theme I (df = 1), and p < .01 for category 4 vs. remainder of Theme I (df = 1).
**p < .001, using χ^2 for zero versus nonzero categories (df = 1).

differ at all with regard to mention of Vietnamese deaths or suffering. Thus the greater concern of women for the pain of war seemed to be channeled wholly along national lines. On other themes, the general finding was that men were more critical of the war effort in all ways—both moral and pragmatic. They were more likely to complain that "we were not really trying to win the war"—a hawk type of response—but they were also more likely than women to question the morality of U.S. motives and actions in Vietnam. Women were more apt to phrase their opposition in more passive ways, for example, that "the war goes on and on." (See also Mueller 1973 on the complexity of gender attitudes elicited by closed questions concerning overall support for the war.)

African Americans

The black-white difference on the basic "mistake" closed question was the largest for any social background characteristic, and this finding of greater black opposition held consistently over the course of attitude surveys on the war. But the meaning of the variation by race was much less clear in terms of the reasons for seeing the war as a mistake. Blacks were less concerned than whites about the lack of "victory" in Vietnam, a 19 percentage point

Table 3.5 Percent by race on selected anti-war themes and subthemes

	Black (N = 322)	White (N = 941)	Difference
Theme I: U.S. Not Winning War (1–4)	20	39	−19***
Theme II: People Killed or Injured	42	42	a
Americans only (1 & 2)	31	30	a
Both (3 & 4)	10	10	a
Vietnamese only (5 & 6)	1	2	a
Theme III: Loss of U.S. Resources	22	20	a
Explicit mention of alternative uses	4	3	a
Theme VII: Vietnam Is Internal Conflict	52	44	6
They cause us trouble (3 and 5)	42	32	10***
We cause them trouble (2 and 4)	5	7	a
Theme VIII: U.S. Goals Morally Questionable	10	11	a
Theme IX: The War Is Confusing (1 and 2)	18	6	12***

Notes: Numbers in parentheses refer to specific categories in Table 3.1.
***p < .001, using χ^2 for categories shown versus other categories of same theme (df= 1 in each case).

a. Less than 2% difference.

difference on Theme I that was highly significant, as shown in Table 3.5. Yet this de-emphasis on pragmatic opposition did not appear to translate into a clear moral critique of the war. Nor was it compensated for elsewhere in any single category, though it generally appeared to be reversed in the categories we have called "They cause us trouble" (Theme VII, categories 3 and 5), as well as in other categories indicating uncertainty over what the war was about. Together these findings suggest a picture of the war as a distant and unclear set of troubles belonging to someone else—more a matter of low involvement in the war rather than conscious opposition to it. We are able to clarify this remoteness in a following section by using linguistic analysis based on the same set of responses.

Implications for the Future

Standing back from detailed analysis of the open explanations to the "mistake" question, the Vietnam results had long-term implications for post-Vietnam policy toward other nations seen as enemies of the United States. The questionnaire for the general public included a question on a possible future Communist-inspired revolution in South America (preceding the Vietnam question by several items). As might have been expected, those who regarded the Vietnam War as a mistake were more likely to resist intervening in such a hypothetical situation. But our thematic codes proved useful in distinguishing further among those who believed the War a mistake. Of those who were opposed to the Vietnam intervention simply because we are not winning (Theme I), 50 percent would still intervene in a new war in South America. But of those who criticized the Vietnam War on moral grounds (Theme VIII), only 25 percent would intervene in a new war. This finding had obvious implications for wars in the years following Vietnam, up to and including the initial support that the president received for the invasion of Iraq in 2003—support that was not at first much diminished by the failure to find weapons of mass destruction. A striking drop in support occurred only when, as with the Vietnam War, lack of visible success was combined with mounting U.S. casualties. The reasons people gave for thinking the Vietnam War a mistake were linked to their support for future wars not directly tied to national survival. Although we may not be entirely clear as to cause and effect, the open responses to the Why question about the Vietnam War indicate the value of understanding not only pro and con positions but the reasons for them.[10]

Language as a Further Clue to Motivation

As codes were created for answers to the question "Why do you think [the Vietnam War] was a mistake?" we noticed that some respondents referred to the United States as "we" and some as "they." This difference suggested possible variation among respondents in the psychological distance between themselves and the rest of the country or its government. I recalled that Brown and Gilman (1960) had shown that two forms of the pronoun "you" in several European languages are meaningful in terms of power and solidarity in relationships. Although the we/they distinction is of a different kind, and probably less self-conscious than choice between *tu* and *vous* in French or similar distinctions in other languages, I decided to take advantage of the open responses by coding the use of "we" and "they" in the Vietnam answers (Cramer and Schuman 1975).

Coders found 885 respondents whose open explanations to the Why follow-up allowed them to be classified as either "we-sayers" (82 percent) or "they-sayers" (18 percent).[11] We-saying was usually easy to code, for example:

> It's *our* own fault *we* are in a mess over there. *We* could clean up that mess if *we* wanted to. It was the same in Korea. *We* were afraid of getting into a war with Red China or Russia.
>
> Because the war in Vietnam does not concern *us* and *we* should not have entered. (Probe) Well, there's so many things in this country all of that money could have bought.

"Our" and "us" were also coded as "we" when they seemed to have the same meaning.

They-saying was less frequent and also somewhat more ambiguous. Coding instructions aimed to include only usage referring to the United States or the U.S. government. Examples of coded responses were the following:

> Because I'm against the war. (Probe) I'm against war in general and specifically I don't think the States should have become directly involved—*they* should have stayed out. (Probe) It's none of *their* business.
>
> It has lasted much too long. I don't think *they've* gained too much and *they've* lost a lot of lives. *They* should fight it and get it over.

The relations between we/they choices and standard background variables are shown in Table 3.6. By far the largest and most significant difference concerns race, with blacks more than two and a half times more likely to be they-sayers than whites. Interpreted in the most straightforward way, African Americans identified less with the United States as a collectivity than did white Americans. Because race is clearly the strongest correlate of we/they choice, it has been included as a control in all further analysis.

Education is the next largest correlate of pronoun choice, but in this case only for whites. White respondents with less schooling were more likely to show psychological distance from the United States by using "they" than were whites with greater education. The absence of a similar relation for blacks reflects relatively high they-saying among better educated black respondents rather than lower they-saying among the less educated. Blacks at all educational levels used "they" to an extent well above the highest white levels.

Table 3.6 Relationships between background variables and pronoun choice

Variable	χ^2	df	gamma	More "they"	Percent "they"
Race	48.7***	1	0.56	Blacks	35% of blacks (base N = 196); 13% of whites (N = 687)
Education	14.8**	4	0.21	Low ed.	21% of 0–8 yr of ed.; 12% of 16+ yr of ed.
for blacks	3.6	4	0.07	—	No clear trend
for whites	11.1**	4	0.20	Low ed.	14% of 0–8 yr; 8% of 16+ yr
Age	3.3	3	0.11	Younger	22% of 21–30; 16% of 60+
for blacks	2.8	3	0.17	Younger	40% of 21–30; 29% of 60+
for whites	0.2	3	0.03	—	No clear trend
Social class identification	4.6*	1	0.19	Working class	21% of working and lower; 15% of middle and upper
for blacks	2.1	1	0.26	Working class	38% of working and lower; 26% of middle and upper
for whites	0.1	1	0.04	—	No clear trend
Family income	3.6	5	0.07	—	No clear trend
for blacks	5.4	5	0.08	—	No clear trend
for whites	2.9	5	0.00	—	No clear trend
Sex	1.3	1	0.10	Men	20% of men; 17% of women
for blacks	1.1	1	0.16	Men	40% of men; 32% of women
for whites	1.0	1	0.11	Men	15% of men; 12% of women
Party preference	6.4**	1	0.24	Democrats	20% of Democrats; 14% of Republicans
for blacks	0.0	1	0.00	—	No clear trend
for whites	0.4	1	0.07	—	No clear trend

* .05. ** .01. *** .001.

At the same time that the objective social class indicator of education was a correlate of white they-saying, subjective class identification was related to pronoun use only among blacks. This finding is consistent with evidence from other research that identification as "lower class" among blacks has been associated, at least in the 1960s and 1970s, with racial militancy (Schuman and Hatchett 1974). Thus the two different types of social class location—objective and subjective—point to different bases for they-saying among blacks and whites. Most of the other associations in Table 3.6 are either nonsignificant or probably spurious, but the age trend in the table for younger African Americans to use "they" more than their elders fits an interpretation of black pronoun usage as especially political in character, since younger age was regularly associated during that period with indicators of black militancy (Caplan 1970).[12]

We can draw two broader conclusions from this first effort at linguistic coding and analysis of open responses. First, the psychological distance African Americans showed from the war in the content of their answers to Why questions was limited to the nature and goals of the war, but the we/they coding of language indicates that the distance was broader and tended to apply to the United States as a total society. Second, race of interviewer had been varied randomly for black respondents, and it is important to note that there is no association between pronoun usage by blacks and whether the survey interviewers were black or white (p > .20). This strongly suggests that respondents are unaware of which pronoun they are using and of its meaning.

In sum, since even in the rather crude form employed in this initial effort, use of "they" versus "we" is associated with other indicators of disaffection, estrangement, and alienation from the government, other types of linguistic coding of responses to future open questions offer polls and surveys the possibility of tapping basic but unconscious ways in which people express themselves and communicate with one another.[13]

"Why" Responses and Causality

When we ask respondents "Why do you think the Vietnam War was a mistake?" we may seem to be expecting them to provide a causal explanation for their previous response describing the Vietnam War as a mistake. Nisbett and Wilson (1977) provided arguments and evidence that respondents have no special access to causal explanations for their own behavior and thus produce essentially the same kind of explanation they might offer if

observing the external behavior of others.[14] Bishop (2005) extends this rea-
soning to survey questioning, stating that respondents cannot explain why
they favor a particular candidate or express some other attitude, since they
fail to recognize forces such as question order and response order that have
been shown to shape answers. In addition, they are often willing to give answers to questions about fictional issues.

How then can we treat "Why" probes as a useful way to understand the
forces leading respondents to believe the Vietnam War a mistake? First, it is
important not to exaggerate the impact of order effects and other seeming
artifacts that survey methodologists—including the present writer—have
shown to operate in the question-answer process. Although some respondents are influenced by the order of questions and the order of response alternatives in specific experiments, many respondents do not show such an
influence: we are often speaking of effects that are statistically significant
but seldom large in substantive importance.

Second, when we find respondents who express opinions about fictional
or quasi-fictional issues, this does not mean that they do not express meaningful attitudes when presented with real issues. The crucial point is that
most individuals attempt to interpret whatever task is presented to them,
whether in an interview or in some other context, and try to give a meaningful response (Schwarz 1996; Grice 1975). If the task is a reasonable one
in terms of their knowledge and understanding, their response is likely to be
reasonable as well. However, if they are presented with an impossible task,
they will still do their best to respond and may well succumb to an artifact
that we provide, for example, a primacy effect if presented with a long list
from which to choose, or a positional bias if asked to select the highest-
quality object from a set of four that are actually indistinguishable.[15] Of
course, the Vietnam War by 1971 was at the other extreme: a major issue
that had dominated news in this country for more than five years, and most
Americans were likely by the time of our survey to have thought about its
larger aspects such as casualties and defeats. Thus it was unlike many of the
issues that Wilson and his colleagues have made the focus of their experiments (Wilson, LaFleur, and Anderson 1996; Wilson and Hodges 1992). As
Page and Shapiro (1992, p. 12) have shown: "Familiarity with political matters is strongly related to the amount of attention that particular issues and
political figures receive in the mass media."[16]

In addition, Nisbett and Wilson acknowledge that in answering questions respondents can draw on personal information that is unavailable to

investigators: knowledge of prior reactions to a particular stimulus and also on whether they have been attending to some stimuli and not others. Thus survey respondents, like all of us, may not have access to certain "cognitive processes," such as how they are able to remember so quickly the name of their first pet dog, but they do have access to their own personal memories that others lack—which is why the name of their first pet dog can serve as a useful form of identification in Internet communications where secrecy is important.

The most important point to keep in mind about responses to Why questions is that we do not simply regard the answers as providing direct causal explanations by respondents. Instead, we draw on what respondents say and what they do not say to construct our own causal explanations, as when the mention of American casualties and not of Vietnamese casualties provides evidence for what particularly troubled a respondent about that war. Likewise, the difference between words implying "they cause us trouble" and words implying "we cause them trouble" helped us understand two radically different perspectives on American intervention in Vietnam. Why questions do not depend on causal interpretations by respondents, but on their expression of points of view that *we* can interpret as clues to their motivation.[17]

The Random Probe

To probe all closed choices by all respondents would be impractical in most surveys, if only because of the total time required. In addition, probing every choice would affect respondents' behavior as they came to anticipate that each of their closed answers would require an explanation. An alternative strategy can provide some of the advantages of Why questions by randomly sampling both closed questions and respondents. Each interviewer can be required to ask follow-up probes after a small subset of questions preselected on a chance basis for each respondent. The probes do not replace the regular closed question but follow immediately after the respondent's choice of an alternative. Using the same type of nondirective phrasing as for standard Why follow-up questions, the interviewer asks the respondent "Could you tell me why you say that?" or "Would you explain what you mean by _____?"[18]

I first applied the random probe technique in 1964 in a lengthy interview survey of 1,000 factory workers and cultivators in Bangladesh, then East

Pakistan (Schuman 1966), but later examples will show its value within the United States as well.[19] The lengthy Bangladesh questionnaire included 200 closed attitude items, and each interviewer learned how to use a simple randomly based method prior to each interview to indicate 10 questions for probing from the total set of 200. In this way we obtained an average of 50 randomly probed responses for *each question,* and these open answers could be used to assess what the question had meant to those individuals, treated as a sample from the total 1,000 respondents. From the same 10-item evaluations, we also obtained a measure of overall understanding by each respondent.

The kinds of information provided will be illustrated by several examples from a set of questions concerning religion. Two of the closed questions had been written to determine whether Islamic religious obligations were interpreted to include achievement-related effort as an end in itself, somewhat similar to Max Weber's ([1905] 1958) thesis about the Protestant Ethic. The answers to these questions showed reasonable variation, intercorrelated well, and were significantly related to a number of background variables. But the results of the random probes suggested that the questions were adequately understood by less than half the sample. Most respondents reinterpreted the questions in ways that had little to do with the investigators' original purpose. For example, consider the question:

Do you think that whether a man works diligently every day is:

1. an absolutely essential part of religion?
2. an important but not essential part of religion? or
3. of little importance to religion?

A common interpretation by respondents was captured by the following response to the probe from a man who had chosen the first alternative:

My family depends on me. If there is no food and empty stomachs [because of laziness], then I cannot give attention to prayer.

Respondents who chose the third alternative tended to give even more distant explanations, for example:

It is not good to work hard everyday. It will ruin the health.

The minority of probed respondents (about two-fifths) who did appear to understand the question in the intended frame of reference (e.g., "Allah has written in the Koran that men should work hard each day") were more educated than average, as might have been expected. For those less educated the question must at the very least be treated with caution, and empirical relationships discoverable with it should be subjected to special scrutiny before final interpretation is made. Some researchers might prefer to drop such a question altogether.

Quite the opposite type of probe results were provided by the following question, intended to determine whether ethical actions and religious actions are thought to be separable:

Do you think a man can be truly good who has no religion at all?

When this question was first discussed with local translators and interviewers, their reaction was unanimously negative. No ordinary man, they felt, would understand the point of the question. Whatever might be the case among Westerners, or perhaps among some college-educated Bangladeshis, the average Muslim would see a nonreligious man as by definition devoid of goodness. They all agreed that the question could not lead to meaningful responses and should not be included. It was included, however, and in fact it produced about one-third Yes and two-thirds No choices. Still, was the question misinterpreted in some way? On the contrary, the random probes indicated that understanding was very good indeed. A typical probe explanation for a Yes response was the following:

He may not believe any religion, yet he can render good offices to the people of the land.

Another man said:

He may be good and his heart may be very pure, and he can help people anyway.

The "no" responses were also to the point:

The man who has no faith has no idea of good and bad, so he cannot be good.
The person who has no religion, what good thing may be in him? He is wretched.

More generally, of the 52 random probes obtained to this question, only one was coded as apparently confused. It therefore seemed reasonable to put aside the reservations of local advisors and to interpret Bangladeshi response patterns for the question much as one would for Americans.

The two questions discussed thus far have indicated the usefulness of random probe responses in reaching decisions about the inclusion or exclusion of questions for analysis. But an important additional value of probe responses comes from making us aware of subtle changes in meaning that have occurred between question formulation and later analysis of data. Usually it is not a case of rejecting a question, but rather of bringing into clearer focus the impact the wording has upon respondents and thus interpreting response patterns in a more meaningful way.

The following forced-choice question, for example, was intended to contrast material striving with concern for more spiritual ideals:

> Some people say that the more things a man possesses—like new clothes, furniture, and conveniences—the happier he is. Others say that whatever material things a man may possess, his happiness depends upon something else beyond those.
>   What is your opinion?

The question produced a wide distribution of responses and appeared to be understood without difficulty. However, the Bengali phrase for "something else beyond those" was interpreted in a broader way than the limited religious idea intended when constructing and translating the question. Those who chose the second alternative sometimes did give clear religious justification, such as "It depends upon God's blessing"; but even more frequently they gave other sensible nonmaterial explanations for their responses, as in the following examples:

> Suppose a man has no child, whereas he has all other things; then he is not happy.
> It depends on one's wife. If she is not good, one is not happy.
> I may have much wealth but there are many enemies against me.

The question was clearly well understood. But just as clearly it would be incorrect to use it as a direct indicator of religious versus secular orientation. The probe responses help the analyst understand more precisely what it is he or she has measured—which is, after all, the final goal of "validity."

We also treated the random probe results quantitatively in the Bangladesh research by having coders read each response and attempt to predict from it the respondent's original closed choice. The predictions were scored along a 4-point scale, running from completely accurate to completely inaccurate prediction, and totals could then be calculated to give an overall score for each item and also an overall score for each respondent. (See Table 3.7.) A high question probe score pointed to ambiguity, lack of clarity, or unintended meaning in a question for the entire sample. A high individual score indicated that a respondent had a generally low level of understanding throughout the interview. Based on this method of evaluation we found that 13 percent of the 200 questions probed presented problems that called for caution in further analysis, and examples of these were given above. Coincidentally, the same percentage of respondents (13 percent) showed serious problems with understanding more broadly, and one might consider removing them from most or even all analysis of the data.

Random probe scores of questions may be useful in many surveys in other cultures, whereas random probe scores for individual respondents are probably of value mainly where the level of education is quite low, though we found only small relations between individual scores and a measure of respondent education ($r=.10$) and a measure of verbal aptitude ($r=.21$). However, it is the qualitative examination of probe responses that is most useful, with or without formal scoring, and not only in a foreign country.

Table 3.7 Scale for scoring random probe responses

Code	Interpretation	Points
A.	Explanation is quite clear and leads to accurate prediction of closed choice.	1
B.	Explanation of marginal clarity and leads to accurate prediction of closed choice.	2
C.	Explanation very unclear; cannot make any prediction about closed choice.	4
D(a).	Explanation seems clear, but leads to wrong prediction of closed choice.	5
D(b).	Respondent was unable to give any explanation of his closed choice ("don't know").	5
D(c).	Respondent in course of explanation shifted his closed choice away from original.	5
(R).	(Explanation is simply literal repetition of closed choice; cannot judge respondent's understanding of question.)	(omit)

Random Probes of American Racial Attitudes

I built random probes into a survey of black attitudes carried out in 15 U.S. cities in 1968 for the National Advisory Commission on Civil Disorders, established by President Lyndon Johnson after widespread urban rioting the previous year. The probes served two purposes. First, our report to the commission not only presented tabulations of the closed question answers, but also included probe responses in the text to provide concrete examples of what respondents had in mind when they gave particular answers to the questions (Campbell and Schuman 1968, p. 20). For example, to a question asking whether black "school children should study an African language," one black respondent who agreed explained: "Since all races have a language of their own, it would be good if we had one too. Italians, Germans, Jews have one, why not us?" But more typical of those who agreed with the same item was a respondent who offered a more universalistic explanation: "I feel they should study all languages."

Second, when the 1968 data were included as one part of a later analysis using an index of "Black Alienation from White Society" (Schuman and Hatchett 1974), the probes proved valuable when we confronted puzzling results at several points. Thus, they provided an explanation of a perplexing curvilinear relationship between our main multi-item measure of the Alienation Index and the following question that presented three alternative choices:

> Generally speaking, do you feel blacks have more, less, or the same duty as whites to obey the law?

It made good sense when we found that those who believe blacks to have less duty than whites to uphold the law had higher Alienation scores than those who said "same duty" ($p < .001$). But it was surprising to find also that those who believe blacks have more duty than whites to uphold the law had significantly higher Alienation scores than those who said "same duty" ($p < .001$). Why should high alienation be associated with both upholding and disobeying the law? We attempted to make sense of this strange finding by double-checking the coding, by introducing various controls, by looking for unusual statistical interactions, and even by examining the Alienation items one by one to make sure that the summary index was not somehow presenting a misleading picture. But none of these efforts provided a clue as to what was going on.

Examination of the random probe responses, however, offered a quite plausible explanation for the result. Those respondents who said "same duty as whites" gave expected answers (e.g., "The law is the law and everybody should obey it"). Likewise, the single "less duty" probed response available also made good sense. But the five probed responses to the closed alternative claiming that blacks had "more duty" than whites to obey the law strongly suggested that it was interpreted differently than the investigators had expected:

[Blacks] have to be more careful because of the racial pressures.

Whites can get away with things [blacks] can't . . .

Because we're colored. Because white people make the law, break it, and do like they want.

I do because they get picked up more at night. Also they can't walk downtown at night without being searched.

Because to me that's the way it seems. They expect more from us. Even when you go to court, the judge expect more. You have to have more witnesses and be able to show concrete sound evidence for everything.

Thus the probe explanations indicated that "more duty than whites" was not really heard as "duty" in the normative sense, but rather as "need" to obey the law: blacks have to be more careful to stick to the law because they are more closely watched. Although based on only a small sample of respondent explanations, the probe responses offer such a plausible interpretation that they provide the key to understanding the perplexing survey result, and the otherwise puzzling curvilinearity now made sense.

In a different instance (Schuman and Hatchett 1974, pp. 98–102), we wondered if an unexpected relationship of high Alienation Index scores to low scores on a four-item Efficacy Scale might be due to the efficacy items seeming to have racial content or at least racial connotations, in which case the two indices would have simply been measuring the same construct and therefore the correlation best regarded as spurious. However, when the probes for each of the four efficacy items were examined, only one of the 169 explanations by black respondents was at all racial; all the others fit the broader intended meaning of the efficacy construct (e.g., "Everything lies in the hands of fate"). This finding indicated that the correlation was substantive, not artifactual: alienated racial attitudes on the part of blacks were related to a larger pessimistic view of forces in opposition to individual effort.

Application of the Random Probe to the General Social Survey (GSS)

The 1984 General Social Survey included random probes after 25 questions that had also been selected randomly to represent the total set of suitable closed items in that major national face-to-face survey. Smith (1989) discusses the results in two ways. First, the quantitative approach developed originally in the Bangladesh research indicated that it was almost always possible to predict the original closed response from reading the follow-up explanations given to the probe. In other words, most respondents were able to explain their closed choice in a way that showed they had understood the closed question and answered it meaningfully. The one exception was a seven-point liberal/conservative scale, where many respondents had difficulty explicating their positions, a finding consistent with past research on the same type of question (Conover and Feldman 1981).

More interesting is Smith's discussion of the varied meanings that respondents apparently had in mind when they gave their answers. For example, a GSS question on whether the respondent was afraid to walk alone at night elicited a number of mentions of race, though race was not referred to in the question itself. A question on taxation was usually answered in terms of taxes being too high, but some respondents referred to inequity in the way taxation was implemented, and others focused on wasteful use of money collected through taxation. A question on requiring national service was answered by a few respondents in terms of citizenship and patriotism, by many others with an emphasis on personal gains to the young themselves, and by still others with reference to those old or needy who would benefit from help provided from such a service program. These differences did not invalidate the closed questions as general attitude measures, but did elucidate the ideas that shaped respondents' answers. Smith concludes that the main contribution of random probes in the General Social Survey is to provide insight into the underlying basis of the attitudes being measured by a number of the questions.

Conclusions

Random probes are especially useful when respondents differ from investigators in educational and cultural terms. This includes not only surveys by Americans in other countries but also complex surveys within the United

States that involve regional, social class, and cultural differences. Academic and professional pollsters differ greatly from the general population in terms of knowledge of public affairs, and in many other ways as well, so a case can be made for including random probes in all surveys where the nature of an issue is at all complex or calls on more than everyday knowledge. A small number of follow-up probes do not take a large investment of survey time, and they can alert researchers to interpretations of questions and answers that might otherwise be missed.

However, when a closed question is particularly important for later analysis and writing, it is clearly preferable to obtain Why explanations for all respondents. The full number of cases provides much greater confidence in the interpretation of findings, and at the same time, it allows the deeper type of analysis illustrated with the Vietnam "mistake" responses, as well as further kinds of linguistic coding exemplified by the "we/they" analysis.

Probes and related techniques are now being emphasized for pretesting questions and questionnaires to diagnose and prevent the many problems that can occur in the administration of polls and surveys (Tourangeau, Rips, and Rasinski 2000, ch. 2; Presser et al. 2004). This emphasis is certainly desirable where the problems create serious obstacles to rapport or produce large and unwanted systematic effects on results. However, if one's focus is on survey findings and their meaning, I believe that random or systematic probes built into the survey itself can be more useful than investing substantial resources in special forms of pretesting, especially when these are carried out in artificial laboratory settings or with convenience samples. Rather than trying to prevent every ambiguity or misunderstanding—an impossible undertaking for most polls and surveys—it is more valuable to learn how actual respondents differ in their interpretations of questions and then to draw on that information in understanding the meanings of the final data.[20] If systematic probes are built into the questionnaire, the information obtained can be used as an integral part of the analysis; if only random probes are available, they can still help us understand unusual patterns of answers, as they did for the question on "duty to obey the law" described earlier.

Whether randomly or systematically, in any serious survey it is wise to obtain open explanations for closed responses that are central to the purpose of the investigation. When "moral values" was included as an alternative to a question on issues in the 2004 election, it was valuable (as discussed in Chapter 2) that the Pew Poll asked respondents—both those who chose "moral values" as the issue that mattered most to them and those who did not: "What comes to mind when you think about moral values." It is true that traditional quantitative analysis is the major way in which we try to understand survey data, yet if our goal is to appreciate the meaning of answers to questions (and the meaning of questions to respondents), we will often wish to follow closed response choices by asking those we interview Why they answered as they did and then draw on what they say as an additional form of evidence when interpreting results. Bridging experience-near and experience-distant concepts can prove useful in ways that often cannot be anticipated.

— 4 —

Artifacts Are in the Mind
of the Beholder

Who asks a question and where it occurs in a stream of questions can have a profound effect on the answers people give. We consider both kinds of context in this chapter, starting with the effects of one question on another question, and then turning to effects that involve interviewers and interviewing. Although context effects are sometimes thought of as artifacts, we are not dealing with error in the usual sense of that term, but with how the meaning of a question depends on the context in which it occurs. It is important to take this variation in meaning into account when planning or interpreting a poll or survey. In the end, context effects offer opportunities for deeper understanding of both responses and respondents.[1]

A Dawning Recognition of Question Context Effects

The possibility that questionnaire context (question order) might influence answers was recognized in the earliest days of polls and surveys but was seldom considered a major problem. In their broad review of response effects in surveys, Sudman and Bradburn (1974) concluded tentatively that the order of questions "has by itself . . . a negligible effect for attitudinal items" (p. 33). They referred also to a careful empirical study by Bradburn and Mason (1964), which stated as "its major conclusion . . . that responses to questions such as those tested—questions of self-report and self-evaluation—are relatively unaffected by order of presentation" (p. 57). At the same time, Bradburn and Mason noted mixed evidence from reports by others and acknowledged the impossibility of generalizing from their research "with any degree of confidence to other situations" (p. 61).

91

I was less cautious in a 1974 oral presentation, stating: "What strikes me most . . . is the extent to which respondents apparently consider each question in and of itself, without much attention to the earlier questions presented to them. The well-managed survey interview is more like a slide show than a motion picture, with each item viewed quite apart from what preceded or is to succeed it" (Schuman 1992, p. 5). The reason for my belief was that very few such effects had been reported in the survey literature at that point, and those few came partly from the Dark Ages of quota sampling, inattention to significance testing (which, whatever its limitations, introduces a certain amount of self-discipline into our endless search for positive results), and often inadequate reporting of basic data as well.[2]

These early conclusions by both myself and others remain true today in the sense that subsequent examinations of total survey questionnaires have not found frequent effects attributable to question order (Schuman and Presser ([1981] 1996, pp. 26–27; Smith 1991a).[3] At the same time, my own statement was clearly wrong in the sense that we now realize there are specific types of context effects that are substantial, reliable, and theoretically meaningful. One of the most interesting of these was discovered long ago, in the early days of the Cold War, but was missed by most survey and polling researchers because it was mentioned only in passing in a chapter that Hyman and Sheatsley (1950) wrote on American public opinion for an audience of educators. This effect has taken on a good deal more importance in recent years.[4]

The Norm of Reciprocity in Surveys as in Life

When each of the two questions shown in the top panel of Table 4.1 was asked first to half a national sample in 1948, Hyman and Sheatsley found that almost all Americans favored having American reporters obtain news from within the Soviet Union, but most were opposed to allowing foreign Communist reporters the same privilege within the United States.[5] When asked in sequence, however, the two questions—in either order—had a dramatic effect on answers to whichever one came second. Support for Communist reporters entering the United States rose sharply in the wake of the question about Americans reporting from Russia, and the results for the latter fell sharply when it was asked after the question about foreign Communists reporting from America. I was initially skeptical of the large effect alluded to by Hyman and Sheatsley (1950), but when we replicated the sequence more than three decades later in 1980, the new results proved highly reliable, as shown in the bottom panel and footnote of Table 4.1 (Schuman and Presser 1981). From the standpoint of interpretation, the effect seemed consistent with what has come to be called the norm of reciprocity. Although not the only important type of context effect recognized today, it takes on broader theoretical significance because it connects the question–answer process to phenomena that are of interest to a range of sciences from anthropology to zoology.

Table 4.1 Percent yes to questions on American and Communist reporters

	Question order		Difference
	1st	2nd	
Americans or Russians (1948)			
"Do you think a Communist country like Russia should let American newspaper reporters come in and send back to America the news as they see it?"	90% (635)	66% (567)	−24%
"Do you think the United States should let Communist newspaper reporters from other countries come in here and send back to their papers the news as they see it?"	36% (581)	73% (635)	+37%
Americans or Russians (Replication, 1980)			
"Do you think a Communist country like Russia should let American newspaper reporters come in and send back to America the news as they see it?"	82% (331)	64% (336)	−18%
"Do you think the United States should let Communist newspaper reporters from other countries come in here and send back to their papers the news as they see it?"	55% (342)	75% (335)	+20%

Sources: National Opinion Research Center Survey (1948); University of Michigan's Survey of Consumer Attitudes (May and July 1980 combined).

Notes: Base Ns are shown in parentheses. Small DK percentages are omitted. Using chi square tests, with df = 1, each of the four differences is highly significant (p < .001).

The Nature and Reach of the Norm of Reciprocity

According to Gouldner (1960), the norm of reciprocity refers to the "mutually contingent exchange of benefits between two or more units" (p. 164). More simply, it is the expectation that if A does something that benefits B, B is expected to do something in return of approximately equivalent value. A and B can be individuals or groups, and if groups they can be as small as couples or as large as entire nations. Because there is a sense of obligation to repay a benefit, one felt by both parties involved, as well as perceptible to outside observers, the concept of "norm" in the sense of "prescription" applies. An implicit feature of the exchange is some temporal delay between the giving of a benefit and its repayment, for otherwise the exchange would be an ordinary economic transaction. Thus, Hauser (2006) treats the ability to defer gratification as essential when an exchange is governed by the norm of reciprocity. Furthermore, there must be at least the possibility of no repayment on the part of the recipient, for otherwise the normative—obligatory—aspect would be lacking.

Each discipline approaches the norm of reciprocity from its own perspective and with its own issues. Within anthropology, Malinowski (1926) wrote about the chain of obligations for both practical and ceremonial exchanges between Trobriand fisherman and agriculturalists, while the sociologist Marcel Mauss (1954) drew on ethnographic reports to describe extravagant ritual feasts (the potlatch) where competition for prestige was the central element in both giving and repaying. Sociologists like Simmel (1950) and Gouldner (1960) have stressed the universality of the norm and its importance for social cohesion, while Homans (1950) and Blau (1967) paid special attention to interpersonal relations and stressed the role of social approval more than material gifts. Developmental psychologists like Piaget (1932) have attempted to identify the age at which the norm of reciprocity first influences the behavior of children, especially in their relations to peers (e.g., Rottenberg and Mann 1986).

In addition to the sociological and related approaches, evolutionary biologists like Trivers (1971) have tried to explain how reciprocity can occur at all, in the face of what is frequently seen as the Darwinian emphasis on "fierce competition between individuals [which should] reward only selfish behavior" (Nowak 2006, p. 1560). However, de Waal (2006), quotes from *The Descent of Man* to argue that Darwin believed social instincts shown by humans to be found in some form in other animals, and de Waal himself reports having observed reciprocal actions between chimpanzees that included a clear time delay. Axelrod (1984) developed a widely cited theory of how reciprocal responses among people can lead to long-term cooperation in iterated prisoner dilemma games, and others (e.g., Fehr and Henrich 2003) have tried to explain how reciprocity can appear even in single encounters. The norm also operates in small routinized ways, as when two social scientists sent Christmas cards to a sample of people listed in Polk Directories and found that 20 percent reciprocated by replying with their own card to the unknown sender (Kunz and Woolcott 1976). Indeed, surveys often attempt to make use of the norm of reciprocity by adding either money or a nonmonetary gift to an initial request for an interview, and these actions have been shown repeatedly to improve willingness to participate (Singer 2002).

A Simple View of Context Effects Attributable to the Norm of Reciprocity

Here our concern is with how the norm of reciprocity affects answers to survey questions. It does this not by influencing each of the parties described in the question—for example, Russians and Americans—but instead by influencing the responses given by one of the parties (Americans, in these experiments) when the relevance of the norm is highlighted by the order of questions. This is an important difference from reciprocal actions in real life—a difference that we will need to consider at a later point.[6]

There is no other past experiment quite as clear in its invocation of the norm of reciprocity as the reporters questions, but three further context experiments, also from the 1940s, draw on awareness of an obligation for reciprocity in responding to an attitude question. The norm itself shades into more general issues of equitable treatment or "fairness," as recognized by Hauser (2006) and by Walster, Walster, and Berscheid (1978). Thus, each of the pairs of questions in Table 4.2 should alert respondents to take account not only of their own preference on the issue, but also of the claims for equal treatment on the part of someone holding an opposing position. The three experiments concern both foreign and domestic issues:

1. Friend or Foe
The earliest instance of a context effect attributable to the norm of reciprocity was reported by Rugg and Cantril (1944) for a split-sample experiment carried out by Gallup in 1939 at the outbreak of World

Table 4.2 Percent yes to each question in three context experiments

	Question order		Difference
	1st	2nd	(2nd − 1st)
1. *Friend or Foe* (asked in 1939; from Rugg and Cantril, 1944)[a]			
"Should the United States permit its citizens to join the French and British armies?"	49% (1415)	43% (1570)	−6%
"Should the United States permit its citizens to join the German army?"	23% (1495)	34% (1431)	+11%
2. *Strikes or Lockouts* (Link, 1946)[b]			
"Do you believe that workers and unions have the right to strike when wages and working conditions don't suit them?"	66%	62%	−4%
"Do you believe that businessmen have a right to shut down their factories and stores when labor conditions and profits don't suit them?"	47%	52%	+5%
3. *Political Contributions by Corporations or Labor* (Gallup 1947)[c]			
"Do you think labor unions should be permitted to spend labor funds (money) to help elect or defeat candidates for political offices?"	23% (1376)	16% (1313)	−7%
"Do you think business corporations should be permitted to spend corporation funds (money) to help elect or defeat candidates for political offices?"	14% (1320)	24% (1362)	+10%

Sources: Data for the experiments 1 and 3 are obtainable from the Roper Center. Results for experiment 2 are from Link (1946), with the total sample size said to be 5,000, divided in half for the experiment but with exact N's not given.

Notes: Base N's are shown in parentheses.

a. Each difference is significant at $p < .005$. Percentages differ from those in Cantril (1944) because DK responses are removed here.

b. Exact Ns on which percentages are based were not given, but total N was reported as 5,000, with approximately 2,500 on each of two forms. Each difference is said to be significant at $p < .01$ (Link 1946). Author was not able to locate the original data, which may not have been archived.

c. Each difference is significant at $p < .001$.

War II. One question to a national sample asked whether American citizens should be allowed to join the British or French armies; the other question asked about Americans joining the German army. When each question appeared in the first location, respondents were more favorable to Americans joining the Allied forces than the German army by 2 to 1, but when the same questions were asked in the second location the ratio shrunk to just 1.3 to 1.[7]

2. Strikes or Lockouts

Link (1946) asked one question about the rights of workers to strike and another question about the rights of businessmen to lock out workers. Support for strikes was 19 percentage points greater than support for lockouts when each was asked in the first position, but the difference decreased to 9 percentage points when each was moved to the second position.[8] The differences are reported to be significant at $p < .01$.

3. Political Contributions by Corporations or Labor Unions

Gallup carried out this experiment in 1947, but apparently did not publish it at that time. As with the Link experiment, there was more support (by 10 percentage points) for the union side than for the corporation side when each question was asked first, but support for the corporate side became greater and support for unions lessened when the questions were in the second position. The differences are significant at $p < .001$.[9]

The three experiments, along with the original Hyman and Sheatsley experiment on American and Russian reporters, were all carried out within several years of one another in the middle and late 1940s, but none of the investigators showed evidence of being aware of the other experiments, nor were the several results ever brought together as part of a more general treatment of context effects, or of reciprocity or fairness. Each experiment appears to have been done primarily, or perhaps only, to prevent misinterpretation of substantive results because of question order, without explicit recognition that the context effect comes from the intrinsic connection between related actions and thus omitting one question does not eliminate but simply changes the effect. In none of the four cases did the nature of the context effects become a focus for further experimentation or analysis.[10]

Recent treatments of context effects accept the empirical findings reported in Tables 4.1 and 4.2 as trustworthy, and the explanation in terms of the norm of reciprocity as persuasive (Sudman, Bradburn, and Schwarz

1996; Tourangeau and Rasinski 1988). The basic result, especially as shown by the reporters experiment, has become a standard example of the importance of context in surveys and of a case where both the data and its interpretation are unproblematic (e.g., Weisberg 2005). However, if we go beyond the comparisons of the distributions shown in Tables 4.1 and 4.2, and add further evidence and analysis, complexities arise that point to changes in the way we should view both the data and their meaning.

A More Complex View of Context Effects and the Norm of Reciprocity

INTRODUCING TIME. The 1980 data on the reporter's experiment provided not only a replication, but a replication after a considerable period of time, thus allowing real change along with a test of the reliability of the context effect. Looking more closely at the results for the questions in Table 4.1, we can note that the differences attributable to the norm of reciprocity were not as great in 1980 as in 1948, though if statistically significant effects due to context are one's sole concern, the possible change over time might easily be ignored. This would be even truer if the results were based on two convenience samples, for example, students from a class or volunteers. With probability sampling from the same national population, however, the change encourages fuller consideration of "time" as an important variable. Moreover, the decrease in the size of each context effect between 1948 and 1980 is highly reliable: for the United States allowing Communist reporters item: $\chi^2 = 10.1$, df = 1, p = .001; for Russia allowing American reporters item: $\chi^2 = 5.8$, df = 1, p = .02.

Suppose now that we consider the possibility of attitude change toward Communist and American reporters continuing to move in the same direction, as indicated in Table 4.1. This is not simply idle speculation: it might really have happened if Gorbachev's attempt to reform the Communist system in Russia had been more successful, not only internally but in winding down the Cold War as well. The effect of such further change is easiest to observe if we focus on the question about allowing Communist reporters into the United States when it is asked first. Suppose by, say, the year 2000, with the Cold War much diminished, the response "Yes" had risen another 20 percent to 75 percent, as shown in the hypothetical Table 4.3, and in addition the result when the question is asked second did not change—as it had not changed between 1948 and 1980—then the context effect would have disappeared entirely. In other words, what Tourangeau, Rips, and Rasinski (2000, p. 211) regard as the largest context effect ever discovered in a national survey would no longer exist! It is less easy to imagine that support for American reporters to be let into Russia would have declined enough to erase that context effect completely, but its size and statistical significance might well have faded considerably. More generally, the context effect in the case of the reporter's questions cannot be divorced from attitudes toward the object itself.[11]

Strack and Martin (1987) have proposed that because cognitive scientists are interested in knowledge about processes, rather than knowledge about content, it is unnecessary for them to do experiments in sample surveys of general populations, with all the additional costs and time that such surveys require. Moreover, they go further and argue that it is better to use homogeneous convenience samples so that there is not unwanted variation in responses due to relations between content and social background variables such as education. But in the case of the norm of reciprocity and the reporter's items, process and content are tied together, and I'm not persuaded that it is possible to study the one and ignore the other completely.

Most psychologists who do laboratory-type experiments seldom think of including long-term social change as an important variable. However, if they did, how could they tell that a difference over time that they discover is not due to the particular convenience sample of students used at each point? And even if they controlled sampling well enough to feel confident of real change, how could they know that what was going on with their college students was also happening with the larger public? Studying change calls for probability samples from a well-defined population, and generalizes only to that population (Sears 1986).[12] This is why sample surveys are done when there is interest in studying the content of attitudes. They may be

Table 4.3 Percent yes about Communist reporters: Hypothetical year 2000

| | Question order | |
	1st	2nd
"Do you think the United States should let Communist newspaper reporters from other countries come in here and send back to their papers the news as they see it!"	75% (581)	75% (635)

Notes: Percentages are hypothetical, as described in the text. Base N's in parentheses are from 1948 data for the Russia question.

crucial as well when our concern is with processes such as context effects, and perhaps other response effects as well, especially as our time horizon begins to extend far enough to alter the way such effects are expressed in the intrinsically social medium of language.

A CONSTRUCT REPLICATION.   The findings of context effects attributable to the norm of reciprocity in Tables 4.1 and 4.2 were all reported after the fact, and with some possibility that they were unplanned even by the investigators, other than as a way of preventing possible influence on their substantive concerns.[13] If the operation of the norm of reciprocity is as clear as now believed, we should be able to design a new experiment that will yield an entirely novel context effect.

National trade barriers seemed to provide a particularly suitable form of construct replication, for trade negotiations are often stated explicitly within a framework of reciprocity.[14] Therefore, Schuman and Ludwig (1983) constructed the order experiment in 1982 that is shown in Table 4.4, and predicted an approximately symmetrical context effect similar to the effects shown for earlier experiments in Tables 4.1 and 4.2. Indeed, the prediction seemed so plausible that reviews of context effects have added its supposedly successful outcome to past evidence in support of context effects due to the norm of reciprocity (e.g., Sudman, Bradburn, and Schwarz 1996; Tourangeau, Rips, and Rasinski 2000). But let's look closely at the actual results.

Not surprisingly, when each question was asked first, many more Americans supported trade restrictions by the United States (76 percent) than supported trade restrictions by Japan (48 percent); see Table 4.4. Thus, self-interest prevails when the norm of reciprocity is not made explicit, though it is interesting to note that nearly half the sample agreed to Japan's use of trade restrictions even when that question came first. This is an indication that national self-interest can sometimes be put aside, a finding we return to at a later point.

In accord with our main hypothesis, there is a large and significant context effect on Japan's use of trade limits when that question comes after the question about trade limits by the United States: allowing trade barriers by Japan increases from 48 percent to 70 percent, reaching almost the level of support given to the preceding item about allowing the United States to set barriers against products from Japan (76 percent). Apparently the norm of reciprocity leads nearly a quarter of the American sample to allow Japan to do something that these Americans would otherwise oppose.

Table 4.4 Context effects on American and Japanese trade restrictions

	Question order		
	1st	2nd	Difference
"Do you think that the American government should be allowed to set limits on how much Japanese industry can sell in the United States?" Yes, allowed:	76% (195)	71% (186)	−5%	$\chi^2 = 1.2$, 1 df, p = n.s.
"Do you think that the Japanese government should be allowed to set limits on how much American industry Can sell in Japan?" Yes, allowed:	48% (186)	70% (195)	+22%	$\chi^2 = 20.0$, 1 df, p = .001

Source: University of Michigan's Survey of Consumer Attitudes, February, 1982.
Note: Base N's are shown in parentheses.

There is also a slight decline in support for U.S. trade restrictions when that question appears in second position, but contrary to our hypothesis the effect is quite small (5 percent) relative to the effect in the other direction, and unlike differences in earlier tables, it does not approach statistical significance ($p > .25$). Furthermore, using a telephone survey of American college students, Bishop et al. (1988) report similar findings: a clear context effect on allowing Japan to have trade limits when it follows the American item ($p < .01$), but no reliable effect on reducing U.S. trade barriers when that question follows the Japan question ($p > .25$). Thus, we find that in this case the pull of self-interest is so great that few, if any, Americans would change their position on the U.S. right to restrict imports from Japan, even after indicating unwillingness to allow Japan to restrict American imports. It is likely that economic problems arising out of Japanese–U.S. trade relations at that point in time were perceived by a large number of Americans almost entirely in terms of competition for the U.S. market.[15]

In sum, this new experiment created an asymmetrical context effect that forces us to modify the previous implicit assumption that the norm of reciprocity always has similar implications in both directions in these experiments. We can also now review the pairs of questions in Tables 4.1 and 4.2, and note that for all of the comparisons, the more popular side, as indicated by the larger percentage of Yes responses in first position, has the smaller reduction as a result of the norm of reciprocity, though sometimes the difference is tiny. The first positions also make intuitive sense because a plurality of Americans seems likely to have favored these views in the 1940s and 1980s. Thus, the trade restriction results may simply be an extreme example of a more general competition between the principle of reciprocity and personal preference.

These conclusions provide compelling evidence that the norm of reciprocity in surveys should not be regarded as an abstract principle that can transcend personal preference and self-interest in concrete situations. The results also point up an important difference between survey-based experiments on reciprocity and what goes on in real life where each party in a reciprocal interaction is almost certain to try hard to prevent being disadvantaged in the exchange. Our experiments should not be treated as reproducing exactly what happens in nonsurvey situations—just as dropping two objects having different weights in a vacuum is not the same as dropping them through currents of ordinary air. Yet survey-based experiments do have the advantage of allowing us to explore further issues about reciprocity effects.

Carriers of the Norm of Reciprocity

Narrow self-interest can hardly account for the fact that nearly half the 1982 sample favored allowing Japan to create trade restrictions even when that question was asked first, and in addition a quarter would oppose American trade barriers when it came first.[16] Thus, even when the norm of reciprocity is not made salient, some respondents answer with the norm in mind. To test this assumption, we made use of a separate small national sample of 41 respondents in March 1982, asking only the question about Japanese trade limits, and then for those who said that Japan should be allowed to set limits, we asked: "Could you tell me why you feel that way?" Of the 24 respondents who said Yes, nearly three-quarters (17) gave a reason clearly involving reciprocity. For example, one person said: "We set limits, so they should be allowed to set limits . . . it's only fair." Thus, for some respondents the norm of reciprocity comes to mind without prompting when a question to which it is relevant is posed.[17]

A plausible hypothesis is that it is more knowledgeable and sophisticated respondents who carry with them awareness of the relevance of the reciprocity norm, whereas others recognize the norm only when it is made salient by context, and still others are not affected by the norm at all. Educational attainment can provide an indicator of both knowledge and cognitive sophistication, and might therefore be expected to interact with context meaningfully. Table 4.5 presents results by education for the trade restrictions experiment, with income controlled, and the findings are consistent with this expectation. When a trade question is asked first, more educated respondents are less likely to support U.S. restrictions on Japanese goods, but more likely to support Japan's right to restrict American goods, than are those with less education. Furthermore, the context effect of the norm of reciprocity is greatest for those with the least education.[18] Thus, it is not that the force of the norm of reciprocity necessarily differs for those at different educational levels on this question, but rather that it is more salient ("chronically present") to those with more education, and requires context to bring it to mind for those with less education.

If the overriding factor in determining responses is the power of the norm of reciprocity, we would expect similar results for the three additional experiments where data are available that include measures of both educa-

Table 4.5 Percent yes on trade restrictions, by education and question context

Trade Restrictions Context Effect	Education		
	0–11	12	13+
Yes, Trade Restrictions by Japan			
Order: Restrictions by Japan 1st	39% (31)	45% (69)	56% (86)
Order: Restrictions by Japan 2nd	86% (29)	67% (69)	67% (100)
Odds ratio:	.10	.41	.62
Response × order × education: linear $\chi^2 = 6.4$, df $= 1$, p $< .01$			
Yes, Trade Restrictions by U.S.			
Order: Limits by U.S. 1st	97% (30)	75% (69)	68% (101)
Order: Limits by U.S. 2nd	67% (33)	74% (69)	70% (87)
Odds ratio:	.07	.93	1.09
Response × order × education: linear $\chi^2 = 6.0$, df $= 1$, p $< .02$			

Source: University of Michigan's Survey of Consumer Attitudes, February, 1982.
Note: Base Ns are shown in parentheses.

tion and income: the two reporters experiments from 1948 and 1980 and the experiment on union and corporation political contributions. However, in Table 4.6 none of these shows a three-way interaction similar to that for the trade restriction experiment, as indicated by the odds ratios within each of the tables and also by formal tests of interaction between each question, context, and education, with income controlled.[19]

Yet the reporter experiments do show important regularities that are much the same in both 1948 and 1980. In all eight tests in Table 4.6, as the regression coefficients indicate, there is a highly reliable relation between more education and more support for allowing foreign Communist reporters into the United States and for allowing American reporters into Russia. Based on other evidence (e.g., Stouffer 1955), it seems likely that this is a result of greater support for freedom of expression and greater tolerance for nonconformity by more educated Americans. Furthermore, since this result occurs even when a question is in second position and thus subject to influence by the norm of reciprocity, it is apparently too strong to permit the kind of reversal that appeared in Table 4.5 for trade restrictions.

At the same time, we can see that the norm of reciprocity does continue to be effective within educational categories: each question in second position shows the same direction of influence as appeared in Tables 4.1, 4.2, and 4.4 for the total samples. For example, among those with 0 to 11 years of education in 1948, agreeing to allow Communist reporters into the United States rises from 25 percent when the question comes first to 63 percent when it follows the question about American reporters going to Russia. By the same token, among those with 0 to 11years of education, insistence on American reporters being allowed into Russia drops from 84 percent to 57 percent when that question follows the question on admitting Communist reporters into the United States. There are twelve possible comparisons in Table 4.6, and all twelve are in the direction predicted by the norm of reciprocity.

When we turn to the final experiment on political contributions, we again find that within each educational category the results are in the direction predicted by the reciprocity norm. For example, considering only first positions, there is more support within each of the three educational categories for contributions by unions than by corporations. Given that starting point as an indicator that unions were more favored at that point in time than corporations with regard to making political contributions, we expect support for union contributions to go down when the question is in second position and for support for corporation contributions to rise when it is in

Table 4.6 Percent yes on reporters, by education and question context

	Education		
A. Reporters (1948)	0–11	12	13+
U.S. Allow Communist Reporters			
Order: U.S. 1st	25% (337)	40% (129)	66% (113)
Order: U.S. 2nd	63% (310)	79% (169)	87% (153)
Odds ratio:	.50	.44	.54

U.S. 1st: b=−.73 SE=.13 p<.001; U.S. 2nd: b=−.57 SE=.14 p=.001.

Russia Allows U.S. Reporters			
Order: Russia 1st	84% (311)	93% (168)	97% (153)
Order: Russia 2nd	57% (324)	69% (125)	87% (116)
Odds ratio:	.79	.45	.62

Russia 1st: b=−.74 SE=.23 p=.001; Russia 2nd: b=−.58 SE=.15 p=.000.

B. Reporters (1980)			
U.S. Allow Communist Reporters			
Order: U.S. 1st	24% (70)	43% (122)	78% (141)
Order: U.S. 2nd	54% (69)	76% (105)	84% (153)
Odds ratio:	.50	.44	.54

U.S. 1st b= 1.17 SE=.18, p=.000; U.S. 2nd: b=−0.58 SE=.18 p=.001.

Russia Allows U.S. Reporters			
Order: Russia 1st	68% (66)	84% (104)	88% (153)
Order: Russia 2nd	35% (66)	58% (123)	83% (138)
Odds ratio:	.79	.45	.62

Russia 1st: b=−.53 SE=.20 p=.007; Russia 2nd: b=−1.00 SE=.18 p=.000.

Sources: Data for 1948 reporters experiment are obtainable from the Roper Center; data for 1980 reporters experiment are from the University of Michigan's Survey of Consumer Attitudes.

Note: Base Ns are shown in parentheses.

second position. Each of these predictions is confirmed in Table 4.7 where there are six comparisons to consider.

However, there is not consistent evidence for education as a predictor of responses either in the interactive sense that was true for the trade restriction experiment, or in the simple correlational sense that held for the 1948

Table 4.7 Percent yes on political contributions

Political Contributions	Education		
	0–11	12	13+
Yes, Contributions by Corporations			
Order: Corporations 1st	13% (655)	12% (310)	17% (312)
Order: Corporations 2nd	23% (661)	24% (362)	27% (295)
Odds ratio:	.50	.44	.54
Corp. 1st: b=−.17 SE=.11 p=n.s. Corp. 2nd: b=−.16 SE=.10 p=.09			
Yes, Contributions by Unions			
Order: Unions 1st	21% (671)	23% (367)	27% (294)
Order: Unions 2nd	17% (648)	12% (311)	19% (312)
Odds ratio:	.79	.45	.62
Union 1st: b=−.28 SE=.10 p=.003 Union 2nd: b=−.11 SE=.11 p=n.s.			

Source: Gallup 1947 (Data are obtainable from the Roper Center for Public Opinion Research).

and 1980 reporters experiments. More generally, each of the three subjects about which we have data for analysis (trade restrictions, reporting by a foreigner, and political contributions) shows a distinctive overall relation between respondent education and the norm of reciprocity, though in each case the efficacy of the norm within educational categories is clear and consistent. A full synthesis of these results for education is not at hand, and thus the familiar refrain of a need for more research—and thinking—is appropriate at this point on this problem.

Conclusions about the Norm of Reciprocity and Context Effect

Implications for Reciprocity in Life

The norm of reciprocity is typically discussed as if symmetrical: A does something that benefits B, and B is expected to do something in return of approximately equivalent value, and so on. However, when looked at from the perspective of an individual evaluating both directions of a reciprocal interaction, many respondents see it as more appealing in one direction than in the other, and this may often be the case with reciprocity between two individuals or two groups, with disagreement or conflict resulting.

A related possibility worth testing in the future is that a benefit may be regarded as obligatory to return, but not necessarily in equal amount or quality. This was nicely captured by a cartoon printed in the *Ladies' Home Journal*. As they are leaving a house where they have obviously just been dinner guests, a wife remarks to her husband: "Eggplant casserole doesn't pay back for prime rib."[20] A dinner has been reciprocated, but not in a way judged to be equivalent. There may certainly be such instances in ordinary life where the reciprocation seems inadequate, and it would be useful if a future experiment attempted to measure actions along an ordinal or interval scale. Perhaps what we tap only in terms of percentages of individuals who do or do not favor reciprocity in particular situations would appear differently if degree of support or opposition had been assessed. In much of the social science literature on reciprocity the same assumption of a dichotomy is made.[21]

There are also ways in which close relationships can modify the expression of reciprocity in important respects. In Whyte's classic study of *Street Corner Society* (1943), the author writes:

> Once Doc asked me to do something for him, and I said that he had done so much for me that I welcomed the chance to reciprocate. He objected: "I don't want it that way. I want you to do this for me because you're my friend. That's all." (p. 256)

Not all relationships call for or can tolerate reciprocity that is too blatant. Moreover, any relationship can experience changes in attitudes that make reciprocity difficult to expect or to assess, unless the attitude change itself is taken into account. This applies also to relationships between groups and organizations, so we should not assume that reciprocity once observed is sure to continue cycling on indefinitely.

We were able to explore the influence of the reciprocity norm in relation to educational level in three quite different spheres: trade barriers between nations, support for reporters being admitted into countries seen as enemies, and political contributions by organizations (unions and corporations) with competing agendas. Just as the efficacy of the norm varied over time, its nature seemed to vary across spheres in relation to education and perhaps to other social factors not tested. Much (though not all) of the research on reciprocity approaches the norm as an abstract force, unmodified by other social variables and social settings, but the results of the present analysis suggests that this is too rarified a view.

Implications for Survey Research

There are important implications for surveys from our study of context effects due to the reciprocity norm. First, we must recognize not only that such effects exist and are important, but that they are due to the integral nature of certain attitudes toward other actors. Reciprocity can have a role in survey questions whether it is implicit for some respondents, is made salient to others by question order, or is either missed or rejected entirely by still others. Similar conclusions come from context experiments on how respondents answer questions about general life satisfaction and satisfaction in specific spheres such as marriage: there are effects of one kind or another no matter what particular questions are included or how they are ordered (Schwarz, Strack, and Mai 1991). We are not dealing with a form of "survey error" in any simple sense.

Second, Tourangeau, Rips, and Rasinski (2000) have classified context effects in terms of a four-stage psychological process that most respondents are assumed to go through when answering an attitude question: first, they must interpret the question; second, they try to retrieve relevant beliefs and feelings; third, using what they are able to retrieve they make a judgment about a desired response; and finally they edit the judgment to fit the alternatives offered and their own need for self-presentation. Sudman, Bradburn, and Schwarz (1996) use a similar classification. However, it is not clear how this works with particular context effects. Tourangeau and Rasinski (1999, p. 306) place the effect for the reporters items at the "judgment" stage, but also note that it may possibly affect retrieval ("what respondents consider in making their judgments"), and presumably the same would be true for the trade limits effect. In addition, it seems possible that some respondents arrive at their final response at the reporting stage, once they see the need to appear consistent in the eyes of their interviewer and indeed to themselves. With a little ingenuity, one might even manage to locate reciprocity context effects at the comprehension stage. In addition, to complicate matters more, it is entirely possible that for some respondents the effect is mainly at one stage, for others mainly at a different stage. Thus, rather than the four components of the response process providing a simple a priori solution "by the book," the attempt to apply the classification to real context effects calls for evidence of what actually goes on with different types of effects and perhaps different kinds of individuals.

Third, it is always useful to attempt three types of replication in a study of context effects, as indeed of response effects generally. There is the initial need for literal replication to make certain that what looks to be a reliable finding is really reliable, because significance tests and similar measures from a single survey are seldom if ever sufficient for that purpose. Next, replication over time is valuable to determine whether a conclusion needs to be changed because attitudes have shifted in some way that alters earlier findings in important, even decisive, respects. "Chance" is not the only source of a failure to replicate an earlier result, as we will see even more clearly in Chapter 6. Beyond both types of literal replication, construct replication is essential to distinguish findings due to specific content from findings due to constructs that the content is assumed to represent. We saw that what seemed like a reasonable extrapolation from one experiment (reporters) to another (trade barriers) did not in fact produce the expected results, and the same turned out to be true when we looked at the impact of education on different applications of the norm. There has been a tendency by those writing about response effects to assume on the basis of a single experiment (e.g., the 1948 Hyman and Sheatsley reporter questions) that effects due to the norm of reciprocity are simple and straightforward, but the analysis in this chapter makes it clear that that is not the case.

Fourth, although much research on context effects can be done with convenience samples such as students, at some points it is important to work with probability samples of a well-defined and heterogeneous population. On the one hand, this is important if replication over time is to be carried out to assess change in the nature of context effects. Such replication calls for the population to be the same at different time points, or at least adjustable to take account of differences. On the other hand, the inclusion of important variables like education as part of the analysis is often accomplished most adequately by working with natural populations, for example, the population of American adults. This is of course expensive and time-consuming, but needed nonetheless.

Finally, because important context effects in surveys are always possible, but are also thought to be uncommon, we have another reason for all major surveys to include split-sample question order experiments, especially where attitudes central to an investigation are being studied. This is much like the efforts in the 1940s that may have been done mainly for substantive reasons, but resulted in the first clear findings of important context effects in surveys. Both substantive and methodological goals are addressed by continuing to construct experiments that identify new context effects.[22] Furthermore, it is also desirable to include open-ended Why follow-up inquiries, as discussed in Chapter 3. The open-ended inquiry about trade restrictions in the present study showed that some respondents had the norm of reciprocity in mind even when it was not made salient by question order. The use of experimentation together with open questioning, along with replications across time and analysis of associations with education and other important social variables, brings to bear the strengths of four different methods in pursuit of fuller understanding of the meaning to be found in questionnaire context.

Postscript on Other Context and Wording Effects

Effects due to reciprocity ordinarily involve two questions of equal specificity, with influence assumed to flow in both directions and usually hypothesized to create greater consistency between responses to the questions. Most other context effects discovered thus far involve what Schuman and Presser ([1981] 1996) called "Part-Whole relations," where one question is more general (the Whole) and is intended to contain, summarize, or imply questions that are more specific (e.g., overall happiness and happiness with one's marriage, or support for legalized abortion generally and support for legalized abortion in the case of a fetus with serious defects). In these cases, context effects have been found for the specific question on the general one, but not the reverse. Furthermore, Part-Whole effects can produce either greater consistency or greater contrast in responses. Although some experimentation on these further types of effects was reported by Schuman and Presser, most of the important research has been developed by others. Starting points for what is now a large literature are Tourangeau and Rasinski (1988; see also Tourangeau, Rips, and Rasinski 2000) and Schwarz and Bless (1992; 2007), with the latter's "inclusion/exclusion" model providing probably the most productive theorizing at present.

Context effects often involve radical shifts in interpretations of words, as in the case of the Communist and American reporters: in one context attitudes toward objects (Communist and American reporters) are the focus, but the other context highlights the norm of reciprocity. This shift can produce different patterns of change over time, as shown in Figure 4.1a, which repeats graphically results from Table 4.1 for the United States letting in a

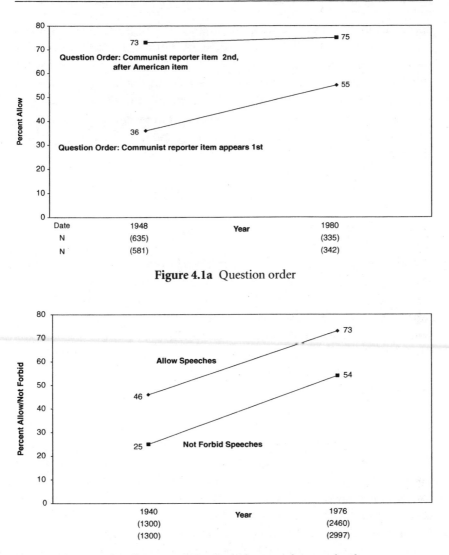

Figure 4.1a Question order

Figure 4.1b Allow versus Not Forbid unpopular speeches by year.
Source: Adapted from Schuman 2002.

Communist reporter.[23] However, in the case of some other types of response effects where a word within a question is altered, there may be a sharp
difference at each point in time, but no difference in the nature (slope) of the
association with time. This is true of the classic wording effect due to the difference between "allowing" an unpopular speech and "not forbidding" the

speech, as shown in Figure 4.1b for two time points (Rugg 1941; Schuman and Presser [1981] 1996). Not only visually, but also statistically, there is little sign of an interaction with year ($\chi^2 = 1.1$, df$= 1$, n.s.), even though the difference in wording has a clear impact at each time point.[24] The alteration of wording in this case evidently involves movement in degree of intensity along a single dimension, but not a radical shift in meaning. The difference between response effects that change meaning and those that do not is fundamental.

The Interviewer as Context

Interviewers are ordinarily expected to serve as transparent intermediaries, for the most part simply asking questions and recording answers. But knowledgeable survey researchers recognized almost from the start that responses to a survey can be affected by who asks the questions. During World War II, Stouffer and his associates in the Research Branch of the War Department compared answers of black soldiers to black interviewers with answers of a matched sample of black soldiers to white interviewers. The black interviewers "tended more than white interviewers to elicit responses reflecting racial protest, unfavorable attitudes toward the war, pessimistic views of postwar conditions, unfavorable reports on the Army, and manifestations of low personal esprit" (Stouffer, 1950, p. 721). Although the differences might possibly have been due to conscious or unconscious biasing behavior by the interviewers, Stouffer added a third sample of black respondents who filled out the same questionnaires in a classroom situation with a black administrator and found that it yielded answers similar to those given to black interviewers, thus providing evidence that it was the soldiers' perceptions and beliefs that influenced their responses, not the interviewers' bias in how they asked the questions or reacted to the answers. Of course, a fourth sample using a white administrator would have clarified the results still further, and more generally the issue of perceived sponsorship of a poll may be as important as who asks the questions (e.g., Presser, Blair, and Triplett 1992).

Similar results by race of interviewer were obtained by Hyman (1954) when he compared African Americans interviewed by black and by white interviewers in Memphis in 1942, but with the additional finding that significantly fewer race-of-interviewer differences occurred when the same design was repeated in New York City. This expanded the interpretation of interviewer effects by emphasizing the importance of local norms in increasing or decreasing the strength of the effects. Hyman's research also added to evidence that interviewer effects in professionally managed surveys come more from respondent attempts to avoid saying things they think are likely to offend interviewers than from direct bias in words or other behavior on the part of the interviewers themselves.[25] Moreover, to the extent that interviewers' own behavior proved important, Hyman provided other evidence that this was not due to ideological bias but because the expectations interviewers hold sometimes leads them to misinterpret answers given by respondents. Thus, on both sides of the interviewer-respondent divide, effects appeared to be due to what the one side assumed—perhaps incorrectly—about the other.

In 1968 Jean Converse and I reviewed a large number of race-of-interviewer effects and noneffects on the answers black respondents gave in a face-to-face survey in metropolitan Detroit. We came to conclusions much like those of Stouffer and Hyman: "To accept a guest into your house and then proceed to explain that you neither trust nor feel friendly toward people of their race probably takes more *chutzpah* than the average respondent possesses" (Schuman and Converse 1971, p. 58). At the same time, we also speculated that with the rise of black militancy at that point in time, it was possible that some black respondents felt a need to exaggerate their anti-white attitudes when the interviewer was black, though no direct evidence of such a phenomenon could be presented based on the available data.[26]

Furthermore, some attitudes can be conceptualized as entirely situational, different but equally valid in different situations. For example, a seemingly neutral question in the 1968 survey asked respondents simply to name their "favorite actors and entertainers" and elicited more black names to black interviewers and more white names to white interviewers. In such cases it is possible that respondent perceptions of the interviewer "primes" racially congruent names without there being a deep-seated motive to please or avoid displeasing the interviewer. The effect is a large one and thus it would be valuable to determine what the correct explanation is.

We also drew the broader conclusion that interviewer effects should be regarded not simply as an artifact of surveys, but as a fact of life in America, with the same effects likely to occur in other spheres where blacks and whites interact. This conclusion in turn suggests that a change over time in race-of-interviewer effects could provide a sensitive barometer of important shifts in the nature of black/white interaction in the United States. With possible future change in mind, we were candid in stressing the time point of our own research by including it in the title of the article: "The Effects of Black and White Interviewers on Black Responses in 1968." A similar measurement over time would be valuable for race-of-interviewer effects on white respondents, since a small survey-based experiment in 1971 indicated that whites were also more likely to express positive racial attitudes to black interviewers than to white interviewers on such issues as racial intermarriage (Hatchett and Schuman 1975–1976), probably for much the same reason of politeness. Unfortunately, later replications were never carried out of either effect to assess long-term change.[27]

Two limitations in most race-of-interviewer findings have been pointed out by Groves (1989). First, since observations are clustered within individual interviewers, calculations of standard errors should take this into account, rather than treating the individual cases as a simple random sample, as was done in my and other earlier studies. This change in calculations means that the differences are likely to be less significant than originally assumed. For the present writing I reanalyzed five items from the 1968 study, with individual interviewers treated as a random factor nested within race of interviewer (Dijkstra 1983), and the original conclusions are essentially unchanged. Furthermore, the effects found in 1968 for black respondents were generally replicated three years later in 1971 with a new sample of interviewers, as well as a new sample of respondents (Schuman and Hatchett 1974), increasing our confidence in the reliability of the original results.

However, a second difficulty with studies of race of interviewer is conceptual: when a physical attribute of interviewers is varied, it is difficult to determine clearly the source of the effect on respondents. Black and white interviewers differ not only in color but in many other ways, including possibly subtle forms of behavior (for example, the tone of voice or facial expression accompanying a question or in reaction to an answer). Thus, it is only an assumption in any particular study that perceptions by respondents of the interviewer's "race" are what influence answers. Groves focuses on the fact that the white interviewers in the 1968 study were young graduate students and the black interviewers were older professional interviewers, but even if this confound was not important, as Schuman and Converse (1971) argue and as later research by others implies (e.g., Davis 1997), the holistic nature of race-of-interviewer as a variable remains a problem.

The same problem occurs when any other physical attribute is varied (e.g., interviewer gender, as in Kane and Macaulay 1993).[28] The power of experimentation—the nature of internal validity as discussed earlier—comes from the extent to which a single variable is manipulated, with all other features held constant where possible, or where not possible, subject to random variation. But "race of interviewer" and "gender of interviewer" are so complex that only in a large and uncertain sense is there an "it" to be manipulated.

The Three Pens Experiment

I carried out a different kind of survey-based experiment on interviewer effects using a design where the single feature manipulated was simpler than a general physical characteristic of interviewers. The occasion was the highly contentious 1990 election in Nicaragua, where the two main candidates were Daniel Ortega, representing the Sandinista (FSLN) party, and Violeta Chamorro, representing the opposing UNO coalition.[29] As a member of a commission that visited Nicaragua in order to examine the quality of the pre-election polling then under way, I heard repeated concerns about the integrity of the polls. Each of the main political parties reported results over the course of the campaign that strongly predicted victory by its side, which cast doubt on whether the polls were being carried out and reported objectively. Yet some of these same surveys (e.g., one for the *Washington Post–ABC News*) were done by reputable firms and appeared to our commission to be administered carefully. Hence one possibility was that respondents were influenced by their *beliefs* about the political sponsorship of a poll. Furthermore, UNO partisans and also some outside observers claimed that many Nicaraguans felt intimidated by the Sandinista government and would be unwilling to express their true voting intentions to interviewers thought to be tied to the government. Indeed, even interviewers who claimed to be doing a nonpartisan poll might be assumed to be connected to the government unless they gave evidence that this was not the case.

To test these claims, I arranged to have what came to be known as the "three pens" experiment administered approximately two weeks before the election, the cut-off point after which polling was not allowed.[30] Each interviewer carried out her interviews in sets of three, administering them identically so far as practical, except for randomly rotating the particular pen she used to record responses. During one interview the interviewer used a pen that displayed the words "DANIEL PRESIDENTE" and was colored red and black, the colors of the Sandinista Party. During another interview the pen displayed the letters UNO and was colored white and blue, the colors of the UNO opposition. During the third interview, intended to be neutral, the pen had no lettering and was red and white, colors that did not have a partisan implication. Interviewers introduced the poll as a college class project and did not mention the pens explicitly, nor make direct reference to personal party affiliation or beliefs, so it was up to respondents to draw whatever conclusions they wished from seeing the pens. The experimental design made for a much simpler manipulation of the hypothesized causal variable—a partisan connection to the survey—than is the case when an interviewer's physical characteristic such as race or gender is varied. In addition, by having each interviewer rotate across the three pen conditions, we addressed the point raised by Groves about confounding type of interviewer with overall interviewer variance.[31]

The results for the three pens experiment were consistent with predictions based on the assumption that respondents were influenced by their perceptions of the sponsorship of the poll, as shown in Table 4.8.[32] First, each of the pen conditions identified with a party produced results in line with expectations: the UNO pen condition showed a majority of voters favoring the UNO coalition, and the Ortega pen condition showed a majority favoring the Sandinista party. Second and crucially, the neutral pen condition showed results that also favored the Sandinista party, which fit the assump-

Table 4.8 Results of the three pen experiment

	Pen condition		
Vote preference	UNO	Neutral	Sandinista
Chamorro	56%	40%	37%
Ortega	44	60	63
Total	100	100	100
N	(48)	(48)	(57)

Gamma = .26, -SE = .13, p < .025 (one-tailed, as predicted)

Source: The original data on which this table is based appear to have been lost in the course of moves by each of the two authors; percentages are taken from Table 3 of their full report (Bischoping and Schuman 1992).

tion that what was intended as a neutral poll was in fact thought by respondents to be connected to the governing Sandinista party. Third, the UNO pen condition turned out to predict accurately the victory by UNO, indeed almost to the percentage point, whereas the other two pen conditions were wrong about the outcome of the election.

The election itself was carefully monitored by outside organizations such as the United Nations and the Carter Commission, the voting was secret, and there was a consensus among neutral observers that the election was not only fair but was widely believed to be fair. Of course, we cannot be entirely sure that most voters did believe this to be the case, but the successful prediction of the results for the two pens identified with the main parties are clear in any case, and the inference about the result for the neutral pen is quite plausible. The design and outcome with regard to the survey-based experiment itself are strong, even if the associations with the final vote tabulation must be regarded as less certain.

Respondents in each survey condition can be thought to have been influenced by their beliefs about the partisanship of the poll they experienced, and in the case of the UNO pen condition this influence appears to have freed some respondents from apparent intimidation by Sandinista influence and encouraged them to state their actual pro-UNO preference. Paradoxically, bias on the part of a survey organization by indicating its sponsorship may have been necessary to reduce bias on the part of respondents.

The three pens experiment allowed us to study the meaning of responses to polls in a society where the honesty of the polls themselves was not trusted. More generally, polls that attempt to predict a final vote require not so much true attitudes—which are never easy to know for sure—but consistency in the way attitudes are expressed from one setting to another. One might obtain good predictions even in a society where *both* the polls and the election are widely assumed to be rigged—so long as the rigging was in the same direction.

Despite the statistical significance of the results and their plausibility, this investigation is one for which construct replication of some type would be highly desirable. Both the hypotheses and results were unusual, the total sample small because of time and funding constraints, and the supervision necessarily indirect. The design does, however, suggest what might be done in studying elections where there are uncertainties about the pre-election polls, the actual voting, or both.

Conclusions about Context and Interviewer Effects on Responses

Standing back from both questionnaire context effects and interviewer effects, we can see that each of the steps in the survey method introduces the possibility of one or more artifacts. Most of these dangers, however, allow opportunities for deeper understanding once we view them as facts of life. A naïve approach to polls that ignores the context in which the question-answer process takes place is quite likely to trip and fall right on its artifact. But a more disciplined and imaginative approach can treat such effects as an important part of the data, and as an invitation to apply survey-based experimentation, supplemented by interpretive Why questions, to discover larger meaning. "Errors," Isaac Newton wrote in 1686, "are not in the art but in the artificers."

— 5 —

The Survey World and Other Worlds

The eminent psychologist Edward Tolman once reflected on why he had spent so much of his life studying the behavior of rats. Noting their many virtues and few vices, he concluded enthusiastically that rats "are marvelous, pure, and delightful" (1945, p. 166). So also the r(ow) by c(olumn) table to the survey analyst—especially if one or two more variables can be added to enrich the tabulation.

Yet we need to avoid allowing a single set of survey data become our entire way of approaching the social world. It can seem too much a parody of William Blake's "Auguries of Innocence": "To see a world in a grain of sand . . ." This chapter attempts to take note of the connections between the world of a single survey and the evidence available from other worlds. I start at a modest level with the possibility of comparing survey data from one population with survey data from another quite different population, then proceed to consider the linkage of surveys to other methods for studying the social world, and finally end by considering what has come to be known as the attitude-behavior problem. Throughout the chapter I try to keep in mind my broader concern with both method and meaning.

Comparisons across Differently Conceived Populations

Reports of most surveys are based on analysis of responses gathered from a single sample or from repeated samples from the same population over time. Often, however, the overall results of a survey can be illuminated by comparing them with findings based on a survey of a theoretically distinct population. Stouffer's [1955] 1992 book, *Communism, Conformity, and Civil Liberties*, discussed earlier in Chapter 2, provides a classic example. In addition to his innovative design and analysis of a national cross-section sample of nearly five thousand American adults, Stouffer drew a sample of 14 types of "community leaders" (mayors, Republican and Democratic county chairmen, American Legion commanders, etc.) from 123 mid-sized Americans cities—1,533 individuals in all. He apparently was responding to criticisms from Herbert Blumer (1948) and others that surveys are too atomistic in their approach, failing to take account of the structure of public opinion and the influence of individuals in leadership positions at all levels.

Among other findings from his comparison of the two theoretically distinct populations, Stouffer reported that "Without exception, each of the 14 types of community leaders tends to be more willing to respect the civil rights of Socialists, atheists, . . . and self-avowed Communists than . . . the rank and file in the same cities as the leaders" (Stouffer [1955] 1992, p. 57). He then goes on to argue:

> the fact that responsible community leaders are more likely than the rank and file to give the sober second thought to the civil rights of the nonconformists . . . can be of much significance to America's future. If the reverse had been found, the future might look dark indeed to those who view with anxiety current threats to historic liberties. Plans of public education which aim at building more respect for the American tradition should be able to count on strong support from influential civic leadership at the grass roots. (p. 57)

Thus even without an internal analysis of either sample, which does occur in considerable detail elsewhere in the book, Stouffer was able to argue that his data address a larger issue ignored in most surveys: community leaders stand intermediate between the general public and those in power in Washington, and were less likely to be swayed by attacks on civil liberties by Joe McCarthy than was the broader public. And indeed in the case of the anti-Communist frenzy in Washington in the early 1950s, it is interesting that by the time Stouffer's book appeared, the assault on civil liberties inspired by McCarthy had peaked and was losing its grip on the public imagination.[1]

My own analysis of explanations for why the Vietnam War was a mistake, discussed in Chapter 3, gained greatly from linking a general population survey to a second sample of responses from local college students. Although the student sample was not ideal in the sense of providing a probability sample of a clearly defined population, it was nevertheless reasonable to claim that it represented a set of individuals influenced by the arguments of those on major campuses who led resistance to the war. The concerns of the student sample turned out to contrast vividly with the considerations that turned the larger public against the war, and the comparison made it clear how different the latter were from the emphases of the anti-Vietnam protest movement on major campuses. Moreover, the contrast continued after the Vietnam War to have implications for different reactions from different parts of the population to U.S. interventions in later years, probably including the invasion of Iraq.

A second example that shows the value of a cross-population comparison started from the opposite direction: not from a general population sample but from a focus on a small set of politically extreme Americans in the Metropolitan Detroit area. David Duke, a former American Nazi and Ku Klux Klan activist, ran for governor of Louisiana in 1991, and as an articulate and nationally known critic of affirmative action and other racial issues, he solicited and received financial support from a substantial number of individuals from outside his state. I obtained from Louisiana the official list of all contributors to the Duke campaign from Metropolitan Detroit—thus creating an initial sample of "Duke contributors."[2] Together with colleagues, I then located and visited the streets on which the contributors lived, and we created a second sample of their near neighbors (usually three neighbors from each street). We next were able to draw a cross-section sample of white households representative of the entire Metropolitan Detroit area. All three samples (Duke contributors, their neighbors, and the cross-section) were sent the same brief mail questionnaire, and the results led to a number of interesting conclusions:

- Duke contributors were spread around the entire metropolitan area, rather than being clustered in any single neighborhood, and in no case were there two or more contributors living on the same street. Thus they were isolates in terms of residence, connected only by their common affinity for what Duke represented.
- Contrary to our expectation, Duke contributors were not more frequently southern-born than the other two samples, though they were more often male, older, and better educated. They also answered our mail questionnaire at a very high response rate (an astonishing 86 percent, as against 78 percent and 74 percent, respectively, for their neighbors and the cross-section sample), and this despite written comments

suggesting that the Duke contributors saw our survey out of the University of Michigan as quite likely biased in a liberal direction.[3]

- In terms of response content, Duke contributors were more apt to perceive crime in their neighborhoods to be a big problem than were either their neighbors or other whites in the Metropolitan cross-section. They also showed less trust in American institutions such as the presidency, courts, media, and unions and expressed more conservative attitudes generally (e.g., opposition to gun control, support for allowing prayer in schools), mostly in a libertarian direction.
- Although Duke contributors differed from their neighbors in the important ways just indicated, their neighbors did not differ significantly from the larger white Metropolitan population in any way we could discover.

Overall and quite remarkably, a survey investigator could evidently obtain what appeared to be an essentially random sample of the white Metropolitan population by first identifying those outliers who contributed money to an ideologically extreme politician running for governor of a different state over a thousand miles away, and then choosing sets of their near-neighbors to include in a survey. Moreover, these comparisons across three theoretically distinct populations could not have been duplicated by sampling a single population, no matter how large the sample obtained.

Survey Results and Results Based on Other Methods

One of the most difficult challenges social researchers face is to gather data using two or more entirely different empirical methods and then make sense of the findings. Of course, in principle different methods aimed at approaching the same problem should lead to the same or at least reconcilable results, but that is not always the case. In addition, measures developed using different methods may be so distinct that a direct comparison of their findings is impossible. It can sometimes seem like results in physics that show light to have properties of either waves or particles, depending on the kind of experiment carried out.[4]

Yet at times a difference in findings can itself prove illuminating, as was the case reported by Converse, Clausen, and Miller (1965) in their study of the Johnson-Goldwater election in 1964. The authors show that poll results were clear early in 1964 that Goldwater was highly unlikely to win the November election. Next they asked how Goldwater and his backers came to see a quite different reality and pointed to the letters that some of these same survey respondents reported having written to newspapers and public officials during that period of time. If we are willing to assume that answers to factual questions about letter writing are close to what an actual enumeration of such letters would yield, Goldwater held a visible lead in this form of "public opinion"—opinion as reflected in the letters. Thus the two different sources of information about reality or, indeed, the two different realities helped explain how Goldwater could be nominated with high hopes for his election and yet go on to lose by a landslide.

An unusual study by Nisbett and Cohen (1996) drew on a number of different research methods to test a proposition about the location in the southern United States of a "culture of honor." With both secondary analysis of existing survey data and new survey data of their own, they confirm that southern white males are more likely than northern white males to endorse the use of violence when situations are described that involve an insult to oneself. They then support and explicate these findings with additional evidence based on other methods, for example:

- Department of Justice and other data show homicides to be more common for whites in the South than in the North, and specifically in rural southern areas that were settled originally by peoples from the fringes of Britain who had been part of a herding economy and who continued in that tradition in the United States.
- To show that actual behaviors, as well as verbally expressed attitudes, reflect the overall regional difference, actions by university male students from the South are compared to those of male students from the North in an experimental situation that entailed a personal insult. The measured responses included observable facial expressions, completions of stories involving insults, and two relevant physiological indicators (cortisol and testosterone). Almost all of the predictions of South-North differences among students were supported.
- The authors report that both laws and votes of political representatives from southern states are less strict with regard to guns and give more support to violent action in self-defense, provide more backing in

Congress for military actions, are more lenient toward domestic violence, and allow more executions of convicted prisoners. These and other measures are used to point to southern distinctiveness at the level of institutions and institutional representatives.

In short, the Nisbett and Cohen (1996) book, *Culture of Honor: The Psychology of Violence in the South,* is a tour de force from a methodological standpoint, with survey data only one element provided in support of an overall argument.[5]

My own attempt at combining survey data with other types of evidence started from a major effort to use polls to describe and understand changes in racial attitudes between 1942 (the first available measures in national surveys) and the late 1990s (Schuman et al. 1997). On basic issues of racial discrimination ranging from public areas such as employment to more personal spheres such as intermarriage, the trends in surveys over the past several decades pointed clearly toward increased acceptance by white Americans of the principle of equal treatment. Figure 5.1 illustrates the change, using two different questions about racial intermarriage, one having to do with public laws and the other with personal preferences.

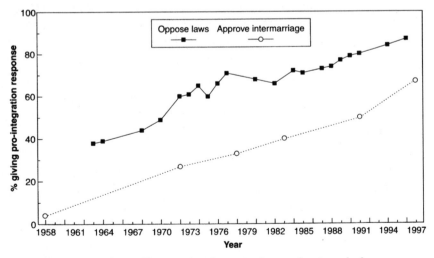

Figure 5.1 Comparison of laws against intermarriage and approval of intermarriage. *Source:* Schuman et al. (1997, p. 118). Copyright © 1985, 1987 by the President and Fellows of Harvard College. All rights reserved.

Although at each time point there was greater support for eliminating laws against intermarriage than there was personal approval of intermarriage, responses to both questions showed essentially the same trends over time (Schuman et al. 1997).[6]

As part of my overall program of research, I was able to obtain entirely different types of data of two kinds. First, Ronald Humphrey and I coded the presence of African Americans in magazine advertisements in two magazines: *Time* and *Ladies Home Journal* from the 1950s into the 1980s (Humphrey and Schuman 1984). During that period blacks were increasingly included in magazine ads and increasingly shown in equal status work situations. However, consistent with the survey data, scenes of blacks and whites in social situations remained relatively rare, and there were other subtle respects in which signs of inequality remained (e.g., white authorities were often shown supervising blacks, but not the reverse).

Second, a much more difficult companion study was an attempt to code actual behavior toward black couples in comparison with behavior toward white couples in a sample of New York City restaurants in 1981 (Schuman et al. 1983) and then to compare what we found at that point in time with the results from a previous investigation three decades earlier (Selltiz 1955). Carrying out a systematic study of social interaction of this type proved to be extremely difficult and was hampered by problems such as the ambiguity of treatment that black couples reported experiencing (e.g., "slow service")—a problem akin to, but more difficult than, coding complex open responses. We also encountered serious racial tensions between the white and black individuals whom we recruited to serve as "testers" of treatment by restaurant personnel. In addition, the study was limited in size because of difficult logistics and minimal funding, though in the end we did find some evidence of a decrease in discrimination between the time points of 1950 and 1981. The research in this case was less instructive for its substantive conclusions than for its lessons in the challenges of systematic social observation of natural behavior that can parallel responses to surveys and polls.[7]

A final example to consider is not a combination of methods already achieved but a set of survey results that demands additional nonsurvey evidence. In a national sample in 1978, Presser and I assessed attitudes toward requiring permits for guns—an issue thought to have influenced some past elections because of the strong feelings of those opposed to any steps toward regulating firearms. One key question was the following:

Would you favor a law which would require a person to obtain a police permit before he could buy a gun, or do you think such a law would interfere too much with the right of citizens to own guns?[8]

Favor	61%
Oppose	39
	100
N	(1,076)

Although the majority of Americans clearly favored requiring gun permits in answer to this question, our main interest was in how supporters and opponents answered two follow-up inquiries, shown in Table 5.1. "Centrality" was intended to provide a subjective measure of attitude strength; "committed action" was included to obtain a self-report of actual behavior. Pro- and anti-permit respondents do not differ greatly in terms of the centrality of this issue, but they do show a large and highly significant difference in their actions: 20 percent of those opposed to gun permits report having written letters, given money, or done both, whereas only 7 percent of those favoring permits say they have done the same—a nearly 3 to 1 ratio. Equally striking is the clear association of attitude centrality to committed action for opponents of gun permits, as shown in Figure 5.2, whereas there is no sign of such an association for those favoring permits.

Thus opponents of gun permits take political action consistent with the degree of strength of their attitudes, whereas those who support requiring permits not only take many fewer actions but the actions they do take show no relation to their attitudes. How can we account for this sharp difference? It seems unlikely that it can be attributed entirely to individual differences in attitudes, since that would not account for the difference in relationships shown in Figure 5.2. What seems more likely, especially based on many reports about the size and efficiency of the primary lobby opposed to gun control—the National Rifle Association (NRA)—is that it has developed highly effective methods of targeting its most committed members at strategic points during elections and legislative processes in order to stimulate letters and contributions. Organizations favoring gun permits and other gun control legislation may be not only smaller and weaker but also less successful at mobilizing those who agree strongly with them about gun

Table 5.1 Centrality and committed action on gun permits

Centrality: "How important is a candidate's position on permits for guns when you decide how to vote in a congressional election—is it one of the most important factors you would consider, a very important factor, somewhat important, or not too important?"

Committed Action: "Have you ever written a letter to a public official expressing your views on gun permits or given money to an organization concerned with this issue?"

	Favor	Opposed
Centrality		
One of most important	5%	8%
Very important	22	26
Somewhat important	39	28
Not important	34	38
Total	100	100
N	(313)	(208)

$$\chi^2 = 6.3, df = 3, p = .10; tau_b = .00$$

	Favor	Opposed
Committed Action		
Written letter	4%	6%
Given money	2	8
Both letter and money	2	6
Neither	93	80
Total	100	100
N	(653)	(417)

$$\chi^2 = 46.4, df = 3, p < .001$$

Source: University of Michigan Survey of Consumer Attitudes, August 1978.

control issues; hence even decisions to send letters and funds remain more with individuals, rather than elicited as part of well-run campaigns.

There is no single way to test the hypothesis just advanced, but one type of useful information could come from a content analysis of pro– and anti–gun control publications, in order to determine when they identify an issue or candidate as calling for action and what steps each takes to mobilize members. It would also be of value to track legislation likely to prompt such efforts. In addition, if respondent cooperation can be obtained, perhaps by using incentives, a panel of individuals could be asked to save dated messages they receive about gun control issues. Letters to the editor in local and

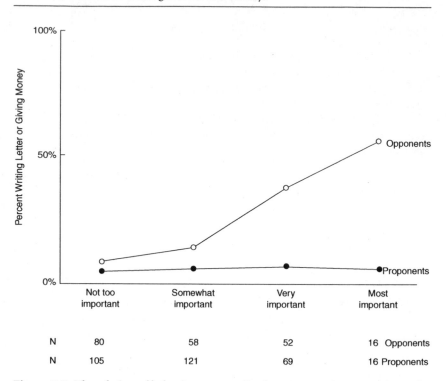

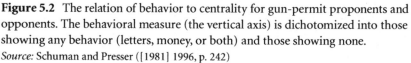

Figure 5.2 The relation of behavior to centrality for gun-permit proponents and opponents. The behavioral measure (the vertical axis) is dichotomized into those showing any behavior (letters, money, or both) and those showing none.
Source: Schuman and Presser ([1981] 1996, p. 242)

national publications could also be reviewed for evidence about the side taken, the specific content, and especially the timing. Once a decision is made to supplement survey data with other evidence, it is likely that other creative steps could be developed to link attitudes to organizational effectiveness, with the goal of explaining the large difference in committed action by those for and against increased control of guns. This study provides a good example of why we need more effort directed at connecting the survey world with evidence from other worlds.

The Relation of Attitudes to Behavior

Concern about different methods of research points to an issue important to almost all attitude surveys: the extent to which attitudes expressed in response to a questionnaire are consistent with directly relevant behavior outside the survey. The issue was raised initially by L. L. Thurstone (1931), the psychologist most responsible for introducing the systematic measurement of attitudes into social science. But the attitude-behavior problem was then given much greater force as the result of a remarkable article by Richard LaPiere (1934), which argued for an almost ineluctable gulf between attitudes as measured by questionnaires and actions as observed in real situations.

LaPiere began with a picturesque thought experiment about a question that he conjectured, perhaps whimsically, might have been put to people in the early 1930s: "Would you get up to give an Armenian woman your seat in a street car?" No matter how carefully the question was constructed and posed, LaPiere claimed that it could obtain only a symbolic response to a symbolic situation:

> The words 'Armenian woman' do not constitute an Armenian woman of flesh and blood, who might be tall or squat, young or old, well or poorly dressed . . . And the questionnaire response, whether it be yes or no, is but a verbal reaction and this does not involve rising from the seat or stolidly avoiding the hurt eyes of the hypothetical woman and the derogatory stares of other street-car occupants. (p. 230)

Having made his primary theoretical point, LaPiere went on to present data from his travels across the country with a foreign-born Chinese couple in the early 1930s. It was a time when discrimination against Chinese, along with many other minorities, was blatant and largely unquestioned in the United States. Yet LaPiere found that his Chinese companions were accommodated without difficulty in all but one of the 250 restaurants, hotels, and tourist homes at which they stopped. Then, six months later, after the completion of his travels, he sent a questionnaire to each place they had visited and asked if it would "accept members of the Chinese race as guests." Of the 128 responses he received, all but one replied No or indicated Uncertainty. (In a useful addition, he also sent questionnaires to a sample of hotels and restaurants that were in the same regions but that they had not visited, and obtained similar results.) LaPiere then concluded that questionnaires, though easy to administer and able to produce quantitative data, yield results that are of no relevance if the goal is to understand actions that occur in real situations. He also notes that the factors that shaped acceptance of his Chinese companions had mostly to do with their clothing, their cleanliness and neatness, and their baggage, and also with their self-confident smiles as they entered an establishment.

Later reviews of LaPiere's 1934 article have pointed out flaws in the design of his Chinese visitors study (e.g., see Ajzen et al. 1970 and Dillehay 1973), but the evidence of almost total inconsistency between attitudes and behavior in LaPiere's report remains a challenge to those of us who expect attitudes measured in surveys to be related to, indeed to predict, later behavior. Moreover, although LaPiere's own theoretical perspective was entirely from the standpoint of a qualitative sociologist, his assumption about the power of immediate situations is consistent with conclusions in contemporary social psychology that have been drawn from a range of experiments, represented by well-known names such as Asch, Latané and Darley, Milgram, Nisbett and Ross, and Zimbardo.

There are several ways to attempt to meet the challenge set forth by LaPiere and others who share his doubts about the value of survey measures of attitudes for learning about nonsurvey behavior. First, even LaPiere acknowledged that polls can predict well how people will vote in the aggregate, and the accuracy of poll predictions close to an election continues to be documented—and this in the face of increasing difficulty in obtaining adequate samples due to new obstacles to contacting respondents and persuading them to take part in surveys (Traugott 2005). LaPiere treated both pre-election polls and actual voting as basically verbal responses to symbolic situations, but his acceptance of such predictions as valid indicates that even for him, the distance between survey responses and at least one kind of nonsurvey behavior is bridgeable.

Within the survey context itself, we can also do more to encourage people to indicate how they are likely to respond to pressures that we and they know can occur in real situations. For example, in a cross-section sample survey of the white population of Metropolitan Detroit at the end of the 1960s, I described the following situation involving racial discrimination, and asked three different follow-up closed questions in sequence (Schuman 1972):

Suppose a good black engineer applied for a job as an engineering executive. The personnel director explained to him: "Personally I'd never given your race a thought, but the two men you would have to work with most closely—the plant manager and the chief engineer—both have strong feelings about blacks. I *can* offer you a job as a regular engineer, but *not* at the executive level, because any serious friction at the top could ruin the organization."[9]

A. Was it all right for the personnel director in this case to refuse to hire the black engineer as an executive in order to avoid friction with the other employees?

B. Should the personnel manager have asked the other men how they would feel about working with a black engineer and then made his decision on the basis of their wishes?

C. In general, do you think employers should hire men for top management without paying any attention to whether they are white or black?

In principle, these three questions should have been answered consistently in terms of either accepting or rejecting discrimination, but instead there was wide variation in responses across the questions:

C. Agrees to racial discrimination in principle.	13% of the sample
A. Agrees to discrimination for sake of harmony.	41% of the sample
B. Agrees to discrimination if majority favor it.	52% of the sample

Depending on the question asked, one could argue that employment discrimination at that point in time was supported by only a small minority of the white population, by two-fifths of that population, or by just over half. This kind of difference, if demonstrated between survey and behavioral data, could readily be interpreted as strong evidence for attitude-behavior inconsistency. Yet these are differences among responses to questions asked not only in the same survey but almost in the same breath! Respondents showed themselves quite capable of taking a different position on the same basic action once the situation itself was portrayed differently, and they did so, according to our interviewers, with little or no sense of embarrassment. Therefore, without claiming that the entire power of real situations can be captured simply by asking the right set of questions, some of the important social pressures that operate in life can be approximated by constructing questions that convey realistic situational forces.[10]

Beyond the conceptual points already made, there is now considerable evidence for what is required to increase consistency between attitude questions asked in a survey and behavior outside the survey. A fundamental starting point is the need to distinguish between "literal consistency" (do people do what they say they will do?) and "evaluative consistency" (are people ordered in the same way on both attitude and behavioral measures?).[11] Literal consistency requires that the survey attempt to measure not an attitude toward an object (e.g., a person or a race or a country), but rather an attitude toward a particular behavior toward the object, and to specify as clearly as possible the time and other contextual factors likely to influence the behavior. This is an important correction to earlier research, which assumed that a broad positive or negative attitude toward an individual or a group implied whatever particular action an investigator happened to measure. The assumption can be seen to be naïve once its implications are thought through, for example, giving a particular gift to one's spouse may show love, but from the knowledge that someone loves their spouse, one could not infer that they will give a particular gift (such as flowers, a puppy, or a vacation in Nepal), for they may express their love in other ways.

Evaluative consistency does assume that an attitude toward an object should be consistent with the overall favorability or unfavorability of actions taken toward the object, even though not necessarily with any particular action. Thus it leads to research that measures a set of behaviors and predicts that a score based on the set as a whole will correlate well with the attitude measure, though recognizing that no specific behavior may be predictable. A fine example of exploring evaluative consistency using a natural population was reported by Weigel and Newman (1976) with a field study in one town that showed a measure of pro-environmental attitudes to relate well to a multi-item measure of pro-environmental behaviors (e.g., actual participation in a roadside litter pickup program). The attitude measure correlated, on average, only .29 with individual environmental behaviors, but the association rose to .62 with an aggregated index of 14 different behaviors. Moreover, in considering the size of these relations, it is important to compare them not with a theoretical maximum of 1.0, but with associations we take seriously in other areas of research. For example, we should note that no more than moderate-sized correlations have been found for the relationship between a father's occupational status and a son's occupational status in America (Blau and Duncan 1967), for the relationship between academic aptitude scores and college grades (Cronbach 1970), and for most other nonartifactual associations of interest to social scientists.

An Attitude-Behavior Field Study

Much of the research examining literal consistency has been done with college students and with measures atypical of surveys, but Brannon and I and a group of graduate students (1973) tested literal consistency between a

Table 5.2 Percent of white respondents supporting either of two laws

"Suppose there is a community-wide vote on the general housing issue. There are two possible laws to vote on. [Present card and read:] Which law would you vote for?"

1. "One law says that a homeowner can decide for himself who to sell his house to, even if he prefers not to sell to blacks."	82%
2. "The second law says that a homeowner cannot refuse to sell to someone because of their race or color."	16
DK, Neither, N.A.	2
Total	100
N	(640)

Source: 1969 Detroit Area Study (Interuniversity Consortium for Political and Social Research).

survey-based attitude measure concerning open housing laws and willingness at a later point to sign a real petition either for or against an open housing law. The research involved a field experiment attached to a standard face-to-face sample survey of the Detroit Metropolitan Area in 1969.[12] White respondents were asked the survey question shown in Table 5.2, and then three months after the survey had been completed, a different person representing a group of "concerned citizens" came to their door and asked the respondent to sign a petition to be sent to the governor and other state officials. The two petitions, only one of which was presented to a respondent, read:[13]

> [*Owner's Rights Petition:*] We believe that it is the right of each homeowner to decide for himself to whom he will sell his house. We urge you NOT to support any law which would force homeowners to sell to someone against their wishes, and if such a law is passed by the current legislature we ask you to veto it.

> [*Open Housing Petition:*] We believe that a person who has a home for sale Does Not and SHOULD NOT have the right to choose buyers on the basis of race, color, or religion. We therefore urge you to support legislation this year which will end racial discrimination in housing, once and for all, in Michigan.

Those who agreed to sign the petition were then asked to perform a still stronger action by allowing their name to be included if the petition was published in one of the two major Detroit newspapers.

More than 80 percent of the respondents in the survey had indicated op-position to an open housing law. These individuals (N=525) were divided randomly into a three-quarters subsample asked to sign the Owner's Rights petition (Condition A), and a one-quarter subsample asked to sign the Open Housing petition (Condition B). Most of the remaining respondents from the original interview had indicated support for an open housing law, and all these people (N=101) were presented the Open Housing petition (Condition C) because the subsample seemed too small to break further. Ideally we would have created a similar random allocation for those favor-ing open housing in the survey, but we thought it better to maintain the group intact for more reliable estimates of their action.[14]

The results of the experiment are shown in Table 5.3. Over two-thirds of the respondents on both sides of the issue (Conditions A and C) were will-ing to affirm their survey-elicited stand by signing a petition ($\chi^2=9.44$, df=1, p<.01). The percentages declined, though not remarkably, in both conditions when stronger action was requested: nearly three-fifths signed with publicity in both conditions. Those espousing owner's rights in the survey showed somewhat more willingness to sign an Owner's Rights peti-tion (85 percent) than did open housing proponents to sign an Open Hous-ing petition (70 percent), but of those who agreed to sign a petition, the open housing proponents were more apt to follow through with stronger action, and thus the two sides did not differ at all if signing with publicity is considered the criterion of action.

Although a high proportion of the sample was consistent in behaving in accord with their survey response, such apparent affirmation could be exag-gerated by the social pressure to sign a petition at all. In Condition B we see that 78 percent of those who had favored owner's rights in the survey were also consistent in refusing to sign an Open Housing petition, though 22 percent did sign that petition opposed to the position they had supported in the prior interview (assuming that reflected their "true attitude"). Thus most respondents did not simply sign whatever was presented to them. Moreover, declining to sign with publicity is much greater as a proportion of overall signing in Condition B than in Conditions A or C, indicating the limit to situational forces in this case.

To estimate overall consistency for owner's rights respondents, one can average those in Condition A who acted consistently and those in Condi-tion B who were consistent in withholding action. If the two conditions are weighted equally, then of those who had originally favored owner's rights,

Table 5.3 Consistency between attitude question in survey and later behavior

| Signing conditions | Attitude preference | Housing petition presented | Percentage taking each action | | | | |
			Refused to sign petition	Signed but declined publicity	Signed and agreed to publicity	Total	N
Condition A	Owner's rights	Owner's rights	15%	26	59	100	293
Condition B	Owner's rights	Open housing	78%	10	12	100	85
Condition C	Open housing	Open housing	30%	12	58	100	76

Source: Survey data and behavioral data are both from the 1968 Detroit Area Study and are available in the same file at the Interuniversity Consortium for Political and Social Research (ICPSR).

85 percent were consistent in signing the Owner's Rights petition, and 78 percent were consistent in refusing to sign the Open Housing petition, which gives an overall average of 82 percent consistency.[15] This average, together with the consistency results for those who supported open housing in the survey, indicates that so far as we can judge from this single field experiment, attitudes can predict behavior to a reasonable extent, though of course not perfectly.

In one sense, of course, LaPiere might have claimed that the attitude-behavior experiment reported here had a large symbolic component, because both in the survey and in the action phase the descriptions of laws were presented in the form of words, though the latter involved presentation by real individuals and carried the implication of wider public knowledge. Before seeing this verbal character of the action as a serious limitation, we should recognize that many highly important actions occur in the form of words stated or written ("I Do" in marriage ceremonies, signatures on checks and contracts and in military enlistments, acts of congress and presidential vetoes), and such actions can clearly entail consequences of a nonsymbolic nature (e.g., prison for failure to live up to military enlistment). Thus the line between symbolic and nonsymbolic actions is not as clear-cut as LaPiere implied.

Yet are there situations for which no survey is likely to be able to predict behavior? Certainly at the extreme this seems likely. How would you behave if a flying saucer suddenly circled around your house? That is probably not predictable, nor are many other unusual events. The main point here can be brought down to earth in the form of a generalization by Fazio (1986, p. 219): when an attitude "is grounded in and based on prior behavior, the attitude-to-later-behavior relation is stronger than when the attitude is based on indirect experience." Fazio presents evidence that supports his finding, which indeed would be supported by our intuition.[16]

Some Concluding Thoughts on Studying More than One World

Asking the same questions to quite different theoretical populations can often be useful, as it was in Stouffer's 1954 survey of the general public and of community leaders. Even without a clear hypothesis, this kind of comparison helps investigators to understand the scope of the findings discovered in their primary sample. Another version of such an extension is replication of the same basic relation within different countries to discover its generality.

For example, in exploring the proposition that national and world events that people recall as important are those that happened during their adolescent and early adult years (discussed in Chapter 2), it has been useful to show that the same basic relation for social memory could be found in samples in both Germany and Japan, with both the same event (World War II) and different events (reunification for Germans, death of the emperor for Japanese)[17].

Use of radically different methods to pursue the same basic investigation is much more challenging, though multimethod studies are now becoming a frequent and admired approach to research. The question arises as to what an investigator should expect in the way of agreement when the methods produce entirely different types of data. In my case, I showed that there is evidence of less racial discrimination today than in the past in survey responses, in magazine advertisements, and in the treatment of customers in restaurants, but beyond that general finding it is difficult to construct comparable variables that can be examined with much precision in three very different sets of data. Nisbett and Wilson argued from federal statistics on violence that the most crucial part of Southern heritage involves rural areas settled originally by peoples from the fringes of Britain who had been part of a herding economy; however, their laboratory experiments on actual behavior compared general samples of students from the "South" and the "North" who happened to be present in a single northern university setting, and the authors do not (and perhaps could not) focus on subregions to fit their earlier theorizing. The challenge of different methods often becomes one of comparing apples and oranges, or perhaps apples and string beans— different in a great many ways. So although the goal of approaching a problem with entirely different methods deserves strong encouragement, I have learned that it should not be undertaken lightly and without considering carefully whether and how it will be possible to synthesize the results.

When we turn to the issue of whether attitudes and actions are related, there is the fortunate possibility of profiting from inconsistencies between different forms of data. LaPiere's travels with a Chinese couple may have presented proprietors with situations even more novel than LaPiere himself had in mind. His goal might have become understanding why hotel and restaurant proprietors rejected reservations for Chinese visitors in question form, but accepted LaPiere's Chinese companions in actuality. When answering questions by mail, did proprietors picture Chinese as laborers in pigtails and coolie hats, speaking an unintelligible tongue, and thus not even recognize the real couple as Chinese? Or did the proprietors act in terms of an overriding belief that the less disturbance the better? LaPiere could have attempted to learn more about these and other possibilities. One good way, not perfect by any means, but among the best available, would have been to ask open-ended follow-up questions, as recommended in Chapter 3, and then to record each proprietor's personal definition of the situation. If he had tried to do this, with the goal of representing a meaningful population of proprietors, of proceeding systematically so as to avoid bias in his inquiry, and of connecting the information to social categories such as age and education, then LaPiere would have reinvented the attitude survey in its richest form. He might have used his negative results not as a stopping point for rejecting the survey approach, but as a starting point for the use of the survey as a method to search for new meaning.

— 6 —

Hunting a Social Science Snark

"Just the place for a Snark," the Bellman cried,
As he landed his crew with care . . .

"Just the place for a Snark! I have said it twice:
That alone should encourage the crew.
Just the place for a Snark! I have said it thrice:
What I tell you three times is true."

. . .

"But oh, beamish nephew, beware of the day,
If your Snark be a Boojum! For then
You will softly and suddenly vanish away,
And never be met with again!"

—LEWIS CARROLL (1874)

"The great tragedy of Science," wrote Thomas Huxley (1870, p. 244) is "the slaying of a beautiful hypothesis by an ugly fact." Tragic perhaps, but essential if progress is to be made in social research. At the same time, it is also true that a highly plausible theoretical conclusion should not be given up lightly in the face of disconfirming data, at least not without careful consideration to make sure the fault does not lie with limitations in the evidence. In a chapter titled "Difficulties of the Theory," Darwin ([1876] 1988, p. 140) wrote: "Some of the [difficulties] are so grave that to this day I can hardly reflect on them without being in some degree staggered . . ." He did his best to address the difficulties, but above all he found his theory of natural selection so persuasive that he could not reject it because of unsolved empirical problems.

No social science theory has anything even faintly resembling the scope and power of the theory of natural selection, but data and theory can at times be competitive in social research in something of the same way, even if on a much smaller scale. The present chapter recounts a case from one part of my earlier research where the competition between meaning and method initially led to compelling data that stimulated what we believed to be a theoretical formulation of very great importance, followed by dismay at the failure of the discovery to hold up as expected when replicated, and finally the sense that something valuable had indeed been learned, though with some uncertainty as to its full meaning.[1]

What is usually published in major journals is research that lays claim to being most successful. What disappoints expectations appears in lesser venues, if at all. Yet even experienced researchers encounter frustrating findings that they must try to turn into positive lessons learned. The present chapter can be seen as such a case study. At the same time, the account makes two important contributions, one conceptual and the second methodological. The first points to the problematic nature of attitude objects, something often ignored in recent theoretical writings about attitudes. The second contribution distinguishes two entirely different explanations for a failure to replicate an original finding, a distinction that is seldom considered as part of methodological instruction. In addition, the chapter draws on methods and meanings already emphasized throughout this book: extensive survey-based experimentation; both literal and construct replication; the importance of keeping in mind social change when interpreting survey data; and open-ended explanations by respondents, though the most revealing explanation come more from a classic study by one of the founders of social psychology than from a specific inquiry of our own.

"Floaters" and Between-Attitude Associations

My account starts from a small set of experiments reported in the course of a chapter, "The Assessment of No Opinion," in the book *Questions and Answers in Attitude Surveys* (Schuman and Presser [1981] 1996). The chapter opens by noting that "To virtually any attitude, opinion, or belief question in a survey, a possible reply is 'I don't know.' Whether the question deals with the performance of the president or the possibility of life after death, respondents may prefer to give what survey investigators call a 'DK response'" (p. 113). Two possible forms of closed questions are then described. One is the typical, or "standard," question where DK is not offered as an alternative, though it is accepted if expressed spontaneously. The other form is a "filtered" question where DK is explicitly offered as one alternative, along with the more substantive choices.[2]

We found that whatever the proportion of DK responses given to a standard question, the filtered form raised that proportion substantially, with a median increment of 22 percent over 19 different experimental comparisons. This finding indicates that on average nearly a quarter of those who gave a substantive response to the standard form of the question would have chosen DK instead if it had been offered. We called these people "floaters," because they move—that is, "float"—between a DK and a substantive response depending upon the form of the question.[3]

My main concern is with what happens when we focus on associations between questions with different content when the form of the question is standard, as against when it is filtered. The two questions that provided key results are shown separately in Table 6.1 in both standard and filtered form. One question deals with Russian-American relations, the other with Arab-Israeli relations. We had no reason to expect the two questions to be correlated either positively or negatively on either question form, there being no necessary connection between beliefs about Russian leaders and beliefs about Arab countries; but when we focused on the associations shown in Table 6.2, they presented an intriguing puzzle. For the standard form of the questions, there is a highly significant positive association between agreeing on the one question and agreeing on the other ($p < .001$). However, for the filtered form, there is no association at all. The highly significant three-way interaction shown at the bottom of Table 6.2 makes chance an unlikely explanation for the striking difference between the two subtables.[4]

To situate the two questions in terms of time, the question on Arab nations was asked in 1974, the year following what came to be known as the "Yom Kippur War," when Israel was attacked unexpectedly by Egypt and Syria and prevailed only after a large loss of soldiers. The year 1974 had no similar large significance for Russian-American relations, though it came shortly after the United States had ended its involvement in the Vietnam War. There was no obvious connection between the content of the two questions, and if their association was substantive, it should have occurred to some extent on both forms of the questionnaire. Hence we initially assumed that the strong association shown on the standard form was artifactual, due in some way to floaters—those respondents who give substantive answers only because DK had been discouraged.

It looked at first as though a likely artifact was close at hand. The Russia and Arab questions are both in agree/disagree format, and therefore susceptible to what is usually called "acquiescence" or acquiescence bias, long recognized as a possible source of correlations in questionnaires of all kinds

Table 6.1 Experiments on two foreign affairs questions

Russian leaders

Standard		Filtered	
"Here are some questions about other countries. Do you agree or disagree with this statement?		"Here are some questions about other countries. Not everyone has opinions on these questions. If you do not have an opinion, just say so.	
The Russian leaders are basically trying to get along with America."		The Russian leaders are basically trying to get along with America.	
		Do you have an opinion on that? [IF YES] Do you agree or disagree?"	
Agree	50%	Agree	39%
Disagree	35	Disagree	23
DK (volunteered)	15	No opinion	38
Total	100	Total	100
N	(499)	N	(510)

Arab nations

Standard		Filtered	
"The Arab nations are trying to work for a real peace with Israel."		"The Arab nations are trying to work for a real peace with Israel.	
		Do you have an opinion on that? [IF YES] Do you agree or disagree?"	
Agree	17%	Agree	10%
Disagree	60	Disagree	45
DK (volunteered)	23	No opinion	45
Total	100	Total	100
N	(492)	N	(513)

Source: Data in Tables 6.1, 6.2, and 6.3 are from the University of Michigan's Survey of Consumer Attitudes, Fall 1974, and are available through the Interuniversity Consortium for Political and Social Research.

(Cronbach 1949; Schuman and Presser [1981] 1996; Krosnick, Judd, and Wittenbrink 2005). This explanation would make good sense because floaters are people who prefer to give DK responses if offered that alternative, but when constrained by the standard form to give a substantive

Table 6.2 Response to Russia item by response to Arab item, for standard and filtered questions

A. Standard Form (DK Not Offered)

	Russian leaders	
Arab nations	Agree	Disagree
Agree	29%	9%
Disagree	71	91
Total	100	100
N	(206)	(142)

$$\chi^2 = 22.0, df = 1, p < .001; gamma = .61$$

B. Filtered Form (DK Offered)

	Russian leaders	
Arab nations	Agree	Disagree
Agree	16%	17%
Disagree	84	83
Total	100	100
N	(144)	(83)

$$\chi^2 = .03, df = 1, p = n.s.; gamma = -.03$$

Russia Response × Arab response × Question Form: $\chi^2 = 8.8, df = 1, p = .003$.

response, they might succumb to acquiescence bias and tend to agree (or in some cases tend to disagree) to statements without paying close attention to the content. An article by Converse (1970) on his classic concept of nonattitudes suggests that this response is just what might happen when people who prefer to say DK are pressured into giving a substantive response.

However, the explanation in terms of acquiescence is inconsistent with two other findings. First, if simple acquiescence is the explanation, we would expect higher agreement to each statement in the standard form than in the filtered form of the question, once percentages are recalculated without DK responses. This does not happen at all on the Russia item, and it happens to only a trivial extent on the Arab item. Second, and even more telling, the 1974 survey was actually divided into three equal-size random samples, with the third subsample similar to the standard form in not offering a DK alternative, but different in that respondents were required to choose between two alternatives, rather than agreeing or disagreeing with a single statement. This forced-choice form of the question, presented in Table 6.3, shows a highly significant positive relation between the Russian and Arab questions, just as did the questions in the standard agree/disagree form. Since acquiescence is ruled out by the forced-choice format, such an artifact cannot be the main explanation for the association between the Russia and Arab items.[5]

It still remains likely that floaters are the source of the association between the Russia and Arab questions in the two forms, standard and forced-choice, that do not offer a DK alternative. Furthermore, there is additional evidence pointing to floaters as the key to this entire set of results. Respondents who received the standard version of the Arab question in the fall 1974 survey were reinterviewed in a February 1975 survey six months later and received the filtered version of the same Arab question. Thus, we were finally able to identify directly those who "floated" between the two question forms—that is, who gave a substantive response in fall to the standard Arab question and a DK response in winter to the filtered Arab question, as well as those who gave substantive responses at both time points.[6] Table 6.4 shows that for those identified directly as floaters in this way, the Arab and Russian questions were reliably associated in the original survey ($p < .001$); for the subsample that did not float on the Arab item between the two time points, there is no Arab-Russian association in the original survey. Therefore,

Table 6.3 Response to Russia item by response to Arab item, for the forced-choice form

"Would you say that the Russian leaders are basically trying to get along with America, or that they are basically trying to dominate America?"

"Do you think the Arab nations are trying to defeat Israel, or are they trying to work for a real peace with Israel?"

	Russian leaders	
Arab nations	Trying to get along	Trying to dominate
Working for peace	21%	8%
Trying to defeat	79	92
Total	100	100
N	(152)	(161)

$\chi^2 = 10.95$, df = 1, $p < .001$; gamma = .50.
Source: See Table 6.1.

Table 6.4 Arab-Russia Associations for floaters and nonfloaters

A. Floaters

	Russian leaders	
Arab nations	Agree	Disagree
Agree	37%	2%
Disagree	63	98
Total	100	100
N	(65)	(47)

$$\chi^2 = 23.6. \; df = 1, p < .001$$

B. Nonfloaters

	Russian leaders	
Arab nations	Agree	Disagree
Agree	18%	16%
Disagree	82	84
Total	100	100
N	(89)	(51)

$$\chi^2 = 0.04, \; df = 1, p = n.s.$$

Russia response $\times$ Arab response $\times$ Floater versus nonfloater: $\chi^2 = 11.5, df = 1, p < .001$.
Source: Survey of Consumer Attitudes, Fall 1974 and February 1975.

Notes: Floaters and nonfloaters are determined from baseline standard form data from fall 1974 and reinterview filtered form data from February 1975. (Floaters are respondents who give a DK response to a filtered question where DK is offered, but a substantive response to a standard question where DK is not offered.) The associations themselves are based on responses to the Arab and Russia questions in the fall 1974 standard questions.

the original split-sample finding was confirmed by this further interview-reinterview analysis.

A New View of Attitudes

As we proceeded step-by-step along the route of identifying floaters as the source of the Russian-Arab association, we also began to develop an interpretation that pointed toward an entirely new theoretical formulation. The explanation of the responses of floaters stemmed, we conjectured, not from a methodological artifact of some common or uncommon variety. Instead, it had to do with the fundamental nature of attitudes and beliefs, and with what happens when these are measured in a general population where respondent knowledge and interest range from almost zero to very great.

The classic conception of an "attitude" developed out of the writings of L. L. Thurstone in the late 1920s. Thurstone acknowledged that "an attitude is a complex affair which cannot be wholly described by any single numerical index" (1931, p. 290), but for purposes of measurement and empirical research he proposed that we can abstract the degree of "favorableness" of an attitude toward an object, just as one can measure the height of a dining room table without claiming to capture in such a measure all the different features of the table. Following this approach, an attitude is widely regarded by social psychologists today as any positive or negative evaluation of an object.[7] However, almost all of the conceptual writing on attitudes focuses on the evaluation or the evaluative process, and almost none on the object of evaluation. For example, the index to the recent *Handbook of Attitudes* (Albarracín, Johnson, and Zanna 2005) includes a large number of entries for "evaluation" and "evaluative," as well as for "attitude" itself, but very few entries appear for "object" and even those few do not refer to conceptual discussions. The same is true of the comprehensive volume by Eagly and Chaiken (1993). The "object" of an attitude seems to be taken for granted and treated as largely unproblematic.

Suppose, however, that people who are at least somewhat knowledgeable about other countries can answer each of the two questions about Arab nations and Russian leaders in terms of what they think is the case for that specific situation. There is no particular reason for the questions to be correlated, because the Russians may be seen as peace loving and the Arabs not, or vice versa. Indeed, that is just what happens on the filtered form where respondents who did not feel they have opinions on the two questions had removed themselves. The correlation between the two filtered questions is essentially zero.

Now suppose that others who would like to avoid offering an opinion— that is, would prefer to give a DK response—are strongly discouraged from doing so, as happens with the standard form of the questions. We surmised that, knowing little or nothing about Arab-Israeli relations, nor perhaps much about the then current stance of Russian leaders toward the United States, they fall back on a more general view of such foreign countries as friendly or unfriendly, a view not based on knowledgeable beliefs about any particular country. Thus the use of a standard question form may tend to create associations between the content of different questions, because each describes a friendly country (one "trying to get along," the other "working for a real peace") as against an unfriendly country. Those who would prefer to give Don't Know responses—ordinarily regarded by survey researchers as a nuisance, or as responsible for meaningless nonattitudes—would therefore be the basis—the "carriers," it might be said—of some important findings in national surveys.

It is embarrassing now to recall and to try to convey the excitement we felt as a result of our increasing confidence in our empirical findings—all based, it must be acknowledged, on associations involving just two survey questions in various forms—and our dawning sense over several weeks of a possibly important new theoretical perspective on attitudes when they are measured in surveys of the general population.[8] We began to look forward to its further generalization and its extension to a range of other survey data.

Furthermore, we were able to test just such an extension ourselves when we realized that if floaters held vague beliefs about Russian leaders and Arab nations, perhaps this applied to political entities or leaders more generally, even American leaders. The same 1974 survey that we had started with happened to include five trust-in-government items, all in standard form (e.g., "Do you think quite a few of the people running the government are crooked, not very many are, or do you think hardly any of them are crooked?"). We summed the five items to create a simple index and looked at its associations with the Arab item that had allowed separation of individual floaters and nonfloaters. Sure enough, the relation proved highly significant for the former ($p < .005$), so that those trusting the Arab nations also showed more trust in American politicians, and, further, as by now we had come to expect, the relation did not approach significance for nonfloaters ($p > .10$). In sum, we felt more and more that we were on the trail of a genuine social science Snark!

Eureka!?

The intricate pattern of confirming cross-checks in the preceding analysis would seem to justify considerable confidence in the initial Arab-Russia difference by form, and it is very hard to believe that the relations were not reliable at that point in time. The two question forms were simply too different in too many ways to consider the findings a matter of chance.[9] We do

"What's the opposite of 'Eureka!'?"

still believe that the two samples were "really" different at that point, but now we come to a great letdown. When we repeated the Russia and Arab experiments in a May 1978 survey, the clear 1974 interaction was no longer in sight and there was simply a small but nonsignificant relation on both forms between responses to the Arab and Russia items. Naturally, our first thought was to search for a problem in the way the data had been coded or analyzed, and we checked carefully all the possibilities we could imagine. But no such easy solution emerged, and we were forced to conclude that the original relation simply did not replicate at a different point in time four years later.[10]

We were deeply disappointed, to put it mildly. Moreover, there was an extremely plausible explanation that argued for the validity of the original results, though it did not provide much support for the idea of a general finding beyond the Arab and Russia items and their association at that earlier point in time. Between 1974 and 1978, major changes occurred in the Middle East: on November 11, 1977, Anwar Sadat, president of Egypt, suddenly surprised the world by announcing to the Egyptian Parliament his willingness to go to Jerusalem to talk with the Israeli government, and just nine days later he spoke directly in the Knesset about his desire for peace between Egypt and Israel. Indeed, at the end of 1977, Sadat was featured as "Man of the Year" by *Time Magazine.* Our May 1978 survey occurred after this extraordinary transformation of the atmosphere in the Middle East, and it is hardly surprising that our own data registered a sharp increase in agreement by the American public that "Arab leaders are trying to work for a real peace with Israel." Whereas only a fifth of the opinion givers had a positive view of Arab nations in 1974, almost half (49 percent) of those offering opinions had that view in 1978 ($\chi^2 = 129.6$, df$= 1$, p$< .001$). This massive shift in attitudes contrasted with the Russian item where there was virtually no change at all.[11]

Ordinarily when an exact replication results in a clear lack of statistical significance, one concludes that the apparent relation found earlier may well have been due to chance—the more so if the original relation had itself been discovered unexpectedly. However, when the failure to replicate occurs after an intervening period that included major events likely to have altered the original association, the failure is ambiguous. In the present case, the pattern of findings discovered originally was so strong and so consistent that an alternative interpretation seems the more likely explanation. We now believe that some floaters on the Arabs question had themselves changed over the four-year period between 1974 and 1978, disrupting the original relation found for the earlier survey.[12] In addition, the changes in the world scene doubtless affected nonfloaters as well, for example, shifting some number of those who would have said Disagree even a year earlier to Agree in the spring of 1978. Thus the nonreplication in this case can be interpreted to show not that the original finding was due to chance, but that it was descriptive of a particular period, rather than a sign of a broader generalization that transcended that point in time.

In addition, we searched our other experiments on standard and filtered questions and found few relations of any kind and none that clearly supported our grand hypothesis about DK floaters as unique "carriers" of associations between attitudes. In that sense, we were forced to consider seriously the possibility that the Snark *was* a Boojum! Except that what "softly and suddenly vanished away" was not the investigators but rather their prized and profound theoretical conclusion.

And yet . . .

The theoretical proposition that objects of attitudes can be responded to in quite different ways and at different levels of abstraction seems so plausible that it is hard to give up, including the sense that the variation may be linked to how familiar we are with an object. It has obvious application when we think of how Americans vote, say, in an election for their representative in Congress or in their state legislature. Some people, perhaps not many, have at least some sense of the candidate's performance on one or more issues important to them and take that into account in their vote decision. But many others, as we well know, vote simply on the basis of political party label, which is not very different from having a general belief about nations being friendly or unfriendly. Or to take a different kind of example, suppose we ask people how they feel about a particular breed of dog, say, Dalmatians, or a particular species of bird, such as a Bittern. Experts on dogs or birds can express an attitude toward the specific type mentioned, but others who choose to answer are likely to do so in terms of their attitude toward dogs or toward birds generally. In fact, the result of learning a lot about virtually any subject is to discover that there are subtypes and sub-subtypes, as well as many other features not previously appreciated, and that one's initial view and initial attitude turns out to have been almost ridiculously superficial.

The problematic nature of objects of attitudes in just this respect was identified many years ago by Solomon Asch (1940), one of the most important figures in the development of modern social psychology. Asch created an experimental situation in which subjects' ratings of "politicians" were influenced by supposed ratings from their peers that indicated either quite positive or quite negative views of politicians. When Asch found that this social influence manipulation did indeed raise or lower the evaluations by his subjects, he rejected the facile explanation that the influence process was simply one of mindless conformity. Instead, he obtained evidence from interviews with his subjects that the different peer reports had stimulated different mental pictures of politicians. Those who received positive peer reports tended to think of political leaders such as George Washington and

Abraham Lincoln, while those who received negative peer reports tended to picture lower level or even corrupt politicians. Thus the judgments of the two sets of subjects were made on the basis of different images of "politicians"—indeed, different meanings to the term "politician." Asch summarized his conclusion in memorable words that still ring true: the process of influence involved "a change in the object of judgment, rather than in the judgment of the object" (p. 458). The term "judgment" in this context has essentially the same meaning as "attitude."

Attitudes toward Objects

The issue for survey researchers then becomes whether such differences in how objects are perceived and responded to are closely connected, on the one hand, to the willingness of people to say Don't Know to a question, and on the other hand, to the extent that survey investigators encourage or discourage admissions of ignorance. A special set of political data that we gathered about two quasi-fictional issues before Congress—the Agricultural Trade Act of 1978 and the Monetary Control Bill of 1979—provides a further hint along both lines. (We call the two issues "quasi-fictional" because we deliberately chose them for their obscurity and were confident that virtually no respondents in our national samples had ever heard of either legislation, though we avoided creating entirely fictitious issues because it seemed better not to lie to respondents.[13])

Both issues were asked about in both standard and filtered form, as shown in Table 6.5. They are typically cited in the survey literature to indicate the proportion of the national population willing to express attitudes toward issues they know nothing about. But our primary interest here is in two further findings. First, if either item is filtered, so that the DK option is explicitly offered, virtually no one gives an opinion: just 10 percent in the case of the Agricultural Trade Act and just 7 percent in the case of the Monetary Control Bill. When the standard form of the questions is used, however, some 31 percent do express attitudes toward the Agricultural Trade Act and 26 percent toward the Monetary Control Bill. For the most part these people consist of "floaters," and all will be treated as such.[14] Thus, the increment in percentage DK created by adding a filter is almost the same as occurs with more typical attitude questions, or looked at from the opposite direction, nearly a quarter of a national sample is willing to offer an opinion when a DK filter is not provided.

Furthermore, based on interviewer recordings of some 35 spontaneous comments by respondents, those who gave substantive answers to the questions did so by interpreting them in ways that made sense to themselves (e.g., one respondent who indicated support for the Agricultural Trade Act explained his response by saying, "We need more trade," whereas a different respondent who opposed the act said, "Shipments from Japan are killing us"). It seems likely that we might have obtained a similar type of meaning-

Table 6.5 Two quasi-fictional issues

A. The Agricultural Trade Act			
Standard		Filtered	
"Congress has been considering the Agricultural Trade Act of 1978. Do you favor or oppose the passage of this act?"		"Congress has been considering the Agricultural Trade Act of 1978. Do you favor or oppose the passage of this act *or* do you not have an opinion on that issue?"	
Favor	19%	Favor	6%
Oppose	12	Oppose	4
DK (if volunteered)	69	No opinion	90
Total	100		100
N	(387)		(787)
B. The Monetary Control Bill			
Standard		Filtered	
"Congress has been considering the Monetary Control Bill of 1979. Do you favor or oppose the passage of this bill?"		"Congress has been considering the Monetary Control Bill of 1979. Do you favor or oppose the passage of this bill *or* do you not have an opinion on that issue?"	
Favor	13%	Favor	3%
Oppose	13	Oppose	4
DK (if volunteered)	74	No opinion	93
Total	100		100
N	(469)		(223)

Source: The data in Table 6.5 panel A are from the University of Michigan's Survey of Consumer Attitudes, November and December 1978, combined. (The different ratio of N's was used for reasons unconnected with this particular experiment, with the division random.) The data in Table 6.5 panel B are from the same survey in April 1979.

ful interpretation for the Russian-Arab associations, if we had encouraged it in the 1974 survey.

These examples of meaning attributed to the questions can be supported further by considering the relation of the Agricultural Trade Act to a different question on economic policy that happened to be included in the same survey (see Table 6.6). Those who favored the Agricultural Trade Act were more likely to feel that the government was doing a good or at least fair job in fighting inflation and unemployment than were those who opposed the act. A similar association occurred for the Monetary Control Bill, and in addition those who favored the latter bill indicated on another question that they thought inflation would be a more serious problem than unemployment in the next year or two. In the case of the Monetary Control Bill, we were also able to carry out reinterviews with respondents six months later and found evidence of reliability over time in supporting or opposing the bill (see Table 6.7). Thus the objects asked about took on real meaning for respondents.

In sum, the investigation of quasi-fictional attitude objects yields results consistent with our earlier assumption with the Russian and Arab items that floaters—those who prefer to say DK, as indicated by their answers on a filtered form, but are persuaded by a standard question to give a substantive response—can create relations between attitude items by developing

Table 6.6 Evaluation of government economic policy by response to the Agricultural Trade Act

"As to the economic policy of the government—I mean steps taken to fight inflation or unemployment—would you say the government is doing a good job, only fair, or a poor job?"

Position on the Agricultural Trade Act	Favor	Oppose
Good job	20%	11%
Only Fair	58	41
Poor Job	22	48
Total	100	100
N	(120)	(73)

$\chi^2 = 13.6$, df $= 2$, p $< .001$; gamma $= .43$.

Source: Data are from University of Michigan's Survey of Consumer Attitudes, November and December 1978, combined.

Table 6.7 Responses to the Monetary Control Bill: Consistency over time

	Time 1: April 1979	
Time 2: October 1979	Favor	Oppose
Favor	62%	33%
Oppose	38	67
Total	100	100
N	(21)	(24)

$\chi^2 = 3.7$, df = 1, p < .03 (one-tailed).
Source: University of Michigan's Survey of Consumer Attitudes, April and October, 1979.

interpretations that connect item content in ways that seem to them sensible. Whereas Converse (1964) showed that real objects can elicit nonattitudes, the present results indicate that what are essentially nonobjects can elicit real attitudes and that these can produce real associations.

High-Energy Particles

We have produced this evidence, it should be acknowledged, by pushing survey questioning to its limit with unfamiliar issues, somewhat like physicists use high-energy particle collisions to produce subatomic entities that cannot be viewed in any other way. The problem remains as to whether we can return to more ordinary survey questioning and discover parallels or, indeed, further examples of the original Arab-Russian associations.

Another finding from a reanalysis of the 1978 replication of the Arab-Russian questions, this time using education rather than question form, yielded results in keeping with the general idea that knowledge about the Arab and Russian items plays a role in whether they are seen as associated or not. If we divide the 1978 sample not in terms of question form, but into four categories by years of schooling completed, 0 to 11, 12, 13 to 15, and 16 plus, the lowest education category shows a highly reliable (p < .01) relation between the Arab and Russia items on both the standard and filtered forms, but none of the other educational categories shows relations approaching significance. In other words, in 1978 education functioned much like question form did in 1974: the Russian and Arab items were seen by the least educated to be associated but not so by those with greater education. There is more than a passing resemblance between operationalizing knowledge by means of education and operationalizing knowledge by means of floating, though we do not as yet fully understand the connection. Since the interaction with education did not occur in the 1974 data, its appearance in 1978 may have been another rare event, whether due to chance or analogous to those events produced by cyclotrons.[15]

At this point, therefore, we have certainly not tracked to its lair a genuine Snark, but we continue to think there is enough evidence that one exists to justify future searching, despite the ever-present danger of stumbling instead upon a Boojum.

Conclusions

This chapter brings together my concerns about both meaning and method, but also highlights the tensions that frequently exist between them. On the one hand, the chapter describes an intensive search for a larger meaning in responses to survey questions, including responses by those who would prefer to opt out of answering and to say Don't Know instead. One appeal of this search is to gain a better understanding of how the objects of attitudes are conceptualized in general populations, which could complement the concentration by surveys over the years on the evaluative nature of attitudes.

At the same time, "method" has been stressed as well, not only reliance on survey-based experiments to identify floaters, but emphasis on literal replication of results and construct replication across different types of questions. Respondents' explanations of their answers also provided clues for making sense of our results, and were even more decisive for Asch's interpretation of his findings. Unless we use all the resources available to researchers, while at the same time testing and retesting our findings to determine their robustness and their scope, we will not understand when and why a replication of an unusual finding will or will not be successful.

The balance between the ambition to discover new meaning and the discipline of attention to method is essential to polls and surveys, as it is to all other branches of science and scholarship. If this leaves conclusions uncertain at times and in need of further research, as is clearly the case for now with regard to effects due to "floaters," so be it.

Conclusion

A Brief Look Back at
Methods and Meanings,
Surveys and Polls

We have to remember that what we observe is not nature in itself,
but nature exposed to our method of questioning.
—WERNER HEISENBERG (1958, P. 58)

A classic example of discovering important meaning in survey responses
dates from Stouffer and his colleagues' development of the concept of "relative deprivation" to explain why "men in the Air Corps, who were on the average most favored by promotions, were also the most critical of promotion
policy" (Stouffer et al. 1949, p. 190). Although the authors were focused on
a paradox in their World War II data, they arrived at a more general interpretation that could be applied to other responses in surveys and in life that
had nothing to do with the Air Corps or even necessarily with promotions.
This kind of insight is not fundamentally different in nature from that in
other sciences, as when Eric Kandel (2006, pp. 194–195) writes of his real-
ization that "For the first time I had identified a motor neuron in *Aplysia*
that controlled a specific behavior! . . . We both were amazed to see the
powerful behavioral consequences of stimulating a single cell and knew it
boded well for identifying other motor cells."

Insights into the meaning of data are first and foremost the product of
thought and imagination, but some methods for discovery can help make
insights more likely. Within surveys, traditional analysis of response data—
whether done by cross-classification of answers, or some form of multiple
regression, or a newer analytic technique—is the basic way of pursuing
meaning, as it was for Stouffer and his colleagues. But in preceding pages I
have emphasized two additional approaches that have often proved of value
for encouraging discoveries of new meaning. One is survey-based experiments that compare two or more different ways of asking questions. The

other is the use of Why inquiries to obtain open-ended explanations of prior answers. Both approaches help us bridge the gap that often exists between experience-near concepts meaningful to respondents and experience-distant concepts that investigators can use in their own interpretations, as discussed in Chapter 3.

Neither experiments nor open-ended probing depend on taking answers to questions literally. Quite the contrary. Experiments look at the effects of varying the way a question is asked, effects that are often beyond the ken of respondents. "Why questions" search for clues as to what a preceding answer implies irrespective of the answerer's intentions. The two approaches also encourage us to make constructive use of the ambiguity that is always inherent in language, learning how the same words can have different meanings for different parts of a population, as we saw in Chapter 3. In addition, each approach helps us avoid the dangers of both "survey fundamentalism" and "survey cynicism," discussed in Chapter 1. If other types of data can be added, including evidence from different populations or from entirely different methods of research, as described in Chapter 5, so much the better.

We all hope that interpretations of survey data will lead at times to new and important discoveries—to finding a genuine Social Science Snark, as attempted in Chapter 6. But because imagination and speculation are so vital to the quest for meaning, it is equally important that we accept the discipline of subjecting our ideas to repeated confrontations with social reality. The initial way to do this is typically through some form of significance testing. Without that kind of routine testing, we are apt to think we see— adapting the title of Henry James's story—a figure in each carpet we come upon. Significance tests are a first protective device, often letting us know that what we think we discover in a particular set of data is better treated as an accidental patterning due to chance.

Yet significance testing is only a crude form of discipline. With small samples we can miss a real finding, and with large samples we can take too seriously results that are trivial. In addition, any serious analyst of survey data is apt to carry out a great many significance tests, so the probability yielded by any one is usually indeterminate. Replication, preferably done independently, is essential for a new finding we wish to claim as genuinely important.

Simple replication is always useful, but two more complex forms are at least equally so. First, since we almost always intend our results to speak to concepts more general than the specific words included in our questions, we need to make sure that the concepts can be shown to work with more than one question form or wording, as explored in Chapter 2. In addition, when studying social attitudes, we should allow for possible change over time, including change that interacts with what we may think of as a timeless proposition, as occurred with a key finding in Chapter 4. For this purpose we must define a clear population and draw adequate samples from it, else we will have no rigorous way to take account of change over time. Of course, much work can be done with convenience samples, such as students in a course, but if we wish our results to have more general implications, it is important to work at some point with samples from a more general population.

The various hypotheses investigated in the course of this book have been at what Merton (1957) referred to as "middle range"—or perhaps even "lower range" at points. No attempt has been made to construct an overall theoretical framework or to advance a sweeping general theory. Others have developed broader approaches in recent years, which I have found both helpful and stimulating, but in each case there has been some feature that kept it from making complete contact with the kinds of propositions I and more than a few others wish to pursue.

For example, an emphasis on "total survey error" (Biemer and Lyberg 2003; Groves et al. 2004; Weisberg 2005) works well where one can conceive of a "true value," and thus it fits probability sampling from a well-defined population, fits asking many questions where objective validation is possible (at least in principle), and fits most other aspects of interviewing, coding, and data processing. But attitudes cannot—even in principle—be connected to objective validation in the sense of a single true value (Bradburn 1983; Duncan 1984; Tourangeau, Rips, and Rasinski 2000), though serious efforts at "construct validation" of an attitude are both possible and desirable (Cook and Campbell 1979; Cronbach 1989). Groves (1991) points out that some questions treated as factual, such as one about current employment asked in U.S. Current Population Surveys, have serious ambiguities (e.g., what does "most" mean in "most of last week"?), and thus he does not like the distinction between "attitudes" and "facts." Groves is certainly correct that some so-called facts ("racial identification") are closer to attitudes, as discussed earlier in Chapter 1.

The crucial distinction is not between "attitudes" and "facts" but between "objective" and "subjective" reports. If a person other than the respondent can decide how to classify "most," perhaps with the help of detailed instructions (e.g., "most" uses "number of hours" and refers to "majority"), we can speak of the information as "objective," and if we wish we can classify the question as concerned with a "fact." However, if the decision hinges on a respondent's self-report (e.g., "I enjoy my work a lot"), then the information is inherently subjective, and we can call it an "attitude" or use a related term such as "belief." The employment question can be said to have a "true value" with which a self-report can be compared, at least in principle; the latter does not, because the self-report is all we have that is definitive, though we can attempt to link the response to objective behaviors (e.g., "she never misses a day of work" or "she always looks happy on her arrival").[1] Finally, there are phenomena like racial identification that are often treated as objective but are closer to subjective, and perhaps Duncan's (1984) use of the term "quasi-fact" is appropriate, though "quasi-attitude" might be just as good. In any case, I do not see how subjective phenomena like attitudes that lack objective true values can fit comfortably within a Total Survey Error framework. Attempts to do so, tend either to ignore the difficulty or to become procrustean.[2]

Another broad theoreticall framework, "cognitive aspects of survey methodology" ("CASM"; Sirken et al. 1991), clearly includes much of what is done in studying the question-answer process. At least part of my own research on the question-answer process can be seen as falling within this movement, even though some was carried out prior to CASM's official christening in 1983 (the date given by Tanur 1999) and with somewhat different terminology. At the same time, an excellent study by Abelson, Loftus, and Greenwald (1992) that reports what is essentially traditional social psychological research is included in a book about "the cognitive bases of surveys" (Tanur 1992). Of course, "cognitive" is a very general term, as when Neisser (1967, p. 4) writes that "every psychological phenomenon is a cognitive phenomenon."[3] Similarly, Gilovich, Keltner, and Nisbett (2006, p. 7) define cognitive psychology as "the study of how people perceive, think about, and remember aspects of the world," hence just about all of the question-answer process and everything related to it can be called "cognitive." What is crucial is to show how particular cognitive concepts and theories lead to specific hypotheses or testable interpretations.[4]

No matter what approach we take as social scientists, it is well to recognize that we are always dealing with data about social reality, not with social reality itself. We are always drawing inferences, making interpretations, testing ideas. Survey researchers, as well as other researchers, may be likened to the men living in the cave in Plato's allegory. Chained to one spot deep within the cave, they could only stare at the wall ahead. Behind them, figures of men and animals and other objects moved along a track, and light from a fire still further back cast the shadows of these objects on the wall in front. For the men, then, the shadows were the only reality they knew—their data, it might be said—and from these shadows they had to infer, as best they could, the true nature of the world.

Plato believed that there is a method that will allow the men to rise, figuratively speaking, and see the true objects, the fire, and in fact the whole world outside the cave, even the sun and the moon and the stars. Some social researchers believe that there is one method that will do the same—the one most often cited by sociologists such as LaPiere is direct observation, because it involves observing interaction in a natural setting with one's own senses. But without doubting the very real advantages of such field studies, we should be wary of assuming that what we perceive most easily with our own eyes and ears is somehow more valid than what we learn through instruments. Else we should insist that the world is flat because it can so clearly look to be flat at the level of ordinary human perception. Nor is viewing the stars with our own eyes somehow truer than looking at them through a telescope or abandoning sight altogether and studying the sky by means of radio waves.

The survey method is also an artificial way of bringing the human scene into focus—where artificial simply means a way created by people. It should be treated with care and skepticism, and as only one of several different methods by which we search for meaning in social life. But polls and surveys will continue to be of great value, not because they are free of artifacts—context effects, interviewer effects, and the like—but because they are able to make use of their own artifacts for illumination.

Notes

References

Index

Notes

Preface

1. For one perspective on Harvard's Social Relations Department, as well as on Antioch College (mentioned later in this Preface), see the first chapter of Clifford Geertz's book *Available Light* (2000). I was fortunate to have spent time in each setting when it was near its zenith.

Introduction

1. For an incisive discussion of subjective phenomena, see Duncan (1984).
2. Applied sampling for surveys confronts major challenges at present, partly because response rates have plummeted, partly because of technological change involving cell phones and use of the Internet, but these are not issues that can be dealt with in this book. One recent source for methodological evidence on nonresponse and its implications for future surveys appears in a special issue of *Public Opinion Quarterly* (Singer 2006). Yet even response rates can be used creatively to provide substantive insights—thus also combining method and meaning—as shown by House and Wolf (1978).
3. I use data from different periods wherever they fit best, regardless of chronology. With Robert Abelson (1995, p. xiv), I also can say: "Many of these examples are somewhat old—but then again, so am I." Where ideas in the book are those I developed over my own career, I have used the first person rather than rewording sentences to sound impersonal.
4. Jean Converse notes that some early commercial and media vehicles used the term "survey," for example, the Crossley Radio Survey and the Fortune Survey (personal communication, but see also Converse 1987). However, "poll" has become the main term for commercial and media reports. Converse (1984) also points out that during World War II, within the Office of War Information the

"Polling Division" was organized by commercial pollsters and the "Surveys Division" was composed mainly of social psychologists with academic ties.

5. Use of the Internet for polls and surveys is growing, but the better Internet surveys are either linked to an earlier sample obtained via a face-to-face or telephone survey, or are used with populations where traditional probability sampling is possible (e.g., members of an organization known to be reachable via the Internet).

6. "Polls" usually concentrate on attitudes or similar subjective phenomena rather than on census-type information, but this emphasis is not an inevitable or failsafe distinction, and "surveys" clearly are used to gather both attitudinal and factual data. Still another point of separation sometimes urged is a focus by polls on single questions, as compared to scales constructed from sets of items that surveys may develop to increase reliability. A distinction between "opinions" and "attitudes" has also been made in these terms (Moser and Kalton 1971), but other writers have been less sure that a profound difference is really involved (McGuire 1985, p. 241).

7. My hypothesis concerning language first appeared in a 1979 University of Michigan newsletter and then with some revision as a piece in the *Public Perspective*, 1997.

8. See Crystal (2004) for the intricate development over time from Old English through the Middle period (which included both Norman French and Parisian French, as well as Latin both early and late) and into Modern English.

9. In addition to more and more polls in other countries carried out by well-known organizations such as ABC News, Gallup, and Pew, the Program on International Policy Attitudes (PIPA) at the University of Maryland now specializes in both American attitudes toward other countries and attitudes in other countries toward issues of importance to the United States.

10. According to Cantril (1944), the "split-ballot" effort was begun by the American Institute of Public Opinion (the Gallup organization) in the late 1930s to address criticisms of poll questions as inadequate or defective in various ways. See also Converse (1987). Bishop and Smith (2001) examined several thousand "split-ballot questionnaires" developed by Gallup, and they then drew on a small subset for a careful analysis of response order effects (Bishop and Smith 2001). See also a more recent analysis Holbrook (2007). In addition, there were a few other, now classic experiments, notably the forbid/allow tone of wording effect first reported by Rugg (1941) and the communist reporters context effect constructed by Hyman and Sheatsley (1950), both of which Schuman and Presser ([1981] 1996) replicated to test the effect after several decades.

11. Also important was Mueller's (1973) analysis of survey data about the Korean and Vietnam wars. Mueller did not have at his disposal actual experiments, but he was sensitive to problems of question wording and made a number of quasi-experimental comparisons that enriched his own analysis and contributed to

later experimental comparisons by others. A similar quasi-experimental approach was taken by Schuman and Duncan (1974) drawing on data from the 1971 Detroit Area Study and emphasizing effects on associations as well as univariate distributions.

12. The "Communist reporter experiment" (Hyman and Sheatsley 1950) is a focus in Chapter 4.

13. One difference between survey-based experiments on questions and other social psychological experiments is that it is often difficult to conceptualize one of the survey conditions (e.g., one order of questions rather than a different order of questions) as a "control condition." For example, in Milgram's (1974) study of obedience to authority, he could treat as the baseline or control condition one in which subjects decided for themselves the level of shock (including no shock) to administer.

14. Sniderman, Crosby, and Howell (2000) report an experiment on a General Social Survey question that has regularly asked which of two hypothetical laws a respondent would vote for:

One law says that a homeowner can decide for himself whom to sell his house to, even if he prefers not to sell his house to blacks.
The other law says that a homeowner cannot refuse to sell to someone because of their race or color.

The authors created two new versions of the question, one that attempted to tilt the balance toward opposition to an open housing law, the other toward support for an open housing law. When they find that the former version does increase opposition, but that the latter version fails to increase support, they conclude that "Opponents have more, or at any rate more readily accessible, arguments to invoke than proponents" (p. 266). But this conclusion assumes that the arguments they devised were equally appropriate for the two sides, which this reader did not judge to be the case (Schuman 2000, p. 316). Others can make their own judgment, but the larger point is that simply because the new wordings are part of a split-sample comparison, they are not freed from the requirement of adducing evidence of validity, which in this particular case imposes the extra burden of determining whether the two new versions are equally appropriate and equally strong.

1. Ordinary Questions, Survey Questions, and Policy Questions

1. I do not know of any attempt in a major survey to discover just what respondents believe will be done with their answers, but this issue would be useful to explore. For interesting qualitative examples of how respondents think of the interview experience, see Converse and Schuman (1974, pp. 22–30, 55–59, 72–75).

2. "Facts" are usually thought of as information ascertainable, at least in principle, by some form of external observation (e.g., an interviewer might count the number of rooms in a house, consulting a book of definitions, with included and excluded spaces noted). "Opinions" can be ascertained only from respondents' reports of their subjective states: attitudes, beliefs, and feelings. But the distinction is not so simple in practice, as the Postscript to this chapter indicates.

3. Schuman and Presser ([1981] 1996) made testing the robustness of relationships in the face of variations in question form, wording, and context a major theme of their book and called it the assumption of "form-resistant correlations." They were able to show such robustness in many cases in their original work, as well as subsequently (Schuman and Scott 1989b; Presser 1990), but by no means in all cases. In Chapter 4 of the present book, we treat one important exception. Others have also reported instances where the assumption does not hold (e.g., Bishop et al. 1980; Bishop 2005; Schwarz 1996).

4. Perhaps the best example of a large change due to a seemingly small alteration in tone of wording is the classic difference between "forbidding" and "not allowing" an action, first reported by Rugg (1941) and later replicated and developed further by others (e.g., Schuman and Presser [1981] 1996; Hippler and Schwarz 1986; Holleman 2000). It is difficult to locate other comparable examples of seemingly insignificant changes in wording that have large effects on distributions or relationships. The forbid/allow experiment also shows that even where marginals are changed considerably by an alteration in tone of wording, each version of the question can reveal much the same change over time, consistent with the principle of "form-resistant correlations" (Schuman and Presser [1981] 1996, pp. 276–278).

5. The constraints of a particular interrogative framework can be observed in non-survey situations as well: "A former senior member of the Coalition Provisional Authority in Baghdad occasionally observed President George W. Bush on video-conferences with his top advisers. 'The president would ask the generals: Do you have what you need to complete the mission? as opposed to saying, Tell me, General, what do you need to win? which would have opened up a whole new set of conversations,' says this official . . . the way Bush phrased his questions, as well as his obvious lack of interest in long, detailed discussions, had a chilling effect. 'It just prevented the discussion from heading in a direction that would open up a possibility that we need more troops,' says the official." Evan Thomas and Richard Wolffe, "Bush in the Bubble," *Newsweek,* December 19, 2005, p. 37.

6. In this CBS Poll question and the two that follow, the size of each of the two subsamples is a little under 500. In this first case, the difference by question wording is highly significant ($p < .001$).

7. Neither the difference between the two wordings nor the three-way interaction of Republican versus Democrat by vote by question wording approaches signif-

icance, though when Independents are included, the interaction is just significant: $\chi^2 = 14.3$, df $= 3$, p $< .01$. For most purposes, however, the two subsamples could be combined to do further analysis using the full sample, ideally with some checks back to results with the separate versions. When sample sizes are very large, significance is likely to be attained, but the difference may be too small to be important.

8. The three-way interaction of response by party (Republican vs. Democrat) by question wording is based on a total of 637 cases, approximately half on each form, and yields: $\chi^2 = 22.6$, df $= 1$, p $< .001$.

9. As Lang's early letters make clear, his belief that Lipset's nonsurvey writings were politically biased (especially "Political Controversies at Harvard, 1636 to 1974," pp. 3–278, in Lipset and Riesman 1975) stimulated his distrust of the 1977 questionnaire. In turn, Ladd and Lipset regarded Lang's attack as motivated by political more than scientific concerns. Nevertheless, it is useful to our discussion to concentrate on points bearing on more general issues of survey methods.

10. All following quotations are from *The File*, except where otherwise noted. (The present paragraphs about *The File* are adapted from my review of the book [Schuman 1983]. I sent a draft of the review to Lipset, Ladd, and Lang for their comments; I don't recall whether either Lipset or Ladd responded, but both before and after the review was published, I received extensive communications from Lang pointing out what he believed to be my many mistakes.)

11. Lipset and Ladd sometimes responded to objections about particular question wordings by claiming that they had no interest in single-item distributions, but only in using the items for bivariate and multivariate analysis (*Science*, February 17, 1978). However, some of the Ladd-Lipset reports of results were not consistent with this claim. In the *Chronicle of Higher Education*, January 16, 1978, they gave a number of unqualified univariate findings, for instance, that 81 percent of their sample agreed that "the private business system in the United States, for all its flaws, works better than any other system devised for advanced industrial society." The problem in this case is not simply the univariate nature of the result but the flavor of political bias that may be conveyed by the wording.

12. Exceptions can occur when individuals define themselves as deviant, whether politically or in other ways.

13. Recently a debate occurred within the "net group" of the American Association for Public Research concerning the appropriateness of asking a question about whether the president should be impeached. Opponents argued that, no, this was not at present a serious public issue to be given prominence by a poll, and proponents claimed that it was legitimate to frame the question whether or not it was much discussed at that point. An argument for the latter position is that we may sometimes fail to understand an important change unless we are willing

to invest in measurement when it is barely visible. For example, poll data indicate that white racial attitudes moved in a liberal direction between 1944 and 1946, but we have no way of knowing whether this change was already occurring during World War II or even earlier, or instead was precipitated by events at the close of the war, as some have argued (e.g., Fredrickson 2002). There are no relevant poll data prior to 1944, nor any in 1945 just as the war was ending.

2. The Primordial Distinction between Open and Closed Attitude Questions

1. In this discussion, as throughout this book, my focus is on questions about subjective phenomena: attitudes, beliefs, values, and the like, with "attitude" the shorthand summary term. For a recent review of the issues when "factual information" is sought, see Schaeffer and Presser (2003), though as discussed in Chapter 1, a distinction between attitudinal and factual data is by no means always clear-cut. But especially where respondents are asked to report where their own behavior fits along a scale of possible behaviors (e.g., number of hours spent watching television or number of sexual partners), a closed set of alternatives may seem to convey information about the normal range and central tendency for the population, and this information can easily affect answers. Thus open questions may to be preferred for such inquiries. See also Schwarz (1996, ch. 5).

2. Converse (1987, pp. 72–73) points out that Likert actually included a variety of types of questions in his 1932 dissertation, only one of which was a set of five-point scales, and these ranged from Strongly Approve to Strongly Disapprove. Frequent references to "Likert-type items" to refer to sets of agree/disagree items are not historically correct. Moreover, when Likert first moved into a government research unit, he introduced a degree of standardization not previously followed there, so the "irony" noted here is due as much to the way his contributions have come to be remembered as to his own intellectual development (see also Converse 1987, pp. 157–159).

3. A small sample of the many sources for research on response order effects would include Payne (1951); Schuman and Presser ([1981] 1996); Krosnick and Alwin (1987); Moore and Newport (1996); Sudman, Bradburn, and Schwarz (1996); Bishop and Smith (2001); Holbrook et al. (2007). On primacy and recency effects in other social psychological research, see for example Petty and Wegener (1998).

4. Excluded for the purpose of this chapter are data too far from realistic surveys of a general population to provide clear evidence (e.g., a careful laboratory study by Dohrenwend [1965] of a small number of undergraduates in one university).

5. The October 1986 experiment and also the experiment in Table 2.2 were first reported by Schuman and Scott (1987), but with new analysis added here. (In tables in this and later chapters, I usually round percentages to the nearest whole number, though they may have been given to the first decimal in an original article. Greater exactness can be of value to someone who wishes to reanalyze the data, in which case they should consult the referenced publication, but otherwise serves no useful purpose and implies more precision than is justified.)

6. Bishop (2005) reports an open/closed experiment that is similar except that the closed form did not invite respondents to name a different problem than those listed explicitly, which probably accounts for its smaller proportion of "other" answers—about 20 percent—than presented in Table 2.1. Bishop's experiment also shows little matching between the open and closed responses, and what matching does occur may be because the question was focused on election issues.

7. Note that the closed question in Table 2.2 was constructed quite differently from the closed "most important problem" question in Table 2.1. The latter had offered only infrequently given open categories, but in the present instance exactly the opposite was done, because with the exception of the computer category, the alternatives offered as part of the closed question were based on the most frequently given open responses. Furthermore, in the experiment in Table 2.1, despite the impressive constraint produced by the listing of rare categories in the closed question, nearly 40 percent of the sample did choose to go outside the listed alternatives. In the experiment in Table 2.2 virtually everyone (95 percent) was satisfied to select one of the listed choices, which is consistent with our having purposely included the four choices that were most frequently given spontaneously plus the one hypothesized to be a potentially preferred choice once made legitimate.

8. In addition, mention of computers was not significantly associated with age in the open "events and changes" question, though it had seemed likely to be an answer given by younger respondents. However, on the closed question, selection of the computer response was significantly ($p < .05$) related to younger age.

9. The original data in Table 2.3 were collected through TESS (Time-sharing Experiments for the Social Sciences, National Science Foundation Grant 0094964) and have not been previously published. The survey was carried out by Indiana University's Center for Survey Research.

10. Although the Kennedy response did not show a significant open-to-closed increase in the smaller 1986 experiment, the percentages then were similar to those in the 2003 replication.

11. Foddy (1993, p. 151) objects to the use of open questions on the grounds that respondents may be unable to recall all possible answers they might give to a question before deciding on one, which fits the Kennedy increase. But in this

case the larger problem is the unintended restriction in the frame of reference created by the open question. Both phenomena are important.

12. The term "salience" has also been used to describe the responses given to an open question, but with the same ambiguity as discussed here with regard to availability. On the one hand, Cannell and Kahn (1968), Geer (1991), and Foddy (1993) all equate salience with importance. On the other hand, the main use of the term "salience" in cognitive psychology refers to conspicuous but not necessarily important aspects of the external world (for example, an odd hat) that catch a perceiver's immediate attention. Even where the internal world of memory is the reference, the stress is still on the fleeting, so that the phrase "seemingly trivial but highly salient information" (Taylor and Fiske 1978, p. 252) captures the emphasis in much cognitive writing. These different meanings of the term make it confusing and it is therefore avoided here.

13. Although written in a simple and straightforward style, Stouffer's *Communism, Conformity, and Civil Liberties* ([1955] 1992) included a number of important innovations that are well described in James A. Davis's Introduction to its 1992 reprinting. The present reexamination of one part of the book is drawn from Kane and Schuman (1991), with further new analysis included in my discussion. Some inferences made from Stouffer's data would be less difficult if the actual open-ended answers had been preserved; but when the study was carried out in the mid-1950s, only the codes were computerized and, so far as I have been able to determine after inquiries to relevant archives (the ICPSR, NORC, the Roper Center, the Harvard University Archives, and the Archives of the Fund for the Republic, which sponsored the survey), the original questionnaires were not saved, though conceivably they remain in an attic somewhere in Cambridge, Massachusetts, where Stouffer himself lived. I believe that Stouffer would have been sympathetic to the analysis I have carried out, despite its revisionist implication for his treatment of open questions in the book.

14. Not surprisingly the cross section registers a higher "don't know" (DK) percentage (eight percent) than the leaders (one percent), but even if the DK category is retained for the single closed question, the cross section perceives significantly (p < .001) more danger from Communists (43 percent "great" or "very great danger") than the leaders (37 percent).

15. Note that the argument here concerning Stouffer's experiment is not that open responses are necessarily superficial, including even those that are largely the result of recent exposure to media emphasis. (See Smith [1989] and Geer [1991] for such a debate, but it is not directly relevant to consideration of closed versus open questions.)

16. The present account of the five surveys given over a 21-month period from 1982 to 1983 draws from Schuman, Ludwig, and Krosnick (1986), supplemented by additional new analysis. The closed version of the MIP question al-

ways provided explicit legitimation of "other" responses by adding: "*or*, if you prefer, you may name a different problem as most important," but as in past experiments this led to few volunteered additions to the alternatives offered.

17. The sum of the four common category percentages was remarkably constant for the five surveys over the 21-month period studied, varying within the narrow range of 49 to 55 percent, with no discernible trend up or down over time. Thus the open/closed comparisons appear to deal with much the same subpopulation at all five time points, though we need to qualify that conclusion below when we consider correlates of responses to the two question forms.

18. Note that the results of the experiment in Table 2.5 are quite different from those that occurred in the earlier experiments on open questions that dealt with crime as an important national problem and with the invention of the computer as an important past event. In both those experiments, a response seldom given to the open form of the question was chosen frequently when offered as an explicit alternative on the closed form of the question. In the present experiment, the choice of nuclear threat shows the same proportionate increase as the other three alternatives combined.

19. The clearest demographic correlate of these explanations is for men to be nearly twice as likely as women to deny the possibility of a nuclear war ($p < .001$), and for women to be nearly twice as likely as men to say that a nuclear war is beyond anyone's personal control ($p < .01$). Viewing nuclear war as a distant problem is not disproportionately characteristic of either sex, but it is significantly more frequent among younger than among older persons. The same is true for more as against less educated persons, though age is the stronger correlate here. However, none of these correlates modifies the main outcome of the follow-up inquiry: respondents had little difficulty explaining why they do not consider the threat of nuclear war the "most important problem" facing the country.

20. One other possible source of change was the highly publicized television showing on November 20, 1983, of a film, *The Day After*, about the devastating effects of a nuclear war. An estimated 100 million people watched the program, one of the largest television audiences in the country's history (*New York Times*, November 27, 1983, p. 11). Moreover, because of the advance publicity the Secretary of State appeared on television immediately afterwards in order to justify government policy on arms control. Our December survey began just three days after the film was shown, and respondents to the open form of the MIP question were asked if they had seen *The Day After*. Some 51 percent said they had seen all or part of it, but there is little evidence of any important effect from the film on mentions of nuclear war: 26 percent of those who saw the film mentioned nuclear war on the open form, while 21 percent of those who had not seen it gave the same mention ($p = $n.s.). Further, if the data are separated into

10-day periods, the difference between viewers and nonviewers was smallest (a mere one percent) in the first 10-day period. The findings suggest that if there was any effect at all from the program, it was due to the general publicity surrounding the film, not to the actual viewing of it. Thus media attention to a fictional catastrophic event did not have the same impact as media attention to less extreme real events.

21. In a reanalysis of the original data in Table 2.5, I used logistic regression to examine the relations of education, age, gender, and region to giving the nuclear threat response. There are effects with both education and age attributable to question form, though they do not change the basic trends over time described in the text. First, more educated respondents were more likely to mention the nuclear threat on the open question, but this difference disappeared on the closed question where listing nuclear war makes it available to all respondents, and all educational categories increase to about the same level in their mentions. The most plausible interpretation of this difference is that more educated respondents tend to keep the nuclear threat in their minds and thus "available" to them, whereas those less educated need to be reminded of the threat by having it listed as a closed question alternative. Second, older respondents on the closed question chose nuclear threat more than those younger, and this response was somewhat more evident in the fifth month than in the earlier months. However, the change between the first four months and the fifth month occurs for all education and age groups.

22. See Abramowitz (2004); Burden (2004); Campbell (2004); Hillygus and Shields (2005); Langer and Cohen (2005); Abramson, Aldrich, and Rohde (2006). The question could not have been asked with the same alternatives in the 2000 election, but there is relevant evidence using correlates of the moral values response. For example, a comparison of the 2000 and 2004 outcomes indicates that Bush gained more in percentage terms from those who seldom or never attended "religious services" than from those who went weekly or more often (tau beta for "moral values" vs. other responses by attendance was .21, $p < .001$). However, it is essential to distinguish the reasons for the change in candidate percentages between 2000 and 2004 from what may well have been an important source of Bush's support in both years.

23. See the Pew Survey Report, November 11, 2005. The survey results were based on telephone reinterviews November 5–8, 2004, of 1,209 respondents who said they had voted in the election. The sample was selected from respondents identified as registered voters in two previous nationwide surveys of adults 18 years or older, both conducted in October 2004. See the Pew Web site (http://people-press.org) for further details.

24. The percentages in Table 2.6 are based on weighted data to match the percentages in Pew's November 11, 2004, Survey Report. The differences between

weighted and unweighted percentages are very small, at most one percentage point. In later analysis, unweighted data are used.

25. The results for the NEP Exit Poll closed question were the following: moral values, 23 percent; Iraq, 16 percent; economy/jobs, 22 percent; terrorism, 19 percent; health care, 8 percent; education, 5 percent; taxes, 5.5 percent, omitting 487 respondents who skipped the question.

26. The survey used for this comparison was carried out by the Kaiser Foundation/Harvard School of Public Health, October 14–17, 2004. Although the focal respondents claimed to be "absolutely certain" to vote, some may not have done so for whatever reason, whereas the Pew respondents all reported having actually voted just a few days before their interview. Thus the two samples differed in a crucial respect, which compromises any comparison of the results. In addition, the Kaiser survey coded gay marriage under "civil rights" and does not mention stem cell research, and it is possible that these would have added a small amount to the eight percent reported here.

27. Our best estimate of where the increase comes from is an examination of the open categories in Table 2.6(A) that were *not* included as alternatives to the closed form of the question. These open categories tend to be more in the direction of "moral values" than of the other more conventional issues, for example, one of the largest is "honesty/integrity," which shows a nearly two to one ratio in Bush to Kerry votes. (One response—"Iraq"—actually increased slightly on the open form as against the closed form, but its relation to preference for Kerry over Bush of approximately three to one is the same on both forms.)

28. The Los Angeles Times Exit Poll question and alternatives were "Which issues, if any, were most important to you in deciding how you would vote for president today? . . . moral/ethical values; jobs/economy; terrorism/homeland security; situation in Iraq; education; social issues such as abortion and gay marriage; taxes; health care; foreign affairs; social security; Medicare/prescription; none of the above.

29. This conclusion assumes that the difference between the closed and open Pew questions is not due to sampling error ($\chi^2 = 3.45$, df = 1, p = .06, two-sided).

30. In Table 2.7, those giving "moral values" as a response are more likely to be white, to be Protestant, to report greater attendance at religious services, and to have a greater likelihood of being "born again," but these relations occur on both question forms and there is no sign of statistical interaction. Only in the case of region is there borderline evidence of interaction (p = .11), with southerners clearly more likely than those in other regions to choose "moral values" on the closed question, but slightly less so than westerners on the open question. There is no evidence of relations to age, education, or gender for either form of the question.

31. This conclusion contradicts Krosnick, Judd, and Wittenbrink (2005, p. 34), who state that "in practice, past studies show that open-ended questions have higher reliabilities and validities than closed-ended questions." However, the only evidence they cite is from two brief reports of students answering test questions in school situations (Hurd 1932; Remmers et al. 1923). Both studies are far removed in nature from modern surveys of attitudes, as well as being deficient in terms of sampling and other features. In addition, it is not clear whether the authors' mention of "reliabilities" takes into account problems of unreliability in coding, which are often serious with open questions. (Krosnick 1999 makes much the same claim, based on the same two reports by Hurd [1932] and Remmers et al. [1923]).

32. As part of their investigation of open and closed questions, Schuman and Presser ([1981] 1996, pp. 97–99) noted that a closed response about "work values" stated "The work is important and gives a feeling of accomplishment." The word "important" seemed likely to encourage choosing that response, but a specially designed experiment comparing the response with one that stated simply "Work that gives a feeling of accomplishment" yielded no sign of such an effect. In addition, other experiments aimed at detecting social desirability or undesirability effects also found none (Schuman and Presser [1981] 1996, pp. 289–293).

33. The 2004 Election Exit Poll included a question that listed seven issues relevant to vote decision (discussed earlier) in two different orders and the results do show a highly significant order effect, but in this instance the forms were self-administered in a setting having considerable time pressure, making them more vulnerable to such effects. In any case, response order effects can be both controlled and examined by randomizing order across questionnaires. The exit poll effect did not change the main analytic findings with the item reported earlier.

34. In addition to problems already discussed, open responses are often ambiguous. See the attempt by Schuman and Presser ([1981] 1996, pp. 88–104) to clarify a question on "work values," especially the distinction between respondents who stressed their wish for a steady income and those who emphasized a desire for high income. The distinction was difficult to make with open responses but easier with closed alternatives. (The process of revision in this case also provides a good example of drawing on previously obtained open responses to sharpen the alternatives to a closed question, so that it in turn will do a better job of capturing distinctions than did the original open or closed versions of the question. The attempt was partly successful, because administration of the new closed version as part of a split-sample comparison with the open form led to a decreased proportion of responses falling outside the categories common to both forms.)

35. The western proportion of the total mentions of the "food and energy crisis" was 15.4 percent, only slightly less than the proportion (17.7 percent) of the total sample (N = 1206) that came from the western region.

36. A notable example of the need to recognize substantial change over time in the meaning of words is a Gallup question from 1954: "Which American city do you think has the gayest night life?" (Smith 1987a).

37. For World War II, the rise for the open question among young respondents has occurred in previous research and has been attributed to recent school experience where World War II is emphasized in history and social studies courses and also has been the subject of widely seen films and television programs.

3. Interpretive Survey Research

1. Geertz notes that he borrowed these concepts from the psychoanalyst Heinz Kohut but does not give a reference. I am indebted to Jeffrey Prager for locating and explicating Kohut's main discussion in his 1984 book, *How Does Analysis Cure?* Kohut's focus is on a patient's subjective experience and its connection to theories developed by the analyst. Geertz's use of the concepts to apply to ethnographers and their informants is a substantial transformation, but one that is inspired with new meaning.

2. My emphasis in this chapter is on open questions following a closed question, thus combining the advantage of the relative simplicity and reliability of closed questioning with the fullness of expression found through open questioning. However, as noted earlier, the inclusion of self-contained open questions can provide a similar opportunity for discovering how people think about features of their social world, as occurs with Philip Converse's analysis of levels of conceptualization, based on such open questions as "Is there anything in particular that you like about the Democratic Party?" (Converse 1964; Campbell et al. 1960, ch. 10). The main point is that a response was not treated as a self-explanatory end in itself but was drawn on by Converse in terms of his own analytic goals.

3. The percentages in Figure 3.1 have been recalculated without "no opinion" responses, which dropped from 16 percent in 1966 to 11 percent in 1971.

4. The protest was centered on a relatively few elite campuses like the University of Michigan and was less pervasive at the much larger set of non-elite state and private universities, colleges, and junior colleges, though this has not always been recognized in later accounts. It is also important to remember that "college-educated Americans" included a substantial number of people who were well past college age when interviewed in national surveys (see Converse and Schuman 1970). Even on elite campuses there were no doubt many like George W. Bush who were not involved in and probably not sympathetic toward campus protests (Minutaglio 1999). University faculties also had considerably greater

internal variation in attitudes toward the war than usually realized, with the physical sciences leaning in a less dovish direction than the social sciences and humanities,, and there was also considerable variation across the faculties of professional schools (Schuman and Laumann 1967).

5. The 1971 cross-section survey that repeated the Gallup "mistake" question was done through the University of Michigan's Detroit Area Study, and the target population was adults living in the Detroit Standard Metropolitan Statistical Area (SMSA) minus the city of Pontiac and the outlying semi-rural areas of the three-county area; it included about 85 percent of the SMSA population. Comparisons with national survey data at about that point in time showed few differences, especially differences likely to be relevant to the Vietnam question. (See Schuman 1972 for a full account of the research described more briefly in this chapter.)

6. It is by no means certain that order of mentions reflects order of importance (see Schuman and Presser [1981] 1996, p. 88, fn. 9).

7. The remaining five themes, and the percentage coded as mentioning each, were the following:

IV. Vietnam Not Important to American Interests, 28 percent;
V. OK to Intervene, But Handling of War Incorrect, 15 percent;
VI. Entry into War Not Procedurally Correct, 15 percent;
IX. The War Is Confusing, 11 percent;
X. Problems with South Vietnamese Government or People, 6 percent.

In general, these themes tend either to duplicate or to provide additional support for the results presented in the text, though I also draw on two of them at a later point. The coding scheme was developed with the assistance of two graduate students: Elizabeth Martin and Sunny Bradford.

8. Tilly (2006) has developed a classification of answers to Why questions in social interaction generally, and in his terms the U.S. officer's explanation at Ben Tre might possibly be seen as a "technical account." However, I have found it difficult to fit the answers respondents gave to the Vietnam open question into Tilly's four types of reasons (convention, codes, stories, technical accounts), perhaps because respondents are speaking to a neutral interviewer, not to a friend, a doctor, or even a concerned witness.

9. At the same time, we should recognize that almost all young men during the Vietnam period were concerned about either being drafted or at least taking a position on the war. When we consider the differences between the Vietnam and Iraq wars, lack of a draft in the latter case has been critically important. It has almost certainly been responsible for the absence of a more vigorous antiwar protest movement against U.S. military involvement in Iraq.

10. A second example of the value of a systematic Why question occurred in a study of racial attitudes for the National Advisory Commission on Civil Disorders in

1968 and is doubly instructive. A large proportion of white respondents, when told that black Americans lost out in "jobs, education, and housing," asserted to an open question that the problem was lack of motivation—an assumption of "free will" and thus readily changed by blacks themselves (Schuman 1969). Later research by others led to closed questions that reached similar conclusions (e.g., Apostle et al. 1983; Kluegel and Smith 1986; see also General Social Surveys 1972–2000: Cumulative Codebook, RACDIF1–RACDIF4). Thus as indicated in Chapter 2, open questions and well developed closed questions can lead to the same results, though open questions are especially useful for the discovery of new meaning.

11. A number of respondents (108) combined both "we" and "they" in their answers, but use of a three-point scale with we/they combinations as intermediate did not change basic results. A still larger number of respondents (288) had not been recorded as using either pronoun, and in some cases it was likely that pronouns and similar "trivial" linguistic features had probably been omitted by interviewers under time pressure. In future research on language use, interviewers should be instructed to record carefully whatever features are being studied—a task that will be simplified where open responses can be recorded fully by machine or computer. In the present analysis we assume that the omitted cases would not change basic conclusions reported about we/they users. Coding was carried out by a single coder, and a second person check-coded a random subsample of 100 responses, achieving 90 percent agreement. The reliability of respondents themselves over time was not so high: 60 respondents gave "we" or "they" responses to the same questions by telephone several months after the original interview, and there is only a nonsignificant trend for pronoun usage to be consistent across the two occasions. This finding may well be due to reliance on a single question for the coding and to the small number of cases in the reinterview sample. Some associations among categories are so strong and so intuitively meaningful as to make it unlikely that they could have occurred by chance, despite the lack of firm evidence of substantial stability over time at the individual level.

12. Examination of both age and education together for both races fails to reveal any nonadditive patterning of the two variables different from their separate effects. Further evidence for the meaning of the racial difference in pronoun choice by blacks comes from the significant association between they-saying and high scores on an index of Alienation from White Society that had been developed in another analysis (Schuman and Hatchett 1974). Despite the reduction in sample size when only African Americans are considered, they-sayers ($n=127$) were significantly more alienated than we-sayers ($n=69$): $F=4.83$, $p=.03$. In addition, when age was controlled by cross-tabulation within three age categories (21–30, 31–49, 50+), the association between racial alienation

and pronoun usage was especially strong among younger black adults (21–30 years of age) and among those with greater education (some college or more).

13. Without knowledge of my use of the we/they distinction in analysis, Cialdini, et al. (1976) developed similar coding (we versus non-we) in an experiment on student identification with victory or nonvictory of their school's football team. Whereas my interest was in differences by race, education, and social class identification, along with possible interviewer effects, Cialdini, et al. were concerned with variation in response to good and bad outcomes for both subjects themselves and their school teams.

14. Wilson (2002) has revised this argument to distinguish between conscious and unconscious responses, with only processes having to do with the latter being inaccessible, though he is not entirely clear on the implications of his revision.

15. This last finding is an example reported by Nisbett and Wilson (1977): subjects were asked to choose which of four indistinguishable pairs of stockings were of best quality, and their responses showed a position effect (they most often chose the one on the far right). Suppose, however, that three of the four pairs of stockings had been obviously torn and the fourth pair was brand new, would we still expect subjects to show the same position effect? I doubt it.

16. Because Wilson and Hodges (1992) find that people more expert in an area are less easily changed by reflecting on their reasons for a judgment, this also suggests that issues that are prominent and already much discussed are less likely to see changes when people reflect on them.

17. My conclusion fits well with Wilson's further explication of the original Nisbett and Wilson (1977) argument (see Wilson 2002, ch. 5). Wilson argues that a third person—in this case, the survey investigator—can sometimes have as good or even better understanding of the reasons for a subject's responses. In the case of a survey, the investigator is able to obtain knowledge of the content of the respondent's conscious thoughts by asking questions and then to use that information to develop explanations that the respondent may not have been fully aware of or able to conceptualize.

18. Random probes are easiest to implement in surveys using interviewers, because respondents will not be aware of which questions will be probed. However, adaptation to self-administered surveys is possible, so long as the questionnaire can be varied across respondents to maintain the basic goal of sampling questions.

19. My Bangladesh survey was part of a larger cross-national study directed by Alex Inkeles (see Inkeles and Smith 1974). I was particularly concerned in Bangladesh about the gap between the abstract concepts we were attempting to operationalize and the poorly educated population we were studying, accentuated by my own need to work mostly through interpreters and translators. It seemed to me essential to find some way of understanding more fully what our

questions meant to respondents and what they in turn intended by their closed choices.

20. In most polls and surveys, eliminating small response effects on final results has little impact because we are often not concerned with percentage differences of one or two points, let alone differences in decimals. The challenge is quite different for some government surveys where much greater precision is called for (e.g., Martin and Polivka 1995; Martin 2006) and is possible because of very large sample sizes.

4. Artifacts Are in the Mind of the Beholder

1. There are other types of context as well as those considered in this chapter: the location of an interview, for example, whether in a home or a workplace, and the mode of administration, whether face-to-face, telephone, Internet, or some other medium or combination of media. For recent treatments, see Groves et al. (2004) and Weisberg (2005). Furthermore, as Bishop et al. (1988) and Schwarz and Hippler (1995) indicate, questionnaire context may have different effects in self-administered questionnaires than in interviews, since in the case of self-administration, respondents can read ahead and be influenced by a question that comes after, as well as before, another. Thus, there are meta-contexts within which question contexts can vary.

2. For example, a textbook by Duverger (1964) reports a percentage difference due to questionnaire context but provides neither N's nor standard errors. In the absence of other evidence, the reported difference had little more credibility than individual sightings of the Loch Ness Monster.

3. Smith (1991a) wisely qualifies this conclusion by pointing out that in both of these examinations, sets of associated items tended to be varied as a whole between the split-sample forms. Since context effects ordinarily occur among items related in content, the randomization procedure probably led to underestimation of potential effects due to question order. Balancing the underestimation, however, is the likelihood that some number of order effects may have little substantive importance. A difference itself may be small and its effect on associations "benign," as O. D. Duncan once put it in a personal communication, changing the strength of relations but not their direction. Of course, even the finding of "statistical significance" in such cases depends on the size of the sample, with very large samples identifying context effects trivial in importance.

4. Hyman and Sheatsley (1950) had not published their full results, but had simply mentioned in their chapter the percentages for one of the two contexts, without giving the number of cases or any other information that would allow readers to judge reliability. The 1948 survey data were archived at the Roper Center for Public Opinion Research, but the data set did not include a variable

to allow separation of the sample into the two experimental halves and thus the experiment was not accessible. While preparing the present book, I discovered a 1980 memo that indicated how the experimental forms might be disentangled, and this permitted analytic use of the data. I am grateful to Marc Maynard and Marilyn Milliken of the Roper Center for crucial help in solving the puzzle presented by the data, which had been transferred from the original punch cards without further change. The Roper Center now includes information on how the experimental results can be obtained from the 1948 data.

5. The full 1948 results were first published by Schuman and Presser ([1981] 1996, p. 29) and are shown here with percentages rounded. A confusing problem when working with the two items is the appearance of the word "Communist" in each one. To keep straight which item is being referred to, I will use the opening phrase to reference each item (i.e., "the U.S. allowing . . ." and "Russia allowing . . ."). This is a different way of referencing the questions than used in Schuman and Presser, and a direct comparison of the two sources should attend to the full wording.

6. For this reason, I used the term "even-handed" rather than "reciprocity" to describe the experiments in previous writing (Schuman and Ludwig 1983). This now seems too fine a distinction, and because it loses the connection to broader social science concerns posed by Gouldner (1960) and others, it seems better to employ the theoretically useful term "reciprocity." However, the perspective of a single party, indeed even an outside observer, remains important because it indicates that the moral nature of the reciprocity principle is apparent even to someone who may not be directly involved in terms of personal self-interest, while at the same time providing an explanation for the asymmetry that appears in analyses to be considered shortly.

7. Germany invaded Poland on September 1, 1939, and this Gallup poll was in the field September 1–6, 1939. Apparently Gallup anticipated but was not certain of the war's beginning, because the questionnaire was headed with the instruction: "THIS BALLOT TO BE USED ONLY IF AND WHEN WAR STARTS IN EUROPE" and was called "SPECIAL WAR BALLOT." (Rugg and Cantril [1944] do not provide sample sizes or significance levels, but these were obtained using the original data from the Roper Center. The recalculated percentages shown here differ somewhat from those given by Schuman and Ludwig [1983], but without change in substantive conclusions.) This context effect was the only one widely available to most survey readers at an early point, but its importance was apparently not fully grasped because it was simply one of a miscellany of question wording effects in the Rugg and Cantril (1944) chapter. In addition, Gallup did not ask for educational level in the poll, which limits our later use of the data for analytic purpose.

8. Link (1946) gives the overall size of his sample as 5,000 and implies that it was divided in half to test order effects, and he also reports the significance of the difference. Unfortunately he does not give exact figures, and I have not been able to locate the original data despite a web search and an inquiry to the successor firm to Link's Psychological Corporation. Thus, the data are not available for later analysis. In Table 4.2, I assume that each half sample was approximately 2,500 in size.

9. The data from this experiment are available from the Roper Center, and they include education, as well as an income measure, thus allowing analytic use later in this chapter.

10. Nor did context effects become a serious concern in broader treatments of survey issues that I have been able to check. For example, Parten's substantial review volume (1950) notes the Link (1946) experiment, but does not discuss any of the others shown in Tables 4.1 and 4.2.

11. It may seem puzzling that attitudes on both reporter questions changed over time when in first position, but that neither question showed a visible change over time when in second position. A possible explanation for this apparent inconsistency is the existence of countervailing pressures on both questions when they are in the second position. This is easier to see with the U.S. allow item. There should have been pressure from the time change toward more Yes, allow Communist reporters into the United States, probably due to much less fear of Communists, as is shown by trend data from the combination of Stouffer (1955) and the General Social Surveys (2000). But at the same time an assumption of reciprocity may have pushed in the opposite direction toward No, because more respondents (18 percent) say No to the question about Russia allowing in American reporters than was the case in 1948 (just 10 percent). If the two pressures balanced out approximately, we would see no significant change over time. The explanation in the case of Russia allowing American reporters question is similar, but more difficult because the motivations for answers on that question are probably not as simple as fear of Communists. Of course, both interpretations are after-the-fact and need further testing in future context experiments that involve change over time. What we do know now is that the lack of change in the second position is a clear finding for both items, just as the change in first position is appreciable and highly reliable in each comparison we make across time in Table 4.1.

12. We need not be rigid on this point. One of the several ways that Milgram's (1974) studies of obedience to authority were so remarkable is that he went to great lengths to show that his findings were not limited to particular convenience samples (or settings). Even though he could not use probability sampling from the general population, he compensated for this limitation in ways that are

reasonably convincing. In addition, although Milgram himself did not focus on change, subsequent replications by others have allowed considerable generalization across cultures and to some extent across time as well (Blass 1999).

13. The 1980 results for the reporters items were an exception, providing convincing evidence of a planned literal replication, though as we have also seen, clear evidence of change in the strength of the original effect.

14. See, for example, the entry "Reciprocal Trade Agreement" in the *Columbia Encyclopedia*, 2000.

15. Bishop et al. (1988) also conducted a parallel study with German students, and in that case the context effect tended to be symmetrical, which they attribute to German "trade relations with Japan . . . not [being] viewed as unbalanced as they are in the United States" (p. 332). Symmetrical findings were also reported for random samples of women from Ghent, Belgium: in both directions ("Europe" and "America") there is evidence of a reciprocity effect (Billiet, Waterplas, and Loosveldt 1992).

16. Possibly some of the latter Americans favored free trade with Japan for either personal or ideological reasons, but it is unlikely that that group is substantial in size, and it is hard to see the same motivation for those wishing to allow Japan to erect its own trade barriers.

17. The small number of cases was due to use of a preliminary cross-section sample drawn for technical purposes in planning a larger telephone sample. Unfortunately, the data from this preliminary sample do not appear to have been saved for later analysis, though with so few cases further analytic use would have been difficult.

18. This is shown by the percentage difference between first and second position for each item, by the odds ratios as well (the further an odds ratio is from 1.0 in either direction, the greater the difference between the two forms), and by the formal tests of interaction (with income included as a control). We can also speculate that those who fail to agree to—or perhaps to recognize—reciprocity even when a trade restriction question comes second might have still lower education than those who do appreciate the need for reciprocity at that point. Looking only at a question in second position, those who show reciprocity on the Japanese item asked second do have more schooling than those who do not ($p = .04$); however, there is only a slight and nonsignificant similar trend on the American question, perhaps again because of the strength of self-interest when imports from Japan are at issue.

19. Chi square results and exact probabilities are not shown, but in all tests for interaction: $p > .10$.

20. The cartoon by Chon Day appeared in the *Ladies Home Journal* (August 1975, p. 128), and is reproduced in Walster, Walster, and Berscheid (1978, p. 156).

21. There are also instances where a small benefit may be reciprocated with one greater in quantity or quality, either as a way of gaining status, as with the potlatch, or in an attempt to encourage future exchanges. Gouldner (1960) speaks of reciprocity as a "starting" act, useful for getting relationships under way, but it can also be an attempt to expand a relationship beyond that wished by the original benefit-provider.

22. What has come to be known as the abortion context effect was discovered entirely accidentally when Schuman and Presser ([1981] 1996) borrowed a general abortion question from the General Social Survey (GSS), found their results using it to differ significantly from the GSS results, and eventually discovered the source of the difference to be due to context.

23. For the reporters items, the interaction of response by context by time is clearly significant: $\chi^2 = 10.1$, 1 df, p = .001 for Communist reporters; $\chi^2 = 5.8$, 1 df, p = .02 for American reporters.

24. The difference between forbidding and not allowing, as shown in Figure 4.2, is almost the same in percentage terms in 1940 and 1976. Of course, the absence of interaction in Figure 4.2 does not preclude a future interaction if the meaning of one or both questions change. (If the upward trend continued strongly in future years, there might eventually be an interaction with time if only because allowing speeches" would presumably approach a ceiling effect at 100 percent before "not forbidding speeches.")

25. Although most of Hyman's questions dealt with attitudes and beliefs, notable were factual differences that went beyond politeness, such as less willingness in Memphis to report ownership of an automobile to white than to black interviewers, which could be interpreted to reflect fear. Detailed results on this question for New York were unfortunately not reported.

26. Some support was found in later research by Anderson, Silver, and Abramson (1988), which pointed to greater validity when reports of voting by blacks were given to white than to black interviewers.

27. The survey vehicle for both the black and white experiments was the University of Michigan's Detroit Area Study (DAS), which allowed random assignment of interviewers by race. Because DAS itself no longer exists, over-time replication is unlikely to be practical in that metropolitan area. Data on this fundamental form of black-white interaction probably requires a new baseline experiment, followed by careful replication after a suitably long stretch of time. However, even a crude comparison at present or in the future with the DAS findings from the late 1960s and early 1970s could be of value, despite using data from a somewhat different population.

28. Groves and Fultz (1985) did make a careful attempt to discover what aspect of gender had effects on attitude content, but the attitudes they had available to

connect to gender were not of direct relevance in the same way as racial attitudes are to race of interviewer.

29. At the time of the three pen experiment, the U. S. government viewed Ortega as
a dangerous leftist and was supporting a rebel force (the "Contras") in the
countryside, as well as hoping for a Chamorro victory.

30. The experiment was carried out by the Nicaraguan polling organization ECO,
with a detailed design developed by Raúl Obregón and Oscar Medrano, and
with Judith Appel serving as liaison with me during the training and field period. For more details of the three pen experiment, as well as supporting analysis that tested other possible hypotheses about the polls and the election, see
Schuman (1990); Bischoping and Schuman (1992).

31. The final total sample size was 299, with nearly 100 in each pen condition, and
with only trivial exceptions the three pen conditions were allocated equally
among the 19 interviewers, as well as across the nine *barrios* in urban Managua
and across 18 rural voting districts. However, in each pen condition approximate half the respondents declined to choose between the UNO and Sandinista
candidates, saying that the ballot was supposed to be secret, or that they did not
know for whom they would vote, or in a few cases opting for another party. The
losses leave the smaller sample sizes shown in Table 4.8. Of course, no field experiment can be as tightly controlled as one carried out in a laboratory, nor was
it possible for the interviewers to be blind to the three conditions. However,
they had been selected and trained to understand and conform to the needs of
a rigorous and nonpartisan experiment.

32. Refusals, Don't Know responses, and minor parties are omitted from Table 4.8,
but were approximately equal across conditions (see Bischoping and Schuman
1992 for the full table). Despite the relatively small subsamples in the table, the
association shown is significant at $p < .025$, using a one-tailed test on grounds
that the hypothesis was clearly stated as to direction, or $p < .05$ on the assumption that it is almost always safer to use a two-tailed test. Of course, like many
one-shot empirical findings, the result may be subject to the "file drawer problem" (e.g., http://skepdic.com/posoutbias.html): the fact that positive results
are more apt to reach publication than are negative results. I doubt that I would
have attempted to publish negative results unless they had shown something of
definite interest.

5. The Survey World and Other Worlds

1. Jackman (1972) reanalyzed Stouffer's data and argued that when education is
controlled, leaders are not more tolerant than the mass public, which implies
that education is the underlying variable. However, St. Peter, Williams, and
Johnson (1977) reanalyzed Jackman's reanalysis and concluded that the leaders'

distinct attitudes could not be explained by education. Others have joined the debate, and so Stouffer can be said to have framed a larger issue for political scientists about elites and the general public. His survey of both leaders and the public was probably the first large-scale effort at a comparison of attitudes across theoretically different but related populations. However, starting with Miller and Stokes (1963), political scientists and others have continued to join two or more surveys as a way of exploring the perceptions and lines of influence between an electorate and its political representatives.

2. See Schuman and Krysan (1996) for further information on sampling and other features and results of the study. The Duke contributors had sent from $2 to $1,000 to the Duke campaign, with $25 the median amount contributed.

3. We followed closely Dillman's (1978) recommendations for maximizing response rates in mail surveys, except that we added a small monetary incentive of $1 as a token of appreciation, as mentioned in Chapter 4 in the discussion of the norm of reciprocity. We also used five sequential mailings, described in Schuman and Krysan (1996).

4. "Truth, Karl Deutsch observed, lies at the confluence of independent streams of evidence" (Putnam 1993, p. 12). Unfortunately, I have not always found this to be as simple as the apothegm suggests.

5. Putnam's (1993) study of civic institutions in different regions of Italy provides another persuasive example of very different types of data brought to bear on a single problem.

6. A similar trend at a lower level has occurred with actual intermarriage between blacks and whites. However, the same trends have not occurred on newer and more complex issues that have arisen, such as affirmative action, which indicates that respondents are candid in giving different answers to different types of questions. The book contains a great deal of evidence and interpretation of the meaning of the changes that did occur over time, as well as of absence of change in various areas and on various types of questions.

7. Recently I also attempted to combine survey results on attitudes toward Christopher Columbus around the time of the 1992 Quincentenary with content analysis of high school textbooks of American history, plus more impressionistic evidence from encyclopedias, films, and congressional debates (Schuman, Schwartz, and d'Arcy 2005). Making comparisons between evidence based on quite different methods again proved difficult, the more so in this case because the different types of evidence were related to radically different populations: e.g., a cross-section sample of Americans asked about Columbus and a sample of textbook authors writing about Columbus. Quite likely also, the orientations in terms of time were different, with the textbooks and encyclopedias written to take account of recent changes in arguments by scholars and political activists looking to the future, whereas the cross-section sample of

Americans consisted largely of people who had grown up in an earlier era and probably expressed beliefs learned at that point.

8. See Schuman and Presser ([1981] 1996) for details, qualifications, and other information about the data drawn on in this discussion. It would, of course, be useful to have more recent data replicating these results from 1978, but there is little reason to expect basic relationships found at that point to be appreciably different today.

9. Here and elsewhere in quoting early research, the word "Negro" has been updated to "black" or "African American."

10. Sniderman and Piazza (1993) later used an approach they called "the counterargument technique" whereby interviewers ask respondents one question, record the response, then present a reason for taking a different position. The authors imply that respondents are influenced by the interviewer as well as by the interviewer's reason for changing, but as we have just seen, respondents are able on their own to respond differently to questions that offer different reasons for taking a position. The more elaborate tactic used by Sniderman and Piazza was not necessary to obtain the basic evidence of inconsistency.

11. I follow here (Ajzen and Fishbein 2005) a chapter that provides an excellent recent synthesis of the attitude-behavior theory and literature. My own earlier synthesis (Schuman and Johnson 1976), which first introduced the term "literal consistency" and distinguished it from "correlational [evaluative] consistency," is also still relevant because it takes account of aspects of the attitude-behavior problem especially important to survey research, such as the impact of interviewer effects. In addition, relevant theory has not changed greatly in recent years.

12. For a full account of this attitude-behavior study, see Brannon and others (1973), which describes in more detail the steps taken to make the research as rigorous as possible.

13. To avoid any reminder of the earlier survey, the petitions used in Brannon and others (1973) were written with somewhat different wording than the two alternatives to the original housing law question, so this study is a quasi-literal rather than completely literal effort. (Unfortunately, in making these changes the term "religion" was included in the Open Housing petition, a regrettable mistake that may conceivably have added some encouragement to signing, though ending "racial discrimination" was clearly emphasized in the wording that people were asked to sign.)

14. Not everyone who had been interviewed could be reached in the follow-up petition phase, but those who could not—144 people classified as "not at home" during the petition phase—did not differ in their earlier interview responses. We had questionnaire information on these individuals, and their loss did not vary significantly across the three main experimental conditions ($\chi^2 = 0.76$, 2 df, n.s.). Furthermore, to distinguish those who refused to consider any petition

from those who signed or rejected the Open Housing petition, petition circulators had first presented an innocuous petition to limit "pollution of our lakes and rivers," before they said that their group had taken "a stand on another public issue" and presented a petition for or against open housing. Only 28 survey respondents refused the screening pollution petition (in most cases refusing to open their door or listen at all), and these people were again distributed equally across the three experimental conditions.

15. Unfortunately, we cannot make the same calculation for Condition C, but since such a high proportion of those who signed also agreed to allow publicity for their open housing position, I suspect that very few would have signed the opposing petition.

16. One major source of attitude-behavior discrepancies occurs when concealment is possible in one but not the other context. It would be foolish to expect to study either crime or sin easily with a questionnaire, though when confidentiality or, better, anonymity, can be guaranteed, people are surprisingly willing to reveal a good deal about actions that are socially disapproved. For a substantial review of evidence on the attitude-behavior problem, see Lord and Lepper (1999), who conclude sensibly that "the closer the match between the representations and perceptions to which a person is responding in different situations, the more consistency there will be in that person's responses to various attitude-relevant stimuli" (p. 295).

17. See Schuman, Akiyama, and Knäuper (1988). See also related studies by Corning (2007), Rieger (1995), Scott and Zac (1993), and Schuman and Rieger (1994).

6. Hunting a Social Science Snark

1. "We" refers to myself and Stanley Presser. Together we went through the highs and the lows described throughout much of this chapter.

2. DK responses tend to be given to poll questions about remote subjects, such as other nations not in the news, as well as by less educated and less knowledgeable respondents generally (Converse 1976–1977).

3. There is no way to identify individual floaters in split-sample experiments. Their existence and proportion are inferred from the difference in DK percentages between filtered and standard forms. Nor could it be easily determined if the same people were floaters on questions having different content. However, the levels of DK on both filtered and standard forms vary greatly across questions with different content, and thus it seems likely that floaters consist of somewhat different people across different questions.

4. The Arab and Russia questions are both measures of attitudes, and neither is conceptualized as the cause of the other. Hence there is no independent variable

in the subtables of Table 6.2, which means that four cell percentages that add to 100 percent might ordinarily be used in each subtable. Such tables are difficult to read, however, and therefore I use column percentages, with the Russia question arbitrarily placed over the columns as though it were the independent variable. Readers are warned that this is merely to enhance readability and that the same conclusions would be drawn if the Arab question were treated as the column variable.

5. An order effect for the forced-choice questions is also not tenable, because the order of substantive alternatives is different for the Arab and the Russia questions.

6. There is some slippage between the set of people identified indirectly as floaters in the first survey and those identified directly through the winter reinterview (e.g., there might have been some true attitude change over the intervening several months, the reinterview sample lost some respondents from the original sample, etc., but it is reasonable to assume that a set of genuine floaters are pinpointed in these data).

7. Thurstone himself spoke of an attitude as "affect" for or against an object (1931), but most later theorists speak in terms of "evaluation," so that an attitude is taken to be any positive or negative evaluation of an object, where the object can be anything at all: a person, idea, political policy, type of food, sunset, and so forth (Schuman 1995). Further, "attitudes" and "beliefs" can be distinguished conceptually, but an attitude can be restated as a belief (X has the attribute of being good or bad), and most nonfactual belief statements can be restated as attitudes (e.g., Democracy is a good system of government).

8. We assumed that findings similar to those in the 1974 survey would not have shown up in most research by social psychologists because they work largely with college students and that few, if any, surveys would have compared standard and filtered questions as we did, though it is true that the National Election Study has used filtered question forms over many years.

9. It is easy to lose sight of the fact that when a relation is tested for significance, it is not simply the single relation that is being tested but the difference between two samples. To the extent that the samples are different, whether due to chance or not, this can show up in many other relations in which they are involved, in addition to the one that led to a significance test. This possibility still leaves open the question of why the samples are different.

10. The reason for the delay in carrying out this replication was that we had not looked closely at inter-item attitude associations for some time after the fall 1974 survey, because that major survey included 20 basic methodological experiments on the full range of issues we were studying and required time for extensive analysis and reporting.

11. Comparison of the full results from the 1978 survey with those of the 1974 survey also showed a drop in the DK proportion for the Arab item from 23 percent to 14 percent on the standard form but no change on the filtered form (45 percent in both years).

12. As Page and Shapiro (1992) suggest, the concentration of the mass media on a particular set of events educates the public and thus leads people previously ignorant of some part of the world to develop new beliefs and attitudes.

13. The distinction between quasi-fictional and fictional issues is one that does not make a difference, as shown by quite similar results reported by Bishop et al. (1980) for an entirely fictitious "Public Affairs Act."

14. Most of the DK respondents were clearly floaters, but the data are not now in a form that readily allows separating floaters from those who say DK even on a filtered form, nor is it likely that the two sets of DK respondents differ greatly. since other experiments reported in Schuman and Presser ([1981] 1996) suggest that by emphasizing the filter even more than was done for these questions, we could reduce the filtered DK percentage to essentially zero for these quasi-fictional items. As Schwarz (1996) notes, a full filter that precedes a question implies to respondents that considerable knowledge will be needed to give an answer to an item.

15. In 2006 we were able to replicate still again the Arab and Russia standard and filtered forms, testing the possibility that because of all the further changes over three decades, still another configuration of attitudes might lead to a restoration of the original 1974 finding. (Eleanor Singer joined us to make this recent replication possible.) Both question forms in 2006 showed trends for agreement with one item to be associated with agreement on the other item, but the associations were almost identical for the two forms (e.g., tau beta = .10 on the standard form and .08 on the filtered form), hence the original 1974 three-way interaction failed again to replicate. The earlier findings using education rather than question form as the third variable also showed only a nonsignificant trend as a replication. A serious limitation of the recent replication attempt, however, was the tiny number of respondents agreeing that Arab nations are interested in peace with Israel (only 13 respondents on the filtered form and 30 on the standard form), which again provides a different social context for the inquiry.

Conclusion

1. Of course, a subjective report may not be accepted by others. For example, a man who abuses and abandons his family may claim to love them and may even convince his psychiatrist of his sincerity, but others are apt to think that if

he is not lying, then he using the word "love" differently from most English speakers.

2. The emphasis by Groves et al. (2004) is indicated by the six examples of surveys they chose for their opening chapter. All but one are government surveys where a conceptualization in terms of true values seems possible, even if difficult in practice, and the single exception (the University of Michigan Survey of Consumer Attitudes) is treated obliquely. No examples are given from the General Social Survey, the National Election Study, the Pew Center, or other major polls and surveys that include substantial sets of questions that involve attitudes or other subjective reports, even though there is a great deal of interest in attitudes and other subjective phenomena on the part of both social scientists and the general public.

3. Neisser adds, however, that the same phenomenon can be looked at from the standpoint of motives ("dynamically") rather than in terms of cognition, which fits well the Abelson, Loftus, and Greenwald (1992) article. The term "cognitive psychology" was developed largely in opposition to behavioristic psychology's rejection of studying mental processes. That battle was won long ago.

4. A number of such hypotheses can be found in Sudman, Bradburn, and Schwarz (1996) and in Tourangeau, Rips, and Rasinski (2000).

References

Abelson, Robert P. 1995. *Statistics as Principled Argument.* Hillsdale, NJ: Erlbaum.

Abelson, Robert P., Elizabeth F. Loftus, and Anthony Greenwald. 1992. "Attempts to Improve the Accuracy of Self-Reports of Voting." Pp. 138–153 in Judith M. Tanur (ed.), *Questions about Questions: Inquiries into the Cognitive Bases of Surveys.* New York: Russell Sage.

Aborn, Murray. 1991. "CASM Revisited." Pp. 21–38 in Monroe G. Sirken, Douglas J. Herrmann, Susan Schechter, Norbert Schwarz, Judith M. Tanur, and Roger Tourangeau (eds.), *Cognition and Survey Research.* New York: Wiley.

Abramowitz, Alan. 2004. "Terrorism, Gay Marriage, and Incumbency: Explaining the Republican Victory in the 2004 Election." *Forum* 2, no. 4. http://www.bepress.com.proxy.lib.umich.edu/forum/.

Abramson, Paul R., John H. Aldrich, and David W. Rohde. 2006. *Change and Continuity in the 2004 Elections.* Washington, DC: CQ Press.

Ajzen, Icek, R. Darroch, Martin Fishbein, J. Hornik. 1970. "Looking Backward Revisited: A Reply to Deutscher." *American Sociologist* 5: 267–273.

Ajzen, Icek, and Martin Fishbein. 1977. "Attitude-Behavior Relations: A Theoretical Analysis and Review of Empirical Research." *Psychological Bulletin* 84: 888–918.

Ajzen, Icek, and Martin Fishbein. 2005. "The Influence of Attitudes on Behavior." Pp. 173–222 in Dolores Albarracín, Blair T. Johnson, and Mark P. Zanna (eds.), *The Handbook of Attitudes.* Mahwah, NJ: Erlbaum.

Albarracín, Dolores, Blair T. Johnson, and Mark P. Zanna (eds.). 2005. *The Handbook of Attitudes.* Mahwah, NJ: Erlbaum.

Alexander, Jeffrey C. 2006. *The Civic Sphere.* New York: Oxford University Press.

Anderson, Barbara A., Brian D. Silver, and Paul R. Abramson. 1988. "The Effects of the Interviewer on Measures of Electoral Participation by Blacks in SRC National Election Studies." *Public Opinion Quarterly* 52: 53–83.

Apostle, Richard A., Charles Y. Glock, Thomas Piazza, and Marijean Suelzle. 1983. *The Anatomy of Racial Attitudes.* Berkeley: University of California Press.

Asch, S. E. 1952. *Social Psychology.* Englewood Cliffs, NJ: Prentice-Hall.

Asch, S. E. 1940. "Studies in the Principles of Judgments and Attitudes: II. Determination of Judgments by Group and by Ego Standards." *The Journal of Social Psychology* 12: 433–465.

Axelrod, Robert. 1984. *The Evolution of Cooperation.* New York: Basic Books.

Biemer, Paul B., and Lars E. Lyberg. 2003. *Introduction to Survey Quality.* New York: Wiley-Interscience.

Billiet, Jaak B., Lina Waterplas, and Geert Loosveldt. 1992. "Context Effects as Substantive Data in Social Surveys." Pp. 131–147 in Norbert Schwarz and Seymour Sudman (eds.), *Context Effects in Social and Psychological Research.* New York: Springer-Verlag.

Bischoping, Katherine, and Howard Schuman. 1992. "Pens and Polls in the 1990 Nicaraguan Election." *American Journal of Political Science* 36: 331–350.

Bishop, George F. 2005. *The Illusion of Public Opinion: Fact and Artifact in American Public Opinion Polls.* Lanham, MD: Rowman & Littlefield.

Bishop, George F., Hans-Juergen Hippler, Norbert Schwarz, and Fritz Strack. 1988. "A Comparison of Response Effects in Self-Administered and Telephone Surveys." Pp. 321–340 in Robert Groves et al. (eds.), *Telephone Survey Methodology.* New York: Wiley.

Bishop, George F., Robert W. Oldendick, and Alfred J. Tuchfarber. 1978. "Effects of Question Wording and Format on Political Attitude Consistency." *Public Opinion Quarterly* 42: 81–92.

Bishop, George F., Robert W. Oldendick, and Alfred J. Tuchfarber. 1983. "Effects of Filter Questions in Public Opinion Surveys." *Public Opinion Quarterly* 47: 528–546.

Bishop, George F., Robert W. Oldendick, Alfred J. Tuchfarber, and S. E. Bennett. 1980. "Pseudo-opinions on Public Affairs." *Public Opinion Quarterly* 44: 198–209.

Bishop, George F., and Andrew Smith. 1999. "Gallup Split Ballot Experiments." *Public Perspective* 2: 25–27.

Bishop, George F., and Andrew Smith. 2001. "Response Order Effects and the Early Gallup Split-Ballots." *Public Opinion Quarterly* 65: 479–505.

Blass, Thomas. 1999. "The Milgram Paradigm After 35 Years: Some Things We Now Know About Obedience to Authority." *Journal of Applied Social Psychology* 29: 955–978.

Blau, Peter M. 1967. *Exchange and Power in Social Life.* New York: Wiley.

Blau, Peter M., and Otis Dudley Duncan. 1967. *The American Occupational Structure.* New York: Wiley.

Blumer, Herbert 1948. "Public Opinion and Public Opinion Polling." *American Sociological Review* 13: 542–549.

Bradburn, Norman. 1983. "Response Effects." Pp. 289–328 in Peter H. Rossi, James D. Wright, and Andy B. Anderson (eds.), *Handbook of Survey Research.* New York: Academic Press.

Bradburn, Norman M. 1982. "Question Wording Effects in Surveys." Pp. 65–74 in Robin M. Hogarth (ed.), *Question Framing and Response Consistency.* San Francisco: Jossey-Bass.

Bradburn, Norman M., and William M. Mason. 1964. "The Effect of Question Order on Responses." *Journal of Marketing Research* 1: 57–61.

Bradburn, Norman M., and Seymour Sudman. 1988. *Polls and Surveys: Understanding What They Tell Us.* San Francisco: Jossey-Bass.

Brannon, Robert, Gary Cyphers, Sharlene Hesse, Susan Hesselbart, Roberta Keane, Howard Schuman, Thomas Viccaro, and Diana Wright. 1973. "Attitude and Action: A Field Experiment Joined to a General Population Survey." *American Sociological Review* 38: 625–636.

Brown, Roger, and Albert Gilman. 1960. "The Pronouns of Power and Solidarity." Pp. 253–276 in T. A. Sebeok (ed.), *Style and Language.* Cambridge, MA: MIT Press.

Burden, Barry C. 2004. "An Alternative Account of the 2004 Presidential Election." *Forum* 2, no. 4. http://www.bepress.com.proxy.lib.umich.edu/forum/.

Camburn, Donald, and Howard Schuman. 1985. "Attitudes of Michigan Residents Concerning the Use of Animals in Medical Research." Unpublished report to the Michigan Society for Medical Research. Survey Research Center, Institute for Social Research, Ann Arbor, MI.

Campbell, Angus, Philip E. Converse, Warren E. Miller, Donald E. Stokes. 1960. *The American Voter.* New York: Wiley.

Campbell, Angus, and Howard Schuman. 1968. "Racial Attitudes in Fifteen American Cities." In *Supplemental Studies for the National Advisory Commission on Civil Disorders.* Washington, DC: Government Printing Office.

Campbell, Donald T., and Julian C. Stanley. 1963. *Experimental and Quasi-Experimental Designs for Research.* Chicago: Rand-McNally.

Campbell, James E. 2004. "The Presidential Election of 2004: The Fundamentals and the Campaign." *Forum* 2, no. 4. http://www.bepress.com.proxy.lib.umich.edu/forum/

Cannell, Charles F., and Robert L. Kahn. 1968. "Interviewing." Pp. 526–595 in Gardner Lindzey and Eliot Aronson (eds.), *The Handbook of Social Psychology,* 2nd ed. Vol. 2. Reading, MA: Addison-Wesley.

Cantril, Hadley. 1944. *Gauging Public Opinion.* Princeton, NJ: Princeton University Press

Caplan, Nahan. 1970. "The New Ghetto Man: A Review of Recent Empirical Studies." *Journal of Social Issues* 26: 59–73.

Carroll, Lewis. [1874] 1962. *The Annotated Snark*. Martin Gardner (ed.). New York: Bramhall House.

Cialdini, Robert B., Richard J. Borden, Avril Thorne, Marcus Randall Walker, Stephen Freeman, and Lloyd Reynolds Sloan. 1976. "Basking in Reflected Glory: Three (Football) Field Studies." *Journal of Personality and Social Psychology* 34: 366–375.

Columbia University Press. 2000. *Columbia Encyclopedia*. 6th ed. New York: Author.

Conover, Pamela J., and Stanley Feldman. 1981. "The Origins and Meaning of Liberal/Conservative Self-Identifications." *American Journal of Political Science* 25: 617–645.

Conrad, Frederick G., and Michael F. Schober. 2000. "Clarifying Question Meaning in a Household Telephone Survey." *Public Opinion Quarterly* 64: 1–28.

Converse, Jean M. 1976–77. "Predicting No Opinion in the Polls." *Public Opinion Quarterly* 40: 515–530.

Converse, Jean M. 1984. "Strong Arguments and Weak Evidence: The Open/Closed Questioning Controversy of the 1940s." *Public Opinion Quarterly* 48: 267–282.

Converse, Jean M. 1987. *Survey Research in the United States: Roots and Emergence 1890–1960*. Berkeley: University of California Press.

Converse, Jean M., and Stanley Presser. 1986. *Survey Questions: Handcrafting the Standardized Questionnaire*. Beverly Hills, CA: Sage.

Converse, Jean M., and Howard Schuman. 1974. *Conversations at Random: Survey Research as Interviewers See It*. New York: Wiley.

Converse, Philip E. 1964. "The Nature of Belief Systems in Mass Publics." In D. E. Apter (ed.), *Ideology and Discontent*. New York: Free Press.

Converse, Philip E. 1970. "Attitudes and Non-Attitudes: Continuation of the Dialogue." Pp. 168–189 in Edward R. Tufte (ed.), *The Quantitative Analysis of Social Problems*. Reading, MA: Addison-Wesley.

Converse, Philip E., Auge R. Clausen, and Warren E. Miller. 1965. "Electoral Myth and Reality: The 1964 Election." *American Political Science Review* 59: 321–336.

Converse, Philip E., and Howard Schuman. 1970. "Silent Majorities and the Vietnam War," *Scientific American* (June): 17–25.

Cook, Thomas D., and Donald T. Campbell. 1979. *Quasi-Experimentation: Design and Analysis Issues for Field Settings*. Chicago: Rand McNally.

Corning, Amy. 2007. "When the Past Is Another Country: The Impact of Emigration on Memory." PhD dissertation, University of Michigan, Ann Arbor.

Cramer, M. Richard, and Howard Schuman. 1975. "We and They: Pronouns as Measures of Political Identification and Estrangement." *Social Science Research* 4: 231–240.

Cronbach, Lee J. 1970. *Essentials of Psychological Testing*. New York: Harper and Row.

Cronbach, Lee J. 1989. "Construct Validation After Thirty Years." Pp. 147–171 in Robert L. Linn (ed.), *Intelligence: Measurement, Theory, and Public Policy: Proceedings of a Symposium in Honor of Lloyd G. Humphreys.* Chicago: University of Illinois Press.

Crystal, David. 2004. *The Stories of English.* Woodstock, NY: Overlook Press.

Darwin, Charles. [1876] 1988. *On the Origin of Species by Means of Natural Selection, or the Preservation of Favoured Races in the Struggle for Life.* In Paul H. Barrett and R. B. Freeman (eds.), *The Works of Charles Darwin.* Vol. 16. New York: New York University Press.

Davis, Darren W. 1997. "Nonrandom Measurement Error and Race of Interviewer Effects among African Americans." *Public Opinion Quarterly* 61: 183–207.

Delli Carpini, Michael X., and Scott Keeter. 1996. *What Americans Know about Politics and Why It Matters.* New Haven, CT: Yale University Press.

Dijkstra, Wil. 1983. "How Interviewer Variance Can Bias the Results of Research on Interviewer Effects." *Quality and Quantity* 17: 179–187.

Dillehay, R. C. 1973. "On the Irrelevance of the Classical Negative Evidence Concerning the Effect of Attitudes on Behavior." *American Psychologist* 28: 887–891.

Dillman, Donald A. 1978. *Mail and Telephone Surveys: The Total Design Method.* New York: Wiley.

Dohrenwend, B. S. 1965. "Some Effects of Open and Closed Questions on Respondents' Answers." *Human Organization* 24: 175–184.

Duncan, Otis Dudley. 1984. " 'Objective and Subjective Phenomena' and 'Subjectivity and Social Facts.' " Pp. 7–14 in Charles F. Turner and Elizabeth Martin (eds.), *Surveying Subjective Phenomena.* Vol. 1. New York: Russell Sage.

Duncan, Otis Dudley, Howard Schuman, and Beverly Duncan. 1973. *Social Change in a Metropolitan Community.* New York: Russell Sage.

Duverger, M. 1964. *Introduction to the Social Sciences.* London: Allen and Unwin.

Dyson, Freeman. 1984 *Weapons and Hope.* New York: Harper and Row.

Eagly, Alice, and Shelly Chaiken. 1993. *The Psychology of Attitudes.* Orlando, FL: Harcourt Brace.

Fazio, Russell. 1986. "How Do Attitudes Guide Behavior?" Pp. 204–242 in R. M. Sorrentino and E. T. Higgins (eds.), *The Handbook of Motivation and Cognition: Foundations of Social Behavior.* New York: Guilford.

Fehr, Ernst, and Joseph Henrich. 2003. "Is Strong Reciprocity a Maladaptation? On the Evolutionary Foundations of Human Evolution." Pp. 54–82 in Peter Hammerstein (ed.), *Genetic and Cultural Evolution of Cooperation.* Cambridge, MA: MIT Press.

Fields, James M. and Howard Schuman. 1976–1977. "Public Beliefs about the Beliefs of the Public," *Public Opinion Quarterly* 40 (Winter): 427–448.

Fishbein, Martin. 1967. "A Consideration of Beliefs, and Their Role in Attitude Measurement." Pp. 257–266 in Martin Fishbein (ed.), *Readings in Attitude Theory and Measurement.* New York: Wiley.

Foddy, William. 1993. *Constructing Questions for Interviews and Questionnaires: Theory and Practice in Social Research.* Cambridge, UK: Cambridge University Press.

Fredrickson, George M. 2002. *Racism: A Short History.* Princeton, NJ: Princeton University Press.

Gallup Poll. 1982. News release. February 7.

Geer, John G. 1991. "Do Open-Ended Questions Measure 'Salient' Issues?" *Public Opinion Quarterly* 55: 360–370.

Geertz, Clifford. 1973. *The Interpretation of Cultures.* New York: Basic Books.

Geertz, Clifford. 1983. " 'From the Native's Point of View': On the Nature of Anthropological Understanding." Pp. 55–70 in *Local Knowledge: Further Essays in Interpretive Anthropology.* New York: Basic Books.

Geertz, Clifford. 2000. *Available Light: Anthropological Reflections on Philosophical Topics.* Princeton, NJ: Princeton University Press.

General Social Surveys: 1972–2006 [Cumulative File and Codebook]. 2006. Chicago, IL: National Opinion Research Center, University of Chicago.

Gilovich, Thomas, Dacher Keltner, and Richard E. Nisbett. 2006. *Social Psychology.* New York: W. W. Norton.

Gouldner, Alvin W. 1960. "The Norm of Reciprocity." *American Sociological Review* 25: 161–178.

Grice, H. Paul. 1975. "Logic and Conversation." Pp. 41–58 in P. Cole and J. L. Morgan (eds.), *Syntax and Semantics.* Vol. 9: *Pragmatics.* New York: Academic Press.

Groves, Robert M. 1989. *Survey Errors and Survey Costs.* New York: Wiley.

Groves, Robert M. 1991. "Measurement Error Across the Disciplines." In Paul P. Biemer, Robert M. Groves, Lars E. Lyberg, Nancy A. Mathiowetz, and Seymour Sudman (eds.), *Measurement Errors in Surveys.* New York: Wiley.

Groves, Robert M., Floyd J. Fowler, Jr., Mick P. Couper, James M. Lepkowski, Eleanor Singer, and Roger Tourangeau. 2004. *Survey Methodology.* Hoboken, NJ: Wiley.

Groves, Robert M., and Nancy Fultz. 1985. "Gender Effects among Telephone Interviewers in a Survey of Economic Attitudes." *Sociological Methods and Research* 14: 31–52.

Hatchett, Shirley, and Howard Schuman. 1975–76. "White Respondents and Race-of-Interviewer Effects." *Public Opinion Quarterly* 39: 523–528.

Hauser, Marc D. 2006. *Moral Minds: How Nature Designed Our Universal Sense of Right and Wrong.* New York: HarperCollins.

Heider, Fritz. 1958. *The Psychology of Interpersonal Relations.* New York: Wiley.

Heisenberg, Werner. 1958. *Physics and Philosophy: The Revolution in Modern Science.* New York: Harper and Brothers.

Hillygus, D. Sunshine, and Todd G. Shields. 2005. "Moral Values and Voter Decision Making in the 2004 Presidential Election." Pp. 201–209 in *PSOnline.* http://www.apsanet.org.

Hippler, Hans-J., and Norbert Schwarz. 1986. "Not Forbidding Isn't Allowing: The Cognitive Basis of the Forbid-Allow Asymmetry." *Public Opinion Quarterly* 50: 87–96.

Holbrook, Allyson, Jon A. Krosnick, David Moore, and Roger Tourangeau. 2007. "Response Order Effects in Dichotomous Categorical Questions Presented Orally: The Impact of Question and Respondent Attributes." *Public Opinion Quarterly* 71: 325–348.

Holleman, Bregje. 2000. *The Forbid/Allow Asymmetry: On the Cognitive Mechanisms Underlying Wording Effects in Surveys.* Amsterdam: Rodopi.

Homans, George C. 1950. *The Human Group.* New York: Harcourt Brace.

House, James S., and Sharon Wolf. 1978. "Effects of Urban Residence on Interpersonal Trust and Helping Behavior." *Journal of Personality and Social Psychology.* 36: 1029–1043.

Humphrey, Ronald, and Howard Schuman. 1984. "The Portrayal of Blacks in Magazine Advertisements: 1950–1982." *Public Opinion Quarterly* 48: 551–563.

Hurd, A. A. 1932. "Comparisons of Short-Answer and Multiple-Choice Tests Covering Identical Subject Content." *Journal of Educational Psychology* 26: 28–30.

Huxley, Thomas Henry. 1897. "Biogenesis and Abiogenesis." Pp. 229–272 in *Discourses: Biological and Geological Essays.* New York: Appleton.

Hyman, Herbert H. 1954. *Interviewing in Social Research.* Chicago: University of Chicago Press.

Hyman, Herbert H., and Paul B. Sheatsley. 1950. "The Current Status of American Public Opinion." Pp. 11–34 in J. C. Payne (ed.), *The Teaching of Contemporary Affairs.* Twenty-first Yearbook of the National Council of Social Studies. Washington, DC: National Council of Social Studies.

Inkeles, Alex, and David H. Smith. 1974. *Becoming Modern.* Cambridge, MA: Harvard University Press.

Jackman, Robert W. 1972. "Political Elites, Mass Publics, and Support for Democratic Principles." *Journal of Politics* 34: 753–773.

Kalton, Graham. 1983. *Introduction to Survey Sampling.* Thousand Oaks, CA: Sage.

Kandel, Eric R. 2006. *In Search of Memory: The Emergence of a New Science of Mind.* New York: W. W. Norton.

Kane, Emily W., and Laura J. Macaulay. 1993. Interviewer Gender and Gender Attitudes. *Public Opinion Quarterly* 57: 1–28.

Kane, Emily W., and Howard Schuman. 1991. "Open Questions as Measures of Personal Concern with Issues: A Reanalysis of Stouffer's *Communism, Conformity, and Civil Liberties.*" *Sociological Methodology* 21: 81–96.

Keeter, Scott. 2007. "Evangelicals and Moral Values." Pp. 80–94 in David E. Campbell (ed.), *A Matter of Faith: Religion in the 2004 Election.* Washington, DC: Brookings Institution Press.

Kish, Leslie. 1965. *Survey Sampling.* New York: Wiley.

Kluegel, James R., and Eliot R. Smith. 1986. *Beliefs about Inequality: Americans Views of What Is and What Ought to Be.* Hawthorne, NY: Aldine.

Kohut, Heinz. 1984. *How Does Analysis Cure?* Chicago: University of Chicago Press.

Krosnick, Jon A. 1991. "Response Strategies for Coping with the Cognitive Demands of Attitude Measures in Surveys." *Applied Cognitive Psychology* 5: 213–236.

Krosnick, Jon A. 1999. "Survey Research." *Annual Review of Psychology.* 50: 537–567.

Krosnick, Jon A., and Duane F. Alwin. 1987. "An Evaluation of a Cognitive Theory of Response-Order Effects in Survey Measurement." *Public Opinion Quarterly* 51: 201–219.

Krosnick, Jon A., and Duane F. Alwin. 1989. "Aging and Susceptibility to Attitude Change." *Journal of Personality and Social Psychology* 59: 416–425.

Krosnick, Jon A., Charles M. Judd, and Bernd Wittenbrink. 2005. "The Measurement of Attitudes." Pp. 21–76 in Dolores Albarracín, Blair T. Johnson, and Mark P. Zanna (eds.), *The Handbook of Attitudes.* Mahwah, NJ: Erlbaum.

Kunz, Phillip R., and Michael Woolcott. 1976. "Season's Greetings: From My Status to Yours." *Social Science Research* 5: 269–278.

Lang, Serge. 1981. *The File.* New York: Springer-Verlag.

Langer, Gary. 2006. "Strife Erodes Afghan Optimism: Five Years After the Taliban's Fall." http://abcnews.go.com/Politics/PollVault/Story?id=2702516&page=1.

Langer, Gary, and Jon Cohen. 2005. "Voters and Values in the 2004 Election." *Public Opinion Quarterly* 69: 744–759.

Langer, Gary, and Jon Cohen. 2006. Letter to the Editor. *Public Opinion Quarterly* 70: 416–418.

LaPiere, Richard T. 1934. "Attitudes vs. Actions." *Social Forces* 13: 230–237.

Latané, Bibb, and John M. Darley. 1970. *The Unresponsive Bystander: Why Doesn't He Help?* Englewood Cliffs, NJ: Prentice-Hall.

Lazarsfeld, Paul F. [1935] 1954. "The Art of Asking Why: Three Principles Underlying the Formulation of Questionnaires." *National Marketing Review* 1: 32–43. Reprinted as Pp. 675–686 in Daniel Katz et al. (eds.), *Public Opinion and Propaganda.* New York: Dryden Press.

Lazarsfeld, Paul F. 1944. "The Controversy over Detailed Interviews—An Offer for Negotiation." *Public Opinion Quarterly* 8: 38–60.

Levi, Primo. 1959. *Survival in Auschwitz.* New York: Collier.

Link, Henry C. 1946. "The Psychological Corporation's Index of Public Opinion." *Journal of Applied Psychology* 30: 297–309.

Lipset, Seymour M., and David Riesman (eds.). 1975. *Education and Politics at Harvard.* New York: McGraw-Hill.

Lohr, Sharon L. 1999. *Sampling: Design and Analysis.* Pacific Grove, CA: Duxbury Press.

Lord, Charles C., and Mark R. Lepper. 1999. "Attitude Representation Theory." *Advances in Experimental Social Psychology* 31: 265–343.

Malinowski, Bronislaw. 1926. *Crime and Custom in Savage Society.* New York: Harcourt Brace.

Malinowski, Bronislaw. 1989. *A Diary in the Strict Sense of the Term.* Stanford, CA: Stanford University Press.

Martin, Elizabeth. 2006. "Vignettes and Respondent Debriefing for Questionnaire Design." Pp. 149–171 in Stanley Presser et al. (eds.), *Methods for Testing and Evaluating Survey Questionnaires.* New York: Wiley.

Martin, Elizabeth, and Anne E. Polivka. 1995. "Diagnostics for Redesigning Questionnaires: Measuring Work in the Current Population Survey." *Public Opinion Quarterly* 59: 547–567.

Mauss, Marcel. 1954. *The Gift: Forms and Functions of Exchange in Archaic Societies.* Glencoe, IL: Free Press.

McGuire, William J. 1985. "Attitudes and Attitude Change." Pp. 233–346 in Gardner Lindzey and Elliot Aronson (eds.), *Handbook of Social Psychology,* 3rd ed. Vol. 2. New York: Random House.

Merton, Robert K. 1957. *Social Theory and Social Structure.* Glencoe, IL: Free Press.

Milgram, S. 1974. *Obedience to Authority: An Experimental View.* New York: Harper and Row.

Miller, Warren E., and Donald E. Stokes. 1963. "Constituency Influence in Congress." *American Political Science Review* 57: 45–56.

Miller, Warren E., et al. 1981. *American National Election Studies Data Sourcebook: 1950–1980.* Cambridge, MA: Harvard University Press.

Minutaglio, Bill. 1999. *First Son: George W. Bush and the Bush Family Dynasty.* New York: Three Rivers Press.

Moore, David W., and Frank Newport. 1996. "Public Policy Questions and Response Order: Prevalence of the Recency Effect." Paper presented at the American Association for Public Opinion Research Conference, May 16–19, Salt Lake City, UT.

Moser, C. A., and Graham Kalton. 1971. *Survey Methods in Social Investigation.* London: Heinemann.

Mueller, John E. 1973. *War, Presidents, and Public Opinion.* New York: Wiley.

Neisser, Ulric. 1967. *Cognitive Psychology.* New York: Appleton-Century-Crofts.

Newton, Isaac. [1686] 1972. Preface to *Philosophiae Naturalis Principia Mathematica.* Cambridge, MA: Harvard University Press.

Nisbett, Richard E., and Dov Cohen. 1996. *Culture of Honor: The Psychology of Violence in the South.* Boulder, CO: Westview Press.

Nisbett, Richard E., and Timothy D. Wilson. 1977. "Telling More than We Can Know: Verbal Reports on Mental Processes." *Psychological Review* 84: 231–259.

Nowak, Martin A. 2006. "Five Rules for the Evolution of Cooperation." *Science* 314: 1560–1563.

Oberdorfer, Don. 1971. *Tet.* New York: Doubleday.

Ogden, Charles K., and I. A. Richards. 1923. *The Meaning of Meaning: A Study of the Influence of Language upon Thought and of the Science of Symbolism.* New York: Harcourt Brace.

Page, Benjamin I., and Robert Y. Shapiro. 1992. *The Rational Public: Fifty Years of Trends in Americans' Policy Preferences.* Chicago: University of Chicago Press.

Payne, Stanley. 1951. *The Art of Asking Questions.* Princeton, NJ: Princeton University Press.

Petty, Richard E., and Duane T. Wegener. 1998. "Attitude Change: Multiple Roles for Persuasion Variables." Pp. 323–390 in Daniel T. Gilbert, Susan T. Fiske, and Gardner Lindzey (eds.), *The Handbook of Social Psychology.* Vol. 1. Boston: McGraw-Hill.

Piaget, Jean. 1932. *The Moral Judgment of the Child.* New York: Harcourt Brace.

Presser, Stanley. 1990. "Measurement Issues in the Study of Social Change." *Social Forces* 68: 856–868.

Presser, Stanley, Johnny Blair, and Timothy Triplett. 1992. "Survey Sponsorship, Response Rates, and Response Effects." *Social Science Quarterly* 73: 699–702.

Presser, Stanley, Jennifer M. Rothgreb, Mick P. Couper, Judith T. Lessler, Elizabeth Martin, Jean Martin, and Eleanor Singer. (eds.). 2004. *Methods for Testing and Evaluating Survey Questionnaires.* New York: Wiley.

Putnam, Robert D. 1993. *Making Democracy Work: Civic Traditions in Modern Italy.* Princeton, NJ: Princeton University Press.

Rasinski, Kenneth A. 1989. "The Effect of Question Wording on Public Support for Government Spending." *Public Opinion Quarterly* 53: 388–394.

Remmers, H. H., L. E. Marschat, A. Brown, and I. Chapman. 1923. "An Experimental Study of the Relative Difficulty of True-False, Multiple-Choice, and Incomplete Sentence Types of Examination Questions." *Journal of Educational Psychology* 14: 367–372.

Rieger, Cheryl. 1995. "Collective Memories in the Late Soviet Union." PhD dissertation, University of Michigan, Ann Arbor.

Ross, Lee. 1977. "The Intuitive Psychologist and His Shortcomings: Distortions in the Attribution Process." Pp. 173–220 in Leonard Berkowitz (ed.), *Advances in Experimental Social Psychology*. Vol. 10. New York: Academic Press.

Ross, Lee, D. Greene, and P. House. 1977. "The 'False Consensus Effect': An Egocentric Bias in Social Perception and Attribution Processes." *Journal of Personality and Social Psychology* 13: 279–301.

Rottenberg, Ken J., and Luanne Mann. 1986. "The Development of the Norm of the Reciprocity of Self-Disclosure and Its Function in Children's Attraction to Peers." *Child Development* 57: 1349–1357.

Rugg, Donald. 1941. "Experiments in Question Wording: II." *Public Opinion Quarterly* 5: 91–92.

Rugg, Donald, and Hadley Cantril. 1944. "The Wording of Questions." Pp. 22–50 in Hadley Cantril (ed.), *Gauging Public Opinion*. Princeton, NJ: Princeton University Press.

Schaeffer, Nora Cate, and Stanley Presser. 2003. "The Science of Asking Questions." *Annual Review of Sociology* 29: 65–88.

Schuman, Howard. 1966. "The Random Probe: A Technique for Evaluating the Validity of Closed Questions." *American Sociological Review* 31: 218–222.

Schuman, Howard. 1969. "Free Will and Determinism in Public Beliefs about Race." *Trans-Action:* 44–48.

Schuman, Howard. 1972a. "Attitudes vs. Actions *Versus* Attitudes vs. Attitudes," *Public Opinion Quarterly* 36: 347–354.

Schuman, Howard. 1972b. "Two Sources of Antiwar Sentiment in America." *American Journal of Sociology* 78: 513–536.

Schuman, Howard. 1983. Review of *The File*, by Serge Lang. *Public Opinion Quarterly* 47: 601–607.

Schuman, Howard. 1990. "3 Different Pens Help Tell the Story." *New York Times*, March 7, op. ed. page.

Schuman, Howard. 1992. "Context Effects: State of the Past/State of the Art." Pp. 5–20 in Norbert Schwarz and Seymour Sudman (eds.), *Context Effects in Social and Psychological Research*. New York: Springer-Verlag.

Schuman, Howard. 1995. "Attitudes, Beliefs, and Behavior." Pp. 68–89 in Karen S. Cook, Gary Alan Fine, and James S. House (eds.), *Sociological Perspectives on Social Psychology*. Boston: Allyn and Bacon.

Schuman, Howard. 1997. "Polls, Surveys, and the English Language." *Public Perspective* 8: 6–7.

Schuman, Howard. 2000. "The Perils of Correlation, the Lure of Labels, and the Beauty of Negative Results." Pp. 302–323 in David O. Sears, Jim Sidanius, and

Lawrence Bobo (eds.), *Racialized Politics: The Debate about Racism in America.* Chicago: University of Chicago Press.

Schuman, Howard. 2002. "Sense and Nonsense About Surveys." *Contexts* 1: 40–42.

Schuman, Howard, Hiroko Akiyama, and Bärbel Knäuper, "Collective Memories of Germans and Japanese About the Past Half Century." 1988. *Memory* 6: 427–454.

Schuman, Howard, and Lawrence Bobo. 1988. "Survey-Based Experiments on White Racial Attitudes toward Residential Integration." *American Journal of Sociology* 94: 273–299.

Schuman, Howard, and Jean M. Converse. 1971. "The Effects of Black and White Interviewers on Black Responses in 1968." *Public Opinion Quarterly* 35: 46–68.

Schuman, Howard, and Otis Dudley Duncan. 1974. "Questions about Attitude Survey Questions." In *Sociological Methodology 1973–74.* San Francisco: Jossey-Bass.

Schuman, Howard, and Shirley Hatchett. 1974. *Black Racial Attitudes: Trends and Complexities.* Ann Arbor, MI: Institute for Social Research.

Schuman, Howard, and Michael P. Johnson. 1976. "Attitudes and Behavior." *Annual Review of Sociology* 2: 161–207.

Schuman, Howard, and Maria Krysan. 1996. "A Study of Far Right *Ressentiment* in America." *International Journal of Public Opinion* 8: 10–30.

Schuman, Howard, and Edward O. Laumann. 1967. "Do Most Professors Support the War?" *Trans-Action:* 32–35.

Schuman, Howard, and Jacob Ludwig. 1983. "The Norm of Even-Handedness in Surveys as in Life." *American Sociological Review* 48: 112–120.

Schuman, Howard, Jacob Ludwig, and Jon A. Krosnick. 1986. "The Perceived Threat of Nuclear War, Salience, and Open Questions." *Public Opinion Quarterly* 50: 519–536.

Schuman, Howard, and Stanley Presser. 1977–78. "Attitude Measurement and the Gun Control Paradox." *Public Opinion Quarterly* 41: 427–438.

Schuman, Howard, and Stanley Presser. [1981] 1996. *Questions and Answers in Attitude Surveys: Experiments on Question Form, Wording, and Context.* New York: Academic Press.

Schuman, Howard, Cheryl Rieger, and Vladas Guidys. 1994. "Generations and Collective Memories in Lithuania." Pp. 313–333 in N. Schwarz and S. Sudman (eds.), *Autobiographical Memory and the Validity of Retrospective Reports.* New York: Springer-Verlag.

Schuman, Howard, and Willard L. Rodgers. 2004. "Cohorts, Chronology, and Collective Memories." *Public Opinion Quarterly* 68: 218–255.

Schuman, Howard, Barry Schwartz, and Hannah d'Arcy. 2005. "Elite Revisionists and Popular Belief: Christopher Columbus, Hero or Villain?" *Public Opinion Quarterly* 69: 2–29.

Schuman, Howard, and Jacqueline Scott. 1987. "Problems in the Use of Survey Questions to Measure Public Opinion." *Science* 236: 957–959.

Schuman, Howard, and Jacqueline Scott. 1989a. "Generations and Collective Memories." *American Sociological Review* 54: 359–381.

Schuman, Howard, and Jacqueline Scott. 1989b. "Response Effects Over Time: Two Experiments." *Sociological Methods & Research* 17: 398–408.

Schuman, Howard, Eleanor Singer, Rebecca Donovan, and Claire Selltiz. 1983. "Discriminatory Behavior in New York Restaurants: 1950 and 1981." *Social Indicators Research* 13: 68–83.

Schuman, Howard, Charlotte Steeh, Lawrence Bobo, and Maria Krysan. 1997. *Racial Attitudes in America: Trends and Interpretations.* Cambridge, MA: Harvard University Press.

Schuman, Howard, Edward Walsh, Camille Olson, and Barbara Etheridge. 1985. "Effort and Reward: The Assumption That College Grades Are Affected by Quantity of Study." *Social Forces* 63: 945–966.

Schwarz, Norbert. 1996. *Cognition and Communication: Judgmental Biases, Research Methods, and the Logic of Conversation.* Mahwah, NJ: Erlbaum.

Schwarz, Norbert, and Herbert Bless. 1992. "Constructing Reality and Its Alternatives: Assimilation and Contrast Effects in Social Judgment." Pp. 217–245 in L. L. Martin and A. Tesser (eds.), *The Construction of Social Judgment.* Hillsdale, NJ: Erlbaum.

Schwarz, Norbert, and Herbert Bless. 2007. "Mental Construal Processes: The Inclusion/Exclusion Model." Pp. 119–141 in D. Stapel and J. Suls (eds.), *Assimilation and Contrast in Social Psychology.* New York: Psychology Press.

Schwarz, Norbert, and Hans-J. Hippler. 1995. *Public Opinion Quarterly* 59: 93–97.

Schwarz, Norbert, Fritz Strack, and Hans-Peter Mai. 1991. "Assimilation and Contrast Effects in Part-Whole Question Sequences: A Conversational Logic Analysis." *Public Opinion Quarterly* 55: 3–23.

Scott, Jacqueline, and Lilian Zac. 1993. "Collective Memories in Britain and the United States." *Public Opinion Quarterly* 57: 315–331.

Scott, W. A. 1968. "Attitude Measurement." Pp. 204–273 in G. Lindzey and E. Aronson (eds.), *The Handbook of Social Psychology,* 2nd ed. Vol. 2. Reading, MA: Addison-Wesley.

Sears, David O. 1986. "College Sophomores in the Laboratory: Influences of a Narrow Data Base on Social Psychology's View of Human Nature." *Journal of Personality and Social Psychology* 3: 515–530.

Selltiz, Claire. 1955. "The Use of Survey Methods in a Citizen's Campaign against Discrimination." *Human Organization* 14: 19–25.

Simmel, Georg. 1950. *The Sociology of Georg Simmel,* trans. and ed. Kurt H. Wolff. New York: Free Press.

Singer, Eleanor. 1978. "Informed Consent: Consequences for Response Rate and Response Quality in Social Surveys." *American Sociological Review* 43: 144–162.

Singer, Eleanor. 2002. *"The Use of Incentives to Reduce Nonresponse in Household Surveys."* Pp. 163–178 in Robert Groves, Don A. Dillman, John L. Eltinge, and Roderick J. A. Little (eds.), *Survey Nonresponse.* New York: Wiley.

Singer, Eleanor (ed.). 2006. "Special issue: Nonresponse Bias in Household Surveys." *Public Opinion Quarterly* 70, no. 5: 637–809.

Singer, Eleanor, and Martin R. Frankel. 1982. "Informed Consent Procedures in Telephone Surveys." *American Sociological Review* 47: 416–426.

Sirken, Monroe G., Douglas J. Herrmann, Susan Schechter, Norbert Schwarz, Judith M. Tanur, and Roger Tourangeau (eds.). 1991. *Cognition and Survey Research.* New York: Wiley.

Smith, Eric R. A. N. 1989. *The Unchanging American Voter.* Berkeley: University of California Press.

Smith, Tom W. 1987a. "The Art of Asking Questions, 1936–1985." *Public Opinion Quarterly* 51: S95–S108.

Smith, Tom W. 1987b. "That Which We Call Welfare By Any Other Name Would Smell Sweeter: An Analysis of Question Wording on Response Patterns." *Public Opinion Quarterly* 51: 75–83.

Smith, Tom W. 1989. "Random Probes of GSS Questions." *International Journal of Public Opinion Research* 1: 305–325.

Smith, Tom W. 1991a. "Context Effects in the General Social Survey." Pp. 57–71 in Paul B. Biemer, Robert M. Groves, Lars E. Lyberg, Nancy A. Mathiowetz, and Seymour Sudman (eds.), *Measurement Errors in Surveys.* New York: Wiley.

Smith, Tom W. 1991b. "Thoughts on the Nature of Context Effects." Pp. 162–184 in Norbert Schwarz and Seymour Sudman (eds.), *Context Effects in Social and Psychological Research.* New York: Springer-Verlag.

Sniderman, Paul M., and Edward G. Carmines. 1997. *Reaching Beyond Race.* Cambridge, MA: Harvard University Press.

Sniderman, Paul M., Grechen C. Crosby, and William G. Howell. 2000. Pp. 236–279 in David O. Sears, Jim Sidanius, and Lawrence Bobo (eds.), *Racialized Politics: The Debate about Racism in America.* Chicago: University of Chicago Press.

Sniderman, Paul M., and Douglas B. Grob. 1996. "Innovations in Experimental Design in General Population Attitude Surveys." *Annual Review of Sociology* 22: 377–399.

Sniderman, Paul M., and Thomas Piazza. 1993. *The Scar of Race.* Cambridge, MA: Harvard University Press.

Stouffer, Samuel A. 1950. "Appendix: Some Notes on Sampling and Questionnaire Administration by the Research Branch." Pp. 709–722 in Samuel A. Stouffer, et al. (eds.), *Studies in Social Psychology in World War.* Vol. 4. *Measurement and Prediction.* Princeton, NJ: Princeton University Press.

Stouffer, Samuel A. [1955] 1992. *Communism, Conformity, and Civil Liberties: A Cross-Section of the Nation Speaks Its Mind.* New York: Doubleday.

Stouffer, Samuel A., E. A. Suchman, L. C. DeVinney, S. A. Star, and R. M. Williams, Jr. 1949. *Studies in Social Psychology in World War II.* Vol. 1. *The American Soldier: Adjustment During Army Life.* Princeton, NJ: Princeton University Press.

St. Peter, Louis, J. Allen Williams, and David R. Johnson. 1977. "Comment on Jackman's 'Political Elites, Mass Publics, and Support for Democratic Principles.' " *Journal of Politics* 39: 176–184.

Strack, Fritz, and Leonard L. Martin. 1987. "Thinking, Judging, and Communicating: A Process Account of Context Effects in Attitude Surveys." Pp. 123–148 in Hans-J. Hippler, Norbert Schwarz, and Seymour Sudman (eds.), *Social Information Processing and Survey Methodology.* New York: Springer-Verlag.

Sudman, Seymour, and Norman M. Bradburn. 1974. *Response Effects in Surveys.* Chicago: Aldine.

Sudman, Seymour, and Norman M. Bradburn. 1982. *Asking Questions: A Practical Guide to Questionnaire Design.* San Francisco: Jossey-Bass.

Sudman, Seymour, Norman M. Bradburn, and Norbert Schwarz. 1996. *Thinking about Answers: The Application of Cognitive Processes to Survey Methodology.* San Francisco: Jossey-Bass.

Tanur, Judith M. 1992. *Questions about Questions: Inquiries into the Cognitive Bases of Surveys.* New York: Russell Sage.

Tanur, Judith M. 1999. "Looking Backwards and Forwards at the CASM Movement." Pp. 13–19 in Monroe G. Sirken, Douglas J. Herrmann, Susan Schechter, Norbert Schwarz, Judith M. Tanur, and Roger Tourangeau (eds.), *Cognition and Survey Research.* New York: Wiley.

Taylor, Shelley E., and Susan T. Fiske. 1978. "Salience, Attention, and Attribution: Top of the Head Phenomena." In L. Berkowitz (ed.), *Advances in Experimental Social Psychology.* Vol. 11. New York: Academic Press.

Thurstone, L. L. 1931. "The Measurement of Attitudes." *Journal of Abnormal and Social Psychology* 26: 249–269.

Tilly, Charles. 2006. *Why?* Princeton, NJ: Princeton University Press.

Tolman, Edward C. 1945. "A Stimulus-Expectancy Need-Cathexis Psychology." *Science* 101: 616–666.

Tourangeau, Roger. 1999. "Context Effects in Answers to Attitude Questions." Pp. 111–131 in Monroe G. Sirken, et al. *Cognition and Survey Research.* New York: Wiley.

Tourangeau, Roger. 2004. "Experimental Design Considerations for Testing and Evaluating Questionnaires." Pp. 209–224 in Stanley Presser, Jennifer M. Rothgreb, Mick P. Couper, Judith T. Lessler, Elizabeth Martin, Jean Martin, and Eleanor Singer (eds.), *Methods for Testing and Evaluating Survey Questionnaires.* New York: Wiley.

Tourangeau, Roger, and Kenneth Rasinski. 1988. "Cognitive Processes Underlying Context Effects in Attitude Measurement." *Psychological Bulletin* 103: 299–314.

Tourangeau, Roger, Kenneth A. Rasinski, Norman Bradburn, and Roy D'Andrade. 1989. "Belief Accessibility and Context Effects in Attitude Measurement." *Journal of Experimental Social Psychology* 25: 401–421.

Tourangeau, Roger, Lance J. Rips, and Kenneth Rasinski. 2000. *The Psychology of Survey Response.* Cambridge, UK: Cambridge University Press.

Traugott, Michael W. 2005. "The Accuracy of the National Preelection Polls in the 2004 Presidential Election." *Public Opinion Quarterly* 69: 642–654.

Triplett, Norman. 1898. "The Dynamogenic Factors in Pacemaking and Competition." *American Journal of Psychology* 9: 508–533.

Trivers, Robert L. 1971. "The Evolution of Reciprocal Altruism." *Quarterly Review of Biology* 46: 35–57.

Turner, C. F., and E. Martin (eds.). 1984. *Surveying Subjective Phenomena.* Vol. 1. New York: Russell Sage.

Tversky, A., and D. Kahneman. 1982. "Judgment under Certainty: Heuristics and Biases." Pp. 3–20 in D. Kahneman, P. Slovic, and A. Tversky (eds.), *Judgment under Uncertainty: Heuristics and Biases.* Cambridge, UK: Cambridge University Press.

Waal, Frans de. 2006. *Primates and Philosophers: How Morality Evolved.* Princeton, NJ: Princeton University Press.

Walsh, Edward J. 1975. *Dirty Work, Race, and Self-Esteem.* Ann Arbor, MI: Institute of Labor and Industrial Relations.

Walster, Elaine, G. William Walster, and Ellen Berscheid. 1978. *Equity: Theory and Research.* Boston: Allyn and Bacon.

Weber, Max. [1905] 1958. *The Protestant Ethic and the Spirit of Capitalism.* New York: Scribner.

Wegner, Daniel M., and David J. Schneider. 2003. "The White Bear Story." *Psychological Inquiry* 14: 326–329.

Weigel, R. H., and L. S. Newman. 1976. "Increasing Attitude-Behavior Correspondence by Broadening the Scope of the Behavioral Measure." *Journal of Personality and Social Psychology* 33: 793–802.

Weisberg, Herbert F. 2005. *The Total Survey Error Approach: A Guide to the New Science of Survey Research.* Chicago: University of Chicago Press.

Whyte, William Foote. 1943. *Street Corner Society: The Social Structure of an Italian Slum.* Chicago: University of Chicago Press.

Wilson, Timothy D. 2002. *Strangers to Ourselves: Discovering the Adaptive Unconscious.* Cambridge, MA: Harvard University Press.

Wilson, Timothy D., Suzanne J. LaFleur, and D. Eric Anderson. 1996. "The Validity and Consequences of Verbal Reports about Attitudes." Pp. 91–114 in Norbert Schwarz and Seymour Sudman (eds.), *Answering Questions: Methodology for*

Determining Cognitive and Communicative Processes in Survey Research. San Francisco: Jossey-Bass.

Wilson, Timothy D., and Sara D. Hodges. 1992. "Attitudes as Temporary Constructions." Pp. 37–65 in A. Tesser and L. Martin (eds.), *The Construction of Social Judgment.* Hillsdale, NJ: Erlbaum.

Wrong, Dennis. 1961. "The Oversocialized Conception of Man in Modern Sociology." *American Sociological Review* 26: 183–193.

Zaller, J. R. 1992. *The Nature and Origins of Mass Opinion.* Cambridge, UK: Cambridge University Press.

Zaller, John R., and Stanley Feldman. 1992. "A Simple Theory of the Survey Response." *American Journal of Political Science* 36: 579–616.

Index

ABC poll, 4, 47, 164n9
Abelson, Robert P., 159, 163n3, 190n3
Abortion issue, 11, 14, 15, 19, 32, 42, 49, 110, 183n22
Abramowitz, Alan, 172n22
Abramson, Paul R., 172n22, 183n26
Acquiescence, 141–144
Afghanistan, 5
Age, 73
Agree–disagree items. *See* Acquiescence
Agricultural Trade Act, 151–154
Ajzen, Icek, 130, 186n11
Akiyama, Hiroko, 187n17
Albarracín, Dolores, 146
Aldrich, John H., 172n22
Alexander, Jeffrey C., 28
Alwin, Duane F., 58, 168n3
Ambiguous questions, 26–27
American Association for Public Opinion (AAPOR), 167n13
Anderson, Barbara A., 183n26
Anderson, D. Eric, 80
Anglo-Saxon, 3, 4
Animals, experiments on, 18–21
Antioch College, 163n1
Apostle, Richard A., 177n10
Arab nations, 141–149
Asch, Solomon E., v, 8, 12, 130, 150, 151
Attitude objects, 146–147, 150–154
Attitude–behavior relation, 128–136
Attitudes. *See* Attitude objects
Availability of responses, 37–43, 59, 170n12
Axelrod, Robert, 95

Bangladesh, 81–85, 88, 198n19
Berscheid, Ellen, 95, 182n20
Bias in questions, 22–27, 55, 117
Biemer, Paul B., 158
Billiet, Jaak B., 182n15
Bischoping, Katherine, 184n30, 184n32
Bishop, George F., 6, 15, 27, 38, 80, 101, 164n10, 166n3, 168n3, 169n6, 179n1, 182n15, 189n13
Black alienation scale, 86
Blair, Johnny, 112
Blake, William, 119
Blaming question form, 43–54
Blau, Peter M., 94, 132
Bless, Herbert, 110
Blumer, Herbert, 120
Bobo, Lawrence, 6
Boojum, 139, 150, 155
Bradburn, Norman M., 1, 91, 97, 100, 108, 158, 168n3, 190n4
Bradford, Sunny, 176n7
Brannon, Robert, 132, 186nn12–13
Brown, Roger, 76
Burden, Barry C., 172n22
Bush, George W., 18, 27, 47–52, 55, 166n5, 172n22, 173n27, 175n4

Camburn, Donald, 20
Campbell, Angus, 86, 175n2
Campbell, Donald T., 6, 158
Campbell, James E., 172n22
Cannell, Charles F., 170n12
Cantril, Hadley, 95, 164n10, 180n7

209

Harvard University Press is a member of Green Press Initiative (greenpressinitiative.org), a nonprofit organization working to help publishers and printers increase their use of recycled paper and decrease their use of fiber derived from endangered forests. This book was printed on 100% recycled paper containing 50% post-consumer waste and processed chlorine free.